How to Be a Waitress and Make Big Tips:

Get a Top Server's Secrets to Maximizing Your Tip Earning Potential

Romana Van Lissum

How to Be a Waitress and Make Big Tips:
Get a Top Server's Secrets to Maximizing Your Tip Earning
Potential

ISBN 10: 1-933817-61-5
ISBN 13: 978-1-933817-61-3

Published by: Profits Publishing
http://profitspublishing.com

Canadian Address
1265 Charter Hill Drive
Coquitlam, BC, V3E 1P1
Phone: (604) 941-3041
Fax: (604) 944-7993

US Address
1300 Boblett Street
Unit A-218
Blaine, WA 98230
Phone: (866) 492-6623
Fax: (250) 493-6603

Dedication

This book is dedicated to all servers past, present, and future. We are an important part of a team that assists in making a successful business flourish!

miss Jolene J.,

all the best to you
for a successful
future!

Your friend,

Romana xx

"Hey Honey, can I take you out for
dinner sometime?
"I'm flattered but I'm married"
"How about coffee then?"

About the Author

Romana Van Lissum has been a successful server for over fifteen years. Starting as a beer barrel and shooter girl in a nightclub, she eventually got employment in a strip bar close to her home as a shooter girl. Working her way up to senior server, over the years she has been training all new servers hired and she shares her tips and tricks with waitresses on pretty much everything you read in this book. It is an industry she is well established in and well known. Over the years, head-hunters would frequent the bar and offer her jobs in their bars and pubs, but as a very loyal employee, she enjoys the people she works with and serves.

In her spare time, Romana enjoys endurance riding with her horses and spending time with friends and family. She is a big advocate for the well being of all animals, and looking after our planet earth is close to her heart.

Romana Van Lissum
www.howtobeawaitress.com

Photo by: Clifton Philpott, CA
bestcpphotos.com
clifton@bestcpphotos.com

Acknowledgements

A few years ago, I flew to Edmonton for my cousin's wedding. After chatting to my aunt Liane about the industry I have worked in for so long, it was she who said to me, "Romana, you know everything about this business. You should write a book!" And THAT was when I felt a spark light within myself. Since then, I started compiling notes and my crazy stories.

This book wouldn't be here if it wasn't for some important people in my life. I want to thank my entire family and all my friends. I am so fortunate to have them all in my life. I couldn't ask for better people to share my life with. An extra special thank you goes to:

My Husband, Rod

He is my rock that supports me in every one of my get-rich-quick schemes and projects that I seem to get myself into. He hands me the baton and lets me run with it. He's my best friend and the one person who knows me inside out. Watching me sit for hours while I'm typing away, he won't forget to tell me how hard I'm working and that this is going to be one hell of a great book! He is one of the rare and few husbands that tells me every single day how beautiful I am and how much he loves me. I'm told by many that I won the "husband jackpot." Yes, they're right! I love you with all my heart, my Roddy. xo

My Illustrator, Ashley Melanson

She is a professional and true artist that I have had the privilege of working with. The drawings add that little extra zest I was looking for of creativity and artistry.

My Daughter, Kelsey

A little social butterfly that makes her parents very proud of her. She's my little "smartie" who's fun to hang out with and is very loyal to her family and friends. My little honor student has helped me with the finalities of the book. I love you dearly, my one and only Girlie.

My Mom, Margit

Playing the mom role, she lets me jabber on and on about my endless stories and ideas every visit and every telephone call we have. She's always there to support and help me.

My Dad, Michael

When I hit a hiccup in my life, he's the one person that will always tell me, "Something bad is for something good. You're not the kind of person that would roll over and play dead. Don't worry! It'll work out."

My Brother, Dan

He's the talented musician who inspired me to move forward with my book writing. He's a true artist who has much respect for music and all instruments. I couldn't ask for a better sibling.

My Aunt, Liane

She's like the older sister I never had and the genius who gave me the idea in the first place.

Mary

The one who hired me fifteen years ago; she believed in a bikini model/shooter girl, giving me a chance to prove that I could be a good waitress.

My Girls

These are the waitresses I serve with everyday, who keep me sane and back me up on a daily basis.

The dancers; many of whom said that I was the perfect server to write this book. If it wasn't for them doing what they do for a living, I wouldn't have a job.

Every single one of my many girlfriends who support me and wish me luck on this new venture.

My Guys

These are the men I have the honor of working with, from the hot bartenders to the talented DJs and masculine doormen; they are true friends and gentlemen.

My Regulars

If it wasn't for these guys and girls, I wouldn't be able to pay my mortgage. Because of these people, I am able to have a book to complete. It is these people whom I've come to know and consider as friends.

Bob Burnham, the author of *101 Reasons Why You Must Write a Book: How To Make A Six Figure Income By Writing & Publishing Your Own Book.*

It is back in November, 2008, that I took a three hour course by Bob Burnham on how to get my book published. This was the day that changed my life!

Ashley Melanson is a Maple Ridge raised independent artist that favors to all mediums of art for self-expressionism.

"Thank you to my Opa and sister for being my life idols in the fine arts."

What Others Say About This Book

"I love this book for one very important reason. Any book that can help people live better lives is number 1 to me. Romana's book shows waiters and waitresses how to dramatically increase their income with simple to follow common sense strategies. If you truly want to dramatically increase your income in the hospitality business you should buy this book."

Bob Burnham
Author of: *101 Reasons Why You Must Write A Book: How To Make A Six Figure Income By Writing & Publishing Your Own Book*

"I found this book very interesting and a fun read. The ideas are presented in a straightforward manner that helps them be understandable. No one idea is very earth shattering but when taken together they provide the blueprint of being a highly successful server.

Romana has been a highly professional server for years and is certainly sought out by clients who find they enjoy their time in the bar more by having her service. I highly recommend this book to anyone who is interested in the service industry."

Roger Welch
President, Maple Ridge & Pitt Meadows Arts Council

"After working with Romana for thirteen plus years, I can think of no one more qualified than her to write this book helping not only new servers, but experienced servers to improve their skills. A very informative read! Way to go Ro!"

Barb MacDonald
Former Server for 28+ years

"Perfectly professional and profound! There are no other words to describe Romana's style at work and her book is the key to your newfound success! As a former waitress turned dancer, I personally recommend this as an exceptionally informative read and her tricks and tips of the trade are exactly what's needed to get the job done right! Working within this industry isn't exactly as easy as it may seem, but with this book added to your collection, you'll be well on your way!"

Charlie
Server for 2 years, turned dancer. Dancer for 6 years.

"I have to say, that I do have a newfound appreciation for waitressing after reading this book. Certain parts of the book made me feel like I was right there in the bar with Romana while she was taking orders and dealing with customers. I loved the line, "If you feel anxious or seem to be in a bad mood, SNAP OUT OF IT QUICK!" Great job Ro."

Ann Marie Gillie
Author of: *If Walls Could Talk: Don't Let Epilepsy Control You!*

"Wow! After reading Romana's book, she has some great information and stories. If only I had a guide to waitressing 16 years ago, I probably would never have started dancing! I was a bartender/waitress 1990-1992 but couldn't deal with the stressful busy rushes."

Anita Margarita
Server/Bartender for 2 years, almost 20 years ago. Dancer for 15 years
Owner of an online bikini business: www.fascinodiva.com

"This book puts everything on the table: an honest and clear truth about serving in a strip club. Romana shows you how to handle sometimes unfavorable situations with grace and ease."

Jolene Jensen
6.5 Years dancing
Currently working towards becoming a nurse

"Thanks for the eye opening read! In this day and age transferable skills make anyone a valued employee—clearly the experience one gains by serving the public can serve anyone in any occupation! The win/win scenario Romana writes about tells us that shining in your role as a server gains the best returns for you, the best for your company's and ultimately the best for your customers as they return again and again—creating that steady stream of business that keeps us all employed! The fun manner in which it is written makes important points easy to remember and the quirky anecdotes serve to punctuate the different points."

Leanne Pearson
Civil/structural designer

"This book will most definitely get you off to a head start in waitressing and is a must read regardless of whether you're just starting out or have been in the industry for some time and are looking for ways to separate yourself from the rest. Not only filled with excellent tips and short cuts that will get you off to a good start, there are also many entertaining stories of what you thought could never happen and how you would deal with these situations successfully. And even if you weren't thinking about getting into waitressing, you will certainly be entertained with the insider's perspective of what it's like to work in a strip bar as a waitress. I mean, how often do we get to have a peek behind the scenes? "

Ronaye Ireland
Author of: *How to Find Trouble Free Horse Boarding, Even If You're
New to Horses*
HorseBoardingSecrets.com

"I found this Book to be an Inspiration! Servers all over the world can use these tactics to make it through any shift imaginable. I believe that every personal experience by Romana is something that one server or another has faced time and time again. It moves me how dedicated a woman can be to her job and how important an eye for detail is. This book is a must read for any starting out server to help them on their feet but also will connect with someone ten or more years into this lifestyle. It is a great laugh and a touching tale."

Kimy Demitor
Serving for 3 years and counting

"*How to be a Waitress and Make Big Tips* is a remarkably easy read, bursting with valuable industry advice. The addition of personal accounts makes the material relatable and engaging. Van Lissum truly delivers an insightful and entertaining tool for everyone currently involved in/or thinking of joining the service industry. Blahopřeji!"

Erin Gourlay, B. Kin
Kinesiologist and server of 6 years

"I found this book to be well thought out and put together. I couldn't stop reading it until I had read it all in one sitting! The anecdotes sprinkled into the general text made it even more interesting. I do believe it will be a valuable "handbook" as some of the tips and ideas work for all types of servers—food, alcohol and even retail sales. After all, it doesn't matter what we're serving, we are still dealing with the public and they can be an interesting and sometimes difficult group.

"I noticed that a lot of things are still basically the same now as back when I first started serving. I first started in the 60's and was only able to serve food. Bars were still segregated, split into beer parlors and cocktail lounges where female bartenders and servers were unheard of—MEN only!

"My first experience working as a bartender was when I moved to Las Vegas in the 70's. I worked in a small bar that was frequented by the Snowbirds flying team and other military personnel from the Nellis Air Force Base. They were a great bunch and were my regulars who took turns coming to stay with me on the nights I closed the bar and made sure I was safely into my car before they left.

"I have my "Serving it Right" License and still volunteer once in a while as a bartender for weddings and New Years dances."

Teresa Leggett
Retail

"I truly enjoyed every aspect of this book! I have been a server for twenty years and I am able to relate to the stories as well as learn from the 'tips' Romana has provided to make even more money! Hilarious read too!"

Kimberly Ann Williams
Server for 20 years, Now a full-time hair stylist

"I have been in the service industry for 6 years now and can fully relate to this book. There are so many little tricks of the trade in this book that will increase your sales and your tips. I wish there was a book like this around when I first started! I had to wait and learn over time. I love it Ro!!!"

Katherine Blackwell
Server and Shooter Girl for 6 years

"Wow, was I surprised! I never thought I could get my questions answered so fast and with so much detail. Romana knows her stuff so well, she taught me so many tricks of the trade that helped me to pick up the pace with my service delivery, how to handle certain clients, and of course earn lots of cash, much more than I could of dreamed. This book will do the same for you."

Antonia Balshaw
Server for 8 years
Now working in the banking industry

"Success in any business can be directly attributed to strong customer service. Good service comes from happy, stable staff. This book gives the readers the tools to be prepared, knowledgeable and profitable which leads to staff loyalty and increased revenues. Romana tells the story of professional servers everywhere, with humor and honesty. It shows both the glamour and the hard work. If I knew any young person looking at serving as a job, I would strongly recommend that they invest in this book. It will make them money!"

Dean Barbour
Executive Director, Chamber of Commerce
serving Maple Ridge/Pitt Meadows

"I love how you break down the art of serving and totally agree the 'simple things' truly work! You cut down on wasted time, unnecessary mistakes, make more money, and I love keeping a clean section. Not only do you draw more customers into your section but getting off shift is a breeze because you have less to clean! It's also a great way to make good money and working hours that work for you! I have a career and still love picking up shifts to have some fun and make a few extra dollars. Serving is one of the best things I ever did because where else can you laugh your ass off, dance at the bar, have a blast, and leave with more money than you came in with and not have a hang-over the next day!

Shawna Johnson
Server for 12 years
Now with B.C. Corrections

"As a chef and a business owner I find Romana's book an invaluable tool for any restaurant owner. Your servers are your direct contact with your customers and your first line of defense. Good service is the key to a successful business. Not only will this book help your staff increase their earning potential but it will increase business in any establishment."

Shon De Vet
Owner of The Bushwood Grill

"The practical knowledge and time-saving suggestions in this book will maximize any server's profits! From beginners to seasoned pros, the detailed chapters cover basic know-how to clever tricks of the trade that will polish serving performance to top-notch quality. Specifically, the first chapter "Yourself: The Server" provides a vivid description of what you can bring to the role of serving to portray yourself in the best light to costumers, your boss, and coworkers, while still maintaining genuine enjoyment of your job. I found the author's personal descriptions of how to convey yourself in a light-hearted, humorous, and personable way to your customers to be very insightful. As well, the author paints a realistic picture of the upsides and downfalls to the industry, which provides the novice server with an established sense of working in this environment. I waitressed for two years in a hotel with a fine dining restaurant and separate lounge, and wish I had read this book at that time, as it would have given me some much needed tools to keep myself organized, moving up the ladder, and raking in the cash, all with a smile on my face. I think we have all had poor service and this book is anything but!!! "

Gia Cartel

Dancing for 3 years

School: B.A. in psychology, currently completing

M.A. in psychology through correspondence while dancing

"Can we ask you a personal question?"
"Well boys, if you're going to ask me if my
boobs are real, they are. No, this is not my
natural hair color. Yes, I'm married. And no,
I will not tell you my age… did I answer
your question?"

About This Book

"I am a cocktail waitress in a strip bar." ~YES, I've said it!~

It's definitely not an easy subject to admit to most people at times.

I've been working for the same bar in the Greater Vancouver area for over fifteen years. There are many reasons as to why I've been there for so long. I love the staff, the customers, and the hours, it's close to my home and, of course, I love the money!

I have probably met almost every type of personality out there and I've had many different serving experiences. Some were upsetting and threw a hiccup into my shift, but I managed to make it through each one and learn from them all. As I think about a bad situation, I realize I could have handled it in a more positive way and, other times, they were situations that I really had not much control in as they were unfortunate circumstances that I experienced on my shift. Waitressing is a job where you're always undergoing new situations. You're dealing with the public, and in dealing with the public it can be extremely challenging at times.

This book is the result of the various experiences I've dealt with over the last fifteen years as a cocktail waitress in a strip bar. This knowledge is turned into advice that I wanted to dissect and put into a very thorough, easy-to-understand format.

I wanted to put a book together that was helpful for all waitresses encountering many different obstacles in our profession, from the newbie that's never held a tray to the old pro that still likes to learn new tricks now and then.

I want this book to be picked up by an individual who has never worked in our industry, and for them to have a clear understanding of what it takes to do this job. Learning to use a till and getting the hang of balancing a full tray of drinks is the easy part. It's the "not knowing how to deal with intoxicated customers," being left with unpaid tabs and a customer who won't take a, "No, I will not go out with you. I told you I'm married for the fifth time!" are a few of the annoyances that a waitress has to deal with.

Yes, there are concerning aspects to the job, but I'm going to tell you how to deal with most of them, so that you are fully aware and prepared for what may lie ahead.

This job has been extremely fun, challenging, and profitable. Some of my greatest friends are the people I work with. My coworkers keep me young at heart and it's not unusual to find us girls being goofy and dancing at the till, or being silly with the customers. We're one big, happy family and we enjoy our jobs and have fun at work.

The Context

As you read this book, most of the time I will be referring to the term *server*, which is a modern definition that is used in the industry today. This book is geared mainly towards a waitress, but a waiter will be able to benefit from most of the information as well. The industry is definitely dominated by women but you will find many excellent waiters in our field. To simplify and shorten my writing even further, I will refer to a server as *she*, a female. As a result of working in a gentleman's club, most of my clientele are men, so I will be referring to customers as *he*, the male.

Almost all names mentioned in this book will be changed for the sake of privacy. Very rarely will a real name even be referred to.

As all of my experiences are collected from the strip bar industry, I will be referring to *my bar* or *our bar* that I work at. It is a shortened version, but I may be referring to any business pertaining to the service industry.

Throughout this book you will come across little anecdotes that read *Romana's Story*, as well as cartoons. These are experiences that have personally happened to me during my years as a server, unless I state otherwise. Periodically, I will put them in a section of a chapter pertaining to that topic.

This book is customized for the cocktail waitress who serves alcohol and food, mainly for the bar industry. The information is geared towards serving men but is helpful to all servers who serve men and women in any serving establishment. Most of the information in this book can be used for any establishment that employs servers.

Use your best judgment and always ask a senior server about house policies on running tabs and other important aspects of the job as every establishment has its own policies and rules.

During the many years of serving, as I came across problems, I figured out how to deal with them on my own if I didn't have the advice or help from others. The more you work and the more of an expert you become in the industry, you will feel what will work for you and what will not.

A personal note to you:

If you have always wanted to try serving, go out there and give it a shot. You may fall in love with it like I did, and if you get very good at it, you can make a lot of money that could change your life. Don't let some of the stories in this book scare you as there is more good to the job than bad. You have the backup of coworkers and there is always someone to help you handle a bad situation.

I've raised my daughter to believe that she should live her life to the fullest. If you're in a job you dislike, get rid of it and try something new. Same goes for anything else you don't like in your life, change it. **If nothing changes, nothing changes!** *Albert Einstein once said, "The definition of insanity is doing the same thing over and over again and expecting different results." Same goes for this line of work. Don't get caught up in the money. If you like the serving part, but you're tired of the establishment, go somewhere new. If you hate the serving part and everything about it, time to get out of the industry. You did it and made some great cash, now it's time to move on.*

I've worked nights for fourteen years and I now have worked the dayshift for the past year. It's the change I'm looking for to make my job seem new and fresh again.

I've worked with many servers over the years. Some have been around for a few months, others a few years. Some have lasted one day and didn't come back. Others liked the job but were very poor at it and were fired. I can usually tell when a server is ready to move on. I can tell when she's unhappy to be there and always complaining. I hear it from the regulars as well. You can't hide energy; people feel it.

My husband Rod told me that while he was listening to his radio station the other day, the topic was on waitressing. A man came onto the radio and reported that his girlfriend works at a well-known, trendy restaurant. He also commented that the public is cheap and on a busy night, his girlfriend makes a measly sixty dollars in tips a night. He feels that she should be making a lot more. A caller called in and remarked that maybe she was a bad server to begin with. There is something to be said about that.

Working in this business is enjoyable and very profitable. I can't imagine a better job where I can make the money I do and have the fun I have.

If you decide to enter the serving industry, read this book, and refer to it many times. Take what you want from it and leave the rest. As a result, I want you to enjoy your road traveled in this interesting profession and make lots of money.

Romana Van Lissum
www.howtobeawaitress.com

A STRANGER IS JUST A FRIEND YOU HAVE NEVER MET
- Author Unknown

Why Do They Like To Hang Out in Strip Bars?!

During the course of writing this book, I started to research some reasons on why people like to hang out in strip bars as often as they do. I knew some of the reasons already, as regulars would tell me over the years as to why they keep coming back. The main reason being the staff (the friendliness and the customers feel like they know them), and the familiarity of the bar (it feels like a second home to them). The quality of dancers is another reason and so is the food.

The "Why's" of Men

During my employment at the strip bar, I would pick my husband's brain on the WHY's of men. Why do guys do this or that? The answer is simple. It always comes down to one thing, and that is sex and naked women. We all know that men are visual creatures and that is basically it.

Recently, I had a nice talk with a couple of my regulars who asked me if I would put a chapter into the book to explain a little more in detail about this industry, as there are many misconceptions on this topic that women have. It got my brain thinking and I decided to do some research on the subject.

I know this book is for the waitress and how to make money, but I wanted to put some light on this subject as this job has been very good to me and got me financially to where I'm at. I don't like to hear people trash on the industry that I have worked so long in. I am here as a spokesperson and have known many of the dancers for years. So, the server is a good person to give the info as we are mainly in the background serving drinks, watching, and seeing what is happening around us.

Most of the readers that will pick up this book will be women and many will have boyfriends or husbands. The info that I know about will shed some light and put some perspective onto this mysterious industry that many know little about.

The majority of the public seem to think that all strip bars are sleazy and seedy. They think that the strippers are all on drugs and want to screw every guy that walks in the room. They probably have an inch more respect for the waitress, but not much.

I'm not a cop or a lawyer and it's not my business as to where the money comes from, so I have no problems with taking money from any of my customers. The clean money and the dirty money! I don't care whether a lawyer or mechanic gives me a tip or a drug dealer or biker does. If you feel like you can't sleep at night taking a tip from the bad boys, maybe you should change your line of work. All money has the EXACT same value and it pays the bills!

The Bars Give Back to the Community

Every year around the holidays, some strip bars give back to the community and do fundraisers to raise money for their local food hampers. It's amazing to read some of the letters that are sent to the local papers from some little bitty that says that all the money we raise is dirty and should not be accepted.

I can imagine them shaking their finger at us with their red face preaching, "How dare you!" and, "Shame on you!"

This past Christmas, we were advertising for our annual fund raiser and a photographer from our local newspaper came to the bar and said she's doing a little story on us. She had also asked us if any of the dancers had a Christmas outfit that she could take some pictures of for the paper. As it was still almost five weeks or so until the holidays, I knew many of the girls wouldn't have anything like that at work. She asked me if I happened to have a Christmas dress and I told her I did, but it was at home. She asked me if I wouldn't mind posing for some pictures if she returned the next day. I agreed.

The end of the week, the picture came out and it ended up being on the front cover of the paper! There was a great little write-up and the picture was very nice and classy. A couple men had written into the paper slamming us by saying that the money is dirty and the hamper society shouldn't accept it. People in the community, as well as staff and customers, were irate! Letters were sent into the paper and it was wonderful how many women, as well as men, were on our side saying how grateful they are that our business goes to the trouble of putting this event on every year and raising as much money as we do. Every single dancer and staff member works for free all day to try and raise as much money as possible for this important cause.

Many Big Misconceptions People Have

So, here it is. Some reasoning on the importance of strip bars and why men and women like to go. The number one reason why strip bars exist is to make *money*! The number one reason why men love to go to strip bars is *naked women*. Put the two together and you got a strip bar that employs naked women so that they make money! It's all really very simple.

Probably the biggest misconception that women have about strip bars is that they could steer their man to infidelity, ruining relationships and families. This is far from the truth. Men are visually stimulated and the reason that the strip bar is there is to make money, not ruin relationships; it's all about business. That is the same reason that dancers and staff are there as well. It comes down to cold hard cash.

This may come as a shock to many people (men and women), but the dancers and the servers don't want to sleep with your man. Hell, if we want sex, we are quite capable of finding our own partner and most of us already have. It basically comes down to us wanting to milk your man of all his money and send him home. It's nothing personal, just business.

As far as I'm concerned, if my husband were out with a bunch of friends, I would prefer him to go to a strip bar and not a normal bar or nightclub. The normal bars have the women out carousing and looking to snag a man. They'll even hit on the married ones and they don't care.

Women cringe at the thought of their man sitting at gyno, throwing money at naked girls. The reason why they throw money at them is that they love the attention they get from the women. When they receive the attention, they may be fantasizing that one of the strippers will leave with them. More upsetting is the thought of hot-looking women, possibly waving their boobs right in your man's face. The reason that the girls do it is to take their money! Men love looking at other naked women because they are visual and they can't help themselves by looking at women's bodies. What do you think happens when your guy is at the beach, on the street, at work, at the gym, or watching a movie on TV? You can't get away from hot girls; they're everywhere! Why do you think there are cheerleaders at football games, or card girls at boxing matches? Why does Snap on Tools put together a calendar with beautiful women in bikinis? Did you ever notice the hot girl straddling a beautiful bike on the cover of a motorcycle magazine? I sure do ... it's on my coffee table right now!

When I used to model, I got hired by a company that sold some kind of part or engine for some industry people. There was a trade fair in Portland, Oregon, and I got hired for two days to go and stand in front of their booth. My job was to say hello to everyone who walked by and ask people (99 percent of them men) if I could pin a button (advertising the company I was working for) on their jacket or shirt. Everyone said yes and I even had guys come to the booth and ask, "I heard you were pinning buttons on people. Could you pin one on me as well?" It was an ingenious marketing plan! While I took a moment and did the pinning, the vultures would swoop in and start up a conversation with the potential, and hopefully future, "client."

If there's a hot-looking girl, of course a guy is going to look at her! Be realistic! When you notice a good-looking guy, you have a second or third look! My husband knows I have the hots for David Beckham, Johnny Depp, and Hugh Jackman. He doesn't get upset that I take a little longer look at them than normal. It's like admiring beautiful shoes in a shoe store window!

Dancers don't want to drag your guy in the back and screw his brains out. I got some crazy news for you, girlfriend, but many of the girls have their own men at home. Let me tell you that some of the guys are pretty hot!

As I said before, the strip bar is there to make lots of money. They are there for catering to men's fantasies. When looking into what other strip bars offer around the world, I found some interesting information.

Some have a built in escort service (found in Europe only), themed rooms to stay in, restaurants, six girls on stage at one time, girls bathing themselves, or girls swinging together in a choreographed laser show. Some strip bars don't even serve alcohol! Others have couch dances, lap dances, private dances, and even bed dances. Others show off the entertainer's aerobic feats.

Did you know that the biggest strip club in the world is The Sapphire Gentlemen's club in Las Vegas, Nevada? It is open 24 hours a day, 7 days a week, and 365 days a year! The size of this place is 70,000 square feet and employs 8,000 exotic dancers.

So, basically it comes down to money. Once in a while, someone will ask me why I think there are no strip bars where women hang out on a daily basis. My answer, "There are no strip bars for women, because the bar would go broke!" Women don't think about sex 24 hours a day, like most men do.

This book is written around the time that the economy went really "wonky" in 2009. I did some reading on the internet and found that there is double the amount of women looking for employment this year as compared to last year and many of those women are looking into this line of work. Strip club dancers and managers said that they're drawing in the same amount of customers but very few high rollers.

This industry is recession-resistant, therefore dancing = job security for the girls.

Table of Contents

**"Hey Sweetheart, you married
or got a boyfriend?"**
"Yes, I'm married"
**"I'd never ALLOW my wife
to work here"**

Chapter 1 – YOURSELF: The Server

Why Waitress?

WHY Do We Serve the Public?

Many people may wonder why a person wants to get into a profession such as serving. Some of the shifts can be pretty long and crazy, you're on your feet at all times, you get hit on, you're dealing with a high-paced job, and there are many different personalities you encounter.

Waitressing is a hard job, but it's very rewarding as well.

You meet some great people, the hours can fit into almost any person's schedule, and the money can be pretty damn good!

It's great to go home at the end of a shift with cash in your pocket, and there's always money for gas or a loaf of bread at the end of a shift. Plus, you still get a pay cheque every couple of weeks.

When the economy is down and people are losing their jobs, you'll find that bars are still busy as ever because when times get tough, people will always drink. When times are good, people will drink to celebrate as well. The hospitality industry rarely will get affected as people will drink when they are happy and when they are sad.

WHEN Are the Hours?

Many people turn to serving because of the hours. If you look around, you will be able to find a pub, restaurant, coffee shop, nightclub, or diner that is open during hours that you need to make some extra money.

Some girls start into it thinking that they'll do it for a few years and then move on to something else, while other girls end up enjoying the hours, the people, and the money. They never leave the industry, like me, and turn into a career waitress.

WHO is Serving?

Professional men and women work office jobs by day and turn to serving at night for extra cash.

Single mothers raise their families on the money they make waitressing and then have the day to spend with their children.

Students go to school during the day and waitress at night to help pay their way through school.

You don't need to take a course or get a degree to learn how to be a waitress.

If you enjoy people, are organized, enjoy a fast-paced work environment, and love cash, this is the industry to get involved in.

For most of my serving years, I've enjoyed working the nightshift, so my daughter didn't have to be raised by a babysitter and I was able to train my horses during the day. It was a bit of a crazy schedule for my husband and me, as our only day off together was Sunday for many, many years. Eventually, we both ended up with Sundays and Mondays as our days off together. Many of our friends and family were amazed that our marriage was strong enough to withstand the crazy bar hours I worked.

WHAT is Being Served?

Servers are needed to serve alcohol, non-alcoholic drinks, and food.

WHERE is a Server Needed?

Looking at our vast industry, you will see that servers are needed for many businesses. You'll find cocktail servers in nightclubs, pubs, gentlemen's clubs, beer gardens, piano bars, and casinos. Food servers are found in diners, family restaurants, high-end restaurants, and tapas bars. Servers are needed for hotels, cruise ships, and golf courses.

Top Qualities a Server Should Have

The amount of money that a server makes depends on a few things. You have to have a talent for this type of work and it helps to be outgoing, quick thinking, and have a lot of stamina.

You can't be intimidated to go up to a big group of people and take over the situation. You may have a loudmouth in the group and a snotty wife darting dirty looks at you. You have to stay on top of your game, take their orders, and keep that smile on your face, while you feel like kicking the loudmouth in the shin and dumping your tray in the lap of the snotty wife.

Quick-thinking girls know how to handle vulgar comments while memorizing a full tray of drinks. They keep on top of checking identification of the young-looking clientele, and keeping a tidy and orderly room all at the same time.

The stamina comes in handy when the bar is full of people and you must keep running out full tray after full tray of drinks while returning back to the bar with a tray of empties, not skipping a beat. You may be weaving and fighting your way through a crowd of people, while avoiding the drunks and keeping them from crashing into your tray.

Sometimes there's no stopping for a breather. You barely have a moment to sip some water, and sometimes you have to wait a while before you have a minute to slip into the restroom.

Unorganized, shy people that get flustered easily don't last long in this job.

There is no shame in being a career waitress. I can definitely say that it has been a fun job that I found very fulfilling and I wouldn't trade it for another. I would suggest going to school and getting some sort of a degree while making money in this industry because one day you'll feel the pressure of not being the hot, young girl anymore. You really can't be doing this job when you're an old timer, as it's very tiring on your body.

A big dilemma to being a career waitress is that you may have trouble with banks as they only look at your wage and not include the tips you've earned to get a loan.

A neat thing about serving is that since you deal with cash most of your shift, you will end up with collector's coins and money from around the world. I have one hell of a big coin collection.

Some Server Drawbacks

As with everything, there are some disadvantages to this line of work. When you're the new person, you will usually get the hours that are the shortest and during the slower times. When you come in for a shift and it's not that busy, you may have to sit on the side lines and wait until the room picks up. Sometimes it never does, and during the dead nights you may not end up working at all. It's silly to put another server on the floor and pay her an hourly wage when there are not even twenty drinkers in the room. I feel bad when I tell a new server to sit and wait, but that's the way it is. As senior waitress, you have to make good business decisions that are advantageous to the bar. When you're new, you will usually be given the section of the room that is perhaps smaller than and not as busy as the other servers'.

In this line of work, you will encounter the unruly customer, the person that commands attention by either starting a fight or yelling. They may have been cut off in another bar and unfortunately ended up at yours. You'll have to cut people off if they've had too much to drink and babysit them until the taxi shows up.

Non-tippers that expect you to get their drinks for them all night long without compensating you with a tip are a few of the people that will make you cringe.

You'll be looked upon as eye candy, especially if you're very attractive or working in a strip bar. Believe me, there are days that you're not in the mood for it, but it comes with the territory.

There is a reason why I like working in a room full of men: some women are difficult to deal with. For more information on this subject, please refer to **Chapter #6, Subchapter #3 on "Women."**

You have to be safe and aware of your surroundings as you leave the bar late at night while going out to your car. For additional information on this subject, please refer to **Chapter #1, Subchapter #4 on "The Essential Aspects of Your Safety at Work as Well as Leaving."**

You can get caught up in the drinking and socializing aspect of this job because it's very entertaining and fun. It's very tempting and, in the beginning, I got roped into it like many do.

Romana's Story... "Get Home!"

As I said above, I got roped into the drinking and socializing aspect part of the bar industry. During the first year, I was asked by one of the other servers if I could give her a ride home at the end of our shift.

"No problem!" I said, as I reached for the phone to call my husband

Rod and tell him that I may get home a little later than normal, as I was going to drive home a different route.

The staff decided to have a cocktail after work and I thought that wouldn't be a problem as I had called Rod earlier and told him I would be home a little late anyways. Well, one drink turned into two, then three and even four. I tried getting out of there a few times but felt pressured into staying.

Three hours later, Rod showed up with a sleeping four-year-old wrapped in her quilt at the door. The bartender from the club next door unlocked the doors and let them in.

That was the first time in our marriage that he raised his voice in front of other people towards me, and I was stunned with embarrassment. My coworkers looked at me with wide eyes and told me to go. I guess the other server found another ride home.

A Typical Shift In the Day of a Server

I would like to give you a taste of a typical shift and the approach to serving customers.

Preparation for Starting Your Shift

I like to arrive at work at least fifteen minutes early, as this will give me enough time to change into my work clothes and footwear. This is the time to use the toilet if I need to or re-apply lipstick.

When I collect my tray, I give it a quick clean if it feels dirty, feels sticky, or smells bad. Our trays are lined with cork and we find that sprinkling a bit of baking soda and some hot water on them, then rubbing the baking soda in with the top side of a glass, gets rid of the stink from the shift before. Baking soda is fantastic to use on all trays to clean them.

I ask the bartender for a float. This is money in bills and coin that is lent to a server to use as change and it's paid back to the bar before the end of the shift. Every server seems to like a different float. I like a roll of nickels (two dollars), a roll of quarters (ten dollars), a roll of loonies (twenty five dollars), three loonies (three dollars), and four fives (twenty dollars). This equals sixty dollars.

I don't bother with dimes as they're a waste of space on my tray and dealing with nickels is a lot easier and I don't have to worry about counting and rolling up dimes at the end of my shift. I like to write a note to myself that I owe the bartender $60.00 for my float and slip it into my waitress box. This way, if he forgets to collect from me, I would know beforehand and not go home at the end of my shift thinking that I was $60.00 richer than I actually was. You would be expected to pay your float next time you come in for a shift if you forgot to pay it back. I wet my rag and fold it neatly, placing it on top of my coins arranged in my ashtray. This way, my change is hidden and basically the only thing taking up any room on my tray is the ashtray. For more information on this subject, please refer to **Chapter #7, Subchapter #2 under "Cash Caddy vs. Ashtray."**

If I'm relieving another server at the end of her shift, I'll ask her how the day went and if anything interesting is going on in the bar. This is the time she'll let me know of patrons that are cut off, any tabs owing to her, stag or birthday parties in the room, etc.

If you feel anxious or seem to be in a bad mood, SNAP OUT OF IT QUICK! People will feel your energy and read your body language. Customers are in there to relax and have a good time and nobody likes to be served by a crab that has a scowl on her face and barely utters a "Hello." I would sooner tip a server that is friendly and slow to bring my drinks than a crabby speed bomb that seems to hate her job.

Onto the floor I go. As I walk through the room, I make sure to smile and greet *every* single customer and ask how they're doing tonight. During the entire time I'm working the floor, I'm picking up empties, wiping tables, and pushing chairs in. This is all very important as it makes the room look clean and neat. If you stay in the habit, it's easy and quick to do. I could never understand servers who would rather trip through or walk around chairs, rather than push them under the table and get them out of the way.

Always remove all empties and garbage as soon as possible when a group has paid their bill and left to go home. If the table is cluttered with empties, newcomers entering the room will think that the table is being used and the occupants are outside having a cigarette or in the restroom. You could be deterring potential customers from sitting in your section by not clearing dirty tables right away.

When picking up empties from a table, I *always* give the spot it was sitting on a quick wipe to get rid of the sticky or wet ring with my damp cloth. The only exception would be if I'm slammed and I can barely keep up to collecting empties in the room. Wiping can be done when I swing by the second time.

As I move through the room, I keep a look-out for accidental spills or empties. As I'm removing the empties or wiping up the spill, I'll mention to the customer, "Let me get rid of the evidence for you!" I always have guys laughing when I make this silly comment to them. It shows your playful and fun side, which may increase your tips.

You don't have to have a fake smile plastered on your face as you mechanically go about your job. You want to look like you're having fun there too. If you're having fun and enjoying your job, your smile will be sincere.

Another fun comment that makes the guys smile is when I drop off a round of drinks. They say, "Thank you" and I respond with, "Thank you for keeping me busy!" It's fun to be a goof!

During the dayshift, I hand out coasters to the dayshift crowd because they're older and I usually have more time than when I work the busier nightshift. Our bar keeps pint glasses in a cooler, so that when draft beer is poured, it is icy cold. Customers are especially grateful for this in the hot summer months. Ice may be clumped at the bottom when the pint is set down, resulting in the icy mug almost sliding into a customers lap. Keep those coasters handy and pay attention if there is ice accumulated at the bottom of the pint. I will either chip the ice away with a bottle opener, or bang the glass firmly on the counter to break off the ice.

As I move around the room and clean tables, there may be change left on a table that I didn't serve. That tip doesn't belong to me, but it does go to the server that was just working. I leave it in her box, or take it to her if she's still in the room. You want to be honest, as Karma will follow you. Let me assure you that cheaters and stealers won't last long in this business.

Make that Sale

As I move through the room, I'm scanning over every single drink on every single table. If the drink is half full or less, I'll ask that customer if they're ready for another. This is an opportunity to make a sale and possibly a tip.

When I take new drink orders and a cocktail or high ball is ordered, I ask if they want to double it up; think higher sales for the bar and a possible bigger tip for you!

I'm also looking for customers that are flagging me down by waving their hand at me, or if they have that longing look in their eyes. You know "the look"... when you walk over and ask, "Did you need another beer?" and with their three-quarter-full beer in their hand they answer with a nod and sigh, "Yes, please!" He's the customer that will be done by the time you swing by with his next drink. He's either very thirsty or in a rush to down a few beers and take off.

I'd like to comment about enunciation and hearing. As a customer is giving you his order and you can't hear him, say "I'm sorry, I can't hear you!" If you still can't hear, don't be shy to repeat yourself. It's happened a few times where someone will order a Kokanee, and I thought I heard "coke." I don't happen to pick up "anee" at the end and usually bring the coke. I just tell him my hearing is really bad from working in the bar for so long. Bud vs. mug is another one. If a person says "Bud," I'll repeat back with "Budweiser?" just to be clear.

Always stick to a pattern or map of the room. You don't want to wander the room aimlessly and miss people sitting at a table in a dark corner. You'll make them mad as it looks like you're avoiding them, and you're missing out on valuable sales and possible tips for yourself!

When I return to the bar, I unload my empties while waiting for any other servers or shooter girls to finish with the till. If there is no room for me, with my tray on my arm I remove the empties and garbage. This way, I make use of valuable time and I can sort out the drink order I have memorized in my head. Don't stand there waiting for the other server to get out of the way. Set your tray down and help her unload her tray while she rings in her order, so it can speed everyone up at the till.

I make sure to always dump any little bit of beer at the bottom of beer bottles, as well as ice in glasses, into the sink. The reason for the beer bottles to be empty is that when you lift the beer case full of empties and if it happens to drop suddenly, you don't get splashed in the face or your shirt with old, stale beer. Take it from a girl who knows. The beer delivery guys appreciate this courtesy as well, as they are the ones moving those cases around.

DO NOT slam empty bottles into the case: place them in gently. I've been in a real rush at times and don't pay attention to this warning, only to get pieces of glass flying out, nearly hitting my eyes!

Keep water by the till and sip on it regularly throughout your shift. I find this very important because if I don't, I end up with a headache. My husband says that I don't seem to have that thirst mechanism in my body to tell me when I'm thirsty. He's right, as I can work in the hot sun for three hours without feeling thirsty and then wonder why my head hurts. So, I make it a point to always keep a drink for myself at the till.

The Drink Order

During a slower dayshift, the bartender may be doing other chores than just standing around. There are limes to be cut, cleaning, restocking, and inventory control. If he's busy doing something with his back facing you, or he's in the back room, I like to ring my order in and call loudly, "Order up!" This is an indication that I'm waiting for him to make my drink order.

When punching a drink order in, there is always an order to punching your drinks into the till. Check with your head waitress or bartender for the order in which they'd like you to ring your drinks in.

At the bar I work at, we ring in our drinks in this order:
- Import beers
- Local beers
- Coolers and ciders
- Bottles of water
- Single high balls, then doubles
- Single cocktails, then doubles
- Shooters (if there's no shooter girl on)
- Pops, juices, and coffees
- Jugs
- Pints
- Glasses

Try to ring everything in order. It can make a bartender leap over the bar for your throat if you ring in orders like this:

- Rum coke
- Stella
- Budweiser
- Double Caesar
- Budweiser
- Jug of dark
- Budweiser
- Bombay tonic
- Pineapple juice
- Miller

The reason why drinks are rung into the till in sequence is to save time. When the bartender looks at the order and starts pulling bottles of beer out of the cooler, he wants to pull out all three Budweisers and the Stella at once.

He wastes time if he pulls bottles onto the counter and then has to turn around and open and shut the cooler doors again if he needs to go back in a few more times. I get very upset at servers that do this because I'm waiting my turn to get my drink order and if another server makes me wait longer than necessary, it reflects on the tips I receive! At my bar, we are told to memorize all drink orders rather than writing them down because it saves time. Yes, you may forget a drink or two or maybe even three. This will happen when you're slammed and feel like you're starting to get out of control. You know what? You're only human! Just apologize, get those forgotten drinks, and move on. If you find that you're starting to get flustered and you need to pull yourself together, move to the side and let the server behind you into the till. I find that retracing my steps and looking back at the room helps a lot.

Have a System for Identifying Your Drinks

While your bartender is working on your order, begin placing your drinks on your tray while putting garnishes and straws into them. He'll make the drinks in order of the way you rang your order in (usually from your right to the left). Always ask the bartender, as each one may have his own system of making drinks.

Always have a plan for marking the drinks on your tray.

Example:

If I have an order that calls for two Caesars, one with no Tabasco, I put two straws into the Caesar with no Tabasco.

If I have an order that calls for a Jack Daniels coke, Rum coke, Vodka coke, and a Vodka diet, I'll put two straws into my Jack Daniels, I'll put a lime twist into my rum, the vodka (with the lime twist sitting on the rim of the glass) goes to the right of the rum and then the vodka diet (lime twist sitting on the rim of the glass) with the two straws goes to the right of the vodka with regular coke. If I have a whole slew of cocktails, I use any system to keep it all organized. If my entire tray is full of cocktails with coke mix, I will even put three straws into a drink if I need to, to be able to recognize it. I'll put them in alphabetical order as well, with two straws signifying a double short. Whatever system you use to keep drinks recognized, use it.

If you put two or three straws into a drink to keep your drinks organized, always remove the extra straws before setting it down in front of your customer.

• As your bartender makes your drinks, *do not* wander away to talk to customers or go to the bathroom. This is irritating for other servers that are trying to juggle their tray and get their drink orders too.

• Some bars may still use the *call order system*. This is where the server calls all her drinks out to the bartender. Look towards the bartender when you call your drinks. Stay a few drinks ahead, as you call loud and not too fast. Don't rattle off the long list as fast as you can. He needs to register in his mind what you are calling out.

If you mix up a couple of drinks, you can still save the situation and switch them if both people didn't drink out of them. If one person sips out of his drink and then complains to you, wait to see if the other person says anything. Most of the time, people won't notice anyways, and you'll just have to replace only one drink instead of two.

For example, customer A at table #12 orders a rye coke and customer B at table #13 orders a rum coke. When dropping off the drinks, you accidentally gave customer A the rum and customer B received the rye.

When grabbing straws to place into your drinks, don't touch them by the end where the customer places his lips. Instead, grab it at the middle. Our hands are extremely unsanitary as we are consistently handling coin, bills, garbage, and empties while touching others' hands. Keep hands away from your face and wash or sanitize your hands as often as you remember. Imagine how many germs are on the mouth end of an empty beer bottle!

Some of my regulars prefer to have a cold frosty mug to go alongside their bottle of beer. I like to take it one step further and pour the contents of their bottle into the glass and deliver it that way. It saves room on my tray, keeps the table from getting more cluttered, and they love the extra special touch that you provide.

Take the frosty glass and give the interior a quick rinse with water before you pour the contents of the bottle into it. This keeps the beer from foaming and spilling over the glass. Tip the glass on its side and pour the beer slowly from the bottle onto the side of the glass. It'll keep the beer from overflowing the glass and foaming like crazy.

When your tray is ready to go and you still need to sign out a tab, move your tray off to the side to do this, as to keep out of the way of other servers. You will be shown how to pre-authorize and advise a credit card from another server. Once you're shown how to do this a couple times, it's easy as pie! To learn more about tabs, please refer to **Chapter #2, Subchapter #3 under "Relevant Tips for Running Tabs."**

*At the end of my bills, I will always finalize it with:
Cheers! Romana

The reason I do this is to make it more personable, and I want them to know my name. So, next time they come in, they'll ask for me by name. Or better yet, maybe they want to get hold of management and tell them that they had the most awesome server ever named Romana and she needs a raise!

As I return to the floor, I stay on the map of the room (or my section, if I'm working with another server), so as not to miss anyone. I stop at my first table and start setting down drinks. At this time I say, "There you go guys. Is that all together or separate?" At this point someone may offer me a credit card to run a tab, or money will be pulled out by individuals to pay for their drinks separately.

Remember your manners and always say "Thank you," whether you get a tip or not. Keep in mind that they may still leave money on the table before they leave.

When I stop at a table and set down a pint of draft beer, sometimes a customer will have a small amount of beer at the bottom of the last purchased pint. Do not dump the leftover into the fresh one without asking him if it's okay to do this. Some guys won't drink the rest and want it taken away.

When picking up empty beer bottles, give the bottle a small shake to tell whether there is any beer still left at the bottom. I have been chased across the bar by customers many times, who complained that he still had a sip full of beer left at the bottom!

When customers leave for the night, I will always call over at them with a "Thanks for coming in, guys!" or "Thanks a lot, guys! Have a great evening!" or "Enjoy the rest of your day, guys!" When you work at a bar long enough and get to know many regulars, don't be surprised if customers come over to hug you or kiss your hand or cheek as they say their good byes.

A Different Kind of Tip

In this line of work, you'll receive other types of tips than monetary. Money is obviously our favorite, but I've been given a fresh salmon, baked goods, homemade jam, chocolates, fresh vegetables from a garden, dozens of roses sent to work (and they weren't from Rod), candles, Scratch and Win lottery tickets, bottles of wine, and a handful of screws to name a few.

Customers have brought me souvenirs from their cruises or trips to Mexico or Hawaii. It's not uncommon that we get a postcard sent to us girls from a customer while on vacation. I wonder if his wife knows?

When tables of people leave, I run over as soon as I can and take away all empties and garbage, straighten and wipe down the table, and push in all the chairs. This clean and neat table looks inviting to a new group that enters the bar. New customers scan the room for a place to sit, and will want to sit at a clean table. I like to keep all my tables more inviting than my coworkers' because this will keep bodies in the chairs in my section, which means my sales are high and I earn more tips.

15

As I near the end of a shift, I make sure I don't have any drinks that I had ordered earlier, and couldn't sell, sitting on ice. I'll collect any open drinks and try to sell them as the bar can't recap opened beers. Please refer to **Chapter #2, Subchapter #2 on "Sales Strategies"** to get tips on how to get rid of drinks that you can't seem to sell.

As customers leave the bar, always thank people for coming in and tell them to have a great night or rest of the day. Pick up all your empties and all garbage. We like to spray down all of our tables with a cleaner to get rid of all spills and stickiness at the end of the night. You will want to find out what cleaning protocol is from your senior servers at your bar. You will also find out what to do with the chairs/bar stools. Are they pushed in or set upside down on the tables so the room is ready for cleaning people?

All cases full of empty bottles are stored away, the sink is cleaned out, and the till area is cleaned up and wiped down. The servers clean their trays and put them away. All dirty rags are put in a bucket for the cleaning people to take away and wash.

As you run all dirty glasswear through the glass washer, add the bar mats and tools that the bartender puts onto the counter as well.

The Structure of Cash-out

You'll check to see if you have any voids to ring in. Ask the coworker responsible to do this.

Do your ring-out. This is the total amount of drinks that you rang in during the course of your shift. Grab your calculator, pen, cash-out paper, and envelope. Pull out all credit card and interac slips, cash, promo cards, and anything else that you need out of your waitress box. Do a thorough check of your box, so a slip or bill is not hiding up in a corner.

As you're adding up all your visa slips, make sure that they're all advised (finalized and put through). I find that during the course of the night, as soon as I'm given the signed pre-authorization slip, I'll advise it almost immediately while I'm placing drinks onto my tray. The slips are stapled together and thrown into my waitress box for safe keeping.

Double check all visa slips so that the advise matches the total on the bill. Scan over and compute everything before you advise it in the first place. If the bill total is $112.00 and the customer wrote $20.00 in the tip line, make sure he wrote $132.00 in the last line and not $122.00 or another total.

Always double check all calculations! If the numbers don't match up, do a third and even fourth tally if you have to. Don't be in a rush to run out the door. Make sure your cash is bang on. Remember to put money aside for your DJ, doorman, kitchen, and especially your wonderful bartender; if it wasn't for him, you wouldn't be able to get your drinks out quickly to your customers (who in turn leave you a big tip!).

Before I leave for the night, I print off an extra copy of my ring-out for that shift and slip it into my waitress bag. Once in a while the till isn't cleared to zero from the day before, so when you print off your sales for a shift and the numbers look a lot higher than normal, you have your correct total from the day before to deduct from.

Romana's Story... "The Packed Restaurant"

A couple of years ago, my daughter Kelsey and I decided to take Rod out for a father's day brunch. We went to a popular family restaurant.

We walked in the door where there were quite a few people waiting to be seated. We told the hostess our name and asked how long the wait would be; she said it was twenty minutes. We looked at one another, nodded, and thought that was ok. Then we waited.

Fifteen minutes went by, and the hostess yelled out, "There is a twenty five minute wait!" The three of us looked at each other and figured that it wouldn't be long now.

Almost fifteen minutes later, we were seated and I was appalled as I looked around our table. There were five tables that were completely empty! As our table was not far from the waiting area, we could hear the hostess as she spoke to customers. She was telling people who were walking in the door that there was a thirty minute wait by then. I wondered why they didn't pack the people into the tables. The only thing I could think of was that they were low on servers and maybe someone called in sick.

Our server came to our table and the first thing we noticed was her filthy white apron hovering above our table, which looked very unappetizing and unprofessional.

If I was a server in that restaurant and there were no bodies at all of my tables, I would be raising some hell! When I'm at work, I want to make money, not waste my time standing around.

It's hard to get customers in the first place, so why turn them away? They may not come back next time.

How to Make Yourself the TOP Earner

Out of all the chapters in this book, this is one of the most lengthy. There are a few points covered here that are repeated (in more detail), as in the chapter *A Typical Shift in the Day of a Server*. I just had many points to cover and it all seemed to roll together.

I must be doing something right when every boss I've had seems to push the new girl at me and says to her, "Romana's going to train you. Do what Ro does." I'm proud of the fact that I am good at my job and others see this as well.

An acronym to keep in mind...

Every Successful Server Needs S.H.O.E.S.

Smile
Honesty
Organization
Enthusiasm/Energy
Sexuality (your persona, your self-carriage, and the way you dress)

I'll explain in detail throughout the book as to why these characteristics are important in this line of work.

Going For the Job and Getting Hired

Do Not Lie to Get the Job.

You picked this book and you're reading it for a reason.

Perhaps you're a girl or guy that has always wondered about the serving industry, thinking that you would enjoy it and heard about the great money that servers make. Maybe you're a rookie server that feels she needs to learn a few tricks to get better and more skilled at her job. Perhaps you're the old pro who's curious if there's anything different or new to learn. Use the tricks in this book and it'll slowly change you into a more efficient and profitable server!

Please don't think that by reading this book (or any other serving book) that you can lie to get a job by saying that you have experience serving. You'll be caught within the first few minutes on the job. It's unfair for the girl who's supposed to train or work with you, and it's unfair to the customers you are to serve.

To become a good server, you need to know how to multi-task. Exposure to all sorts of scenarios and people will help over the years, as well as learning the basics, understanding and working the till, and then basically being thrown to the wolves for the experience.

Cocktail waitressing can be very fast-paced and confusing at times. By the time you memorize a large table's confusing drink order, three people decide to order something completely different, or a table decided to separate their bill after all. You're under pressure, but if you've got it under control, your speed is bang on, and you're moving along efficiently—it's a great feeling!

Here's a story for you to digest…

Romana's Story: This is actually Rod's story, "Please give me a job!"

Around the same time I got into serving, my husband got laid off as an auto mechanic at the dealership he worked at.

As he started to pound the pavement, he dropped his résumé off at six different dealerships he wanted to work at. Three days later he got a call from Toyota and got the job.

Years later, he was told that they had a big stack of résumés around the time he got hired. The reason he got hired was that he put something on his cover sheet that nobody else did; it showed his desire to work there. In his résumé, he stated that he would work for free for two weeks to prove himself to let them judge if he was a good enough mechanic or not to hire on. He got paid from the day he was hired almost fifteen years ago. They send him to Toyota school every few years to update and about ten years ago he became and maintains his master tech status.

If you have your eye set on a place you would kill to work at, you have nothing to lose (except the hourly wage) if you put something similar on your résumé's cover sheet, just as Rod did in the story above. Change the amount of time if two weeks seems a little too long. Just stipulate that you'd like to keep the tips you earn during the shifts so there are no misunderstandings. If you prove to them what a great, reliable server you are, you will get the job and more than likely get paid from day one.

When you go in to apply for a job, you've got one time to make a good first impression. Apply your make-up, do your hair, put on some heels, and dress nice. When girls come into our bar to apply for a job, their résumé is thrown into the garbage if they dress like a slob, or they have spelling mistakes on it. Be friendly, polite, and outgoing, remember your manners, and smile!

When dropping off your résumé, don't go into restaurants and diners during lunch hours, as this is when they have their lunch rush and staff is busy. Don't go in after 11:00 am and before 2:00 pm, and always ask to speak to the manager. If the boss is not in, ask when would be a good time to come by and drop off a résumé. Don't bother leaving your résumé with anyone there. Sometimes they aren't given to the person in charge anyways, are misplaced, or are even thrown into the garbage. You want the manager to meet with you and see what a great asset you would be to his team.

When asked about your serving experience, be honest! If you don't have any type of serving experience, you may have to apply anywhere and everywhere. You'll just have to see who's willing to give you a shot. If you end up getting a call from a dumpy diner, take the job. It doesn't mean you have to work there the rest of your life. Use it to gain some experience and once you feel confident in your serving abilities, try applying for the dream jobs again.

Do you know if your province's laws state that you must have a serving certificate in order to serve alcohol or even food to the public? In British Columbia it is law to have a "Serving it Right" card before anyone can serve alcohol in an establishment. For information on **"Serving it Right,"** please refer to **Chapter #9, Subchapter #2 under "The Legalities"** or check it out on the web. To aid in your chances of getting hired for a job, look into getting a "Serving it Right" certificate if you want to serve alcohol. Put a photocopy of the card or certificate in your résumé. It doesn't take long and you do it online.

Congratulations, You Got the Job! Now you need to impress a lot of people: your new boss, your new coworkers, and the customers.

Why Your Appearance is Always Important

Always do your Make-up and Hair

As you get comfortable at your job and the longer you stay, over the years I've seen some coworkers get lazy and into the bad habit of not applying their make-up or doing their hair before coming to work. Customers don't want to see what you look like on your *day off*, no matter what shift you're working, be it a busy Friday or a slow Tuesday. Put your make-up on, do your hair, shave and be conscious of your cleanliness, and wear well put together clothing every single shift you work.

You're in an environment where you're constantly competing for attention against dancers, other hot servers, and "dolled up" female customers coming into the bar. You don't want to be known as the unkempt waiter or waitress.

Clothing

You're working in the serving industry, so pay special attention to your clothing. Obviously, you'll be told what the dress code is. Usually it's black skirt or pants, white blouse, black hose and shoes, unless you'll be given a uniform to wear. Don't show up to work with a dirty or rumpled looking shirt, or a baggy skirt that is two sizes too big for you. Never show up at work in jeans, no matter how nice they seem. There is nothing wrong with a nice, fitted, flattering low cut top showing great cleavage. Be proud of your looks. Dress for Success.

Treat Your Feet Like Gold

During the winter, black leggings with a skirt and flat heeled black boots are my comfort of choice. The leggings keep my legs warm, and the boots look stylish and sexy. I wear socks in all my boots because the socks keep my feet toasty; they also soak up the sweat and keep my boots from stinking.

As the season starts to change and the weather starts to warm up, keep cooler shoes ready to pull out at work. You'll notice that as you work your shift one day, your feet will start to swell, hurt, and feel overheated. If you're busy and running off your feet, now is the time for a change in footwear. Pulling off the boots, your calves will feel cooler and so will your feet. Pressure points will be changed and you feel that you can walk another ten miles with a change in footwear. If it wasn't for your feet, you wouldn't be able to work and make money, so treat them well!

If you're a woman who wears pantyhose, keep a couple extra pairs at work. It looks really tacky and unprofessional when a server has a big run or hole in them while she's working.

Years ago, we hired a server who would show up on a busy Friday afternoon in stripper shoes! She could barely walk and she struggled to keep balanced with her tray. I had mentioned to her that she should really get some comfortable shoes as she will have no toes left at the end of the week. She mentioned that they were *just for fun*. Not even an hour later she had changed her fun footwear to flip flops she had worn to work in the first place.

Nails

Nails are important as well. This is my weakness as I have horses I train during the summer, but during the winter months when I spend less time with them, I put fake nails on. This is the time I'm showered with comments from guys on what beautiful nails I have. People see your hands when you set drinks down in front of them, give them change, shake their hand, and collect empties. Unfortunately for me, horses and long nails don't go well together.

Other Important Ways to Take Care of Yourself

Rest

Your presentation isn't the only thing you need to keep on top of. Make sure you get a good night's sleep because rest is important. It keeps you awake and energized, and your mental alertness is one hundred percent! Monitor the amount of time you spend in the socializing scene. After a shift, you can end up with coworkers at someone's house for after-work cocktails. Before you know it, the sun is coming up. I know because I've been there! It's easy to get caught up in the Bar Life. You party all night and sleep all day. For some, it just doesn't work. We have personal obligations to fulfill and chores that need to be done. Perhaps you still have another day job as most friends of mine who work in the bar have. Some people (myself included) get headaches or migraines if they don't get their eight hours of sleep.

As you get to know the job, you'll know which days are your busiest and make you the most money. In the past, I worked Friday nights and my shift was nine hours long. It was the best shift of the week as I started early in the afternoon and got the guys getting off work and coming in with their buddies before the weekend. I made some great money because the crowd was older, full of blue collar workers, and regulars were the main clientele during that time of the day. The shift switched gears to the dinner crowd and then the party room. I went home with stupid amounts of money in exchange for sore feet and shoulder/back aches. Often, I would dream of serving that night (the dreams were of me forgetting customer's orders or the bartender taking twenty minutes to get my drinks made for me ... all nightmares). So, I always made sure that before my shift, I didn't do anything too strenuous like doing loads of shopping or tons of errands. I basically hung out at home doing some light housework, reading, or watch TV. I kept my day pretty mellow as I liked to save my energy for work on that long, busy, money-making night. I also made it a point to wear my most comfortable boots, tops, and skirts. I liked to make sure that my hair wasn't falling into my eyes and I didn't have to keep sweeping it off my face, so it would be partially clipped back.

Be On Time

Years ago, we had a DJ who would show up for his shift at least forty-five minutes to an hour late, consistently. I was amazed that he had a job with us as long as he did. We were low on DJs, so there wasn't anyone to take over his shift at the time. Around the same time, I literally freaked out on a waitress who was always ten minutes late from relieving me from my shift so I could go home. I know I was making tips, but it got extremely exhausting. She would saunter into the room at the exact time I was to get off the floor, and then disappear for those ten minutes to sit on the toilet or re-apply her make-up.

23

Don't run into work with a couple minutes to spare. Arrive at least fifteen minutes early, which gives you ample amount of time to prepare for a shift. You'll have time to change your clothing, use the washroom, get your tray ready, collect your float, and talk to the other server you're relieving from her shift to ask her if anyone is cut off or of any problems in the day. Always be on time. You could be inconveniencing a coworker out of a break or going home on time. If you think you may be a few minutes late, call the bar and let them know.

Eating

Eat before going to work so you're not concentrating on your stomach grumbling and wondering when you're able to go on a break to eat. Bars ARE the service industry and if the bar is busy and packed, you may not be allowed to go on a break during your scheduled time. You are there to serve and sell. I've worked nine-hour shifts in the past without a break, because that's how busy the bar was.

If you're diabetic or need to eat, be prepared to eat on the run. Ask your boss where you could keep something to eat that is convenient but out of the way and let him know of your diabetes. Use your best judgment and don't order messy food like a cheeseburger or steak.

If you're new, don't start making demands about eating and needing a break. Go with the flow, and wait for the head waitress or boss to give you the okay to head off for your break.

Watch what you eat before a shift ... I'll say one word and that is gas. If you're gassy, Tums help settle a tummy, but there's not much you can do for the farts. One of my girlfriends would feel the pressure build and run into a big group of people (always "the non- tippers," she explained) and release the pressure, then briskly walked away. It was a good laugh for us and she felt it was kind of a payback to the non-tippers.

Cell Phones

Cell phones are a big part of almost everyone's life. Keep your cell phone in your purse and don't bring it near the bar. It's distracting and you will not be able to concentrate on your job if you're answering calls or if you keep reading and sending text messages. If you're checking your cell at the bar, you'll end up standing in the way of other servers trying to get to the till, and this is annoying to a server like me. I'm there to work and make money, not waste precious time on my cell phone. If the boss walks in and sees you on your cell, it doesn't look good. If customers see you on your phone while their drinks are empty, you might as well say good bye to any tips, and you may even make them so mad that they won't come back.

Same goes for the business line in the bar. Don't hand out your work number to friends. The only people that have my work number are my husband, my daughter, and my parents. They know that it is for emergency purposes only.

Tips to Become a Well-Rounded Server

As you get comfortable at your bar and you're learning all the ins and outs of cocktail waitressing, you'll want to learn more about this job.

Study your bartenders and ask questions when neither of you are very busy. When customers order drinks like Harvey Wallbangers or B52 shooters and you don't know what they contain, ask your bartender. The more information you know the better, because it could speed things up at the bar. One day, you could end up working with a new bartender who might not know what a Dirty Hooker shooter is, but you will.

About eight years ago, I went to the Dollar Store and picked up a recipe card holder and recipe cards. I spent a slow Tuesday dayshift writing out all our cocktails and shooters that we make in the bar. It is kept behind the bar, and when a new person works and doesn't know a recipe, help is close at hand. It has become a life saver more times than I can remember and is still used to this day. Don't feel threatened and feel like you need to memorize a trillion drinks if you buy a bartending recipe book. Most people order common drinks like screwdrivers, long islands, and beer anyways.

When customers ask me, "Could you please bring me four *pink caboose* shooters?" I'll ask what is in them and the response is usually, "I don't know, but they make them at the *Yippee Kiay Bar* down the street." A lot of people don't know that bartenders make up their own drinks and shots and throw a name at them. So, unless you know what's in it, you may be out of luck.

Learning to bartend comes in handy. If your bartender leaps over the bar to help the doorman break up a fight, you'll be able to grab your own drinks or help out customers standing in the line. I came into work one Tuesday dayshift and I had no bartender for the first hour of my shift as he didn't know he was on the schedule. I served and bartended by myself until help arrived.

Ask the bartender to show you how to change the keg and the boxes of syrup during slow times. Know where to get extra stock such as coffee filters, shot glasses, till tape, etc. Everything new you learn to do can help out a fellow coworker or a new person when they're busy and need help. It makes you more valuable as an employee.

Know what drinks to add your garnishes to. Lime or lemon twists will usually be added to drinks that contain alcohol such as rum, gin, vodka, and even tequila. Corona bottles should have a lime twist popped into the mouth as well. Some customers will specifically let you know, "No twist" if they don't want it.

Being the low man on the totem pole (the new server), you may be required to fill in the "not so popular shifts." You'll have to be pretty flexible in taking what's available and needs filling in. This may mean weekends, late evenings, or long weekends. Coworkers may need their shifts covered for concerts, holidays, or some short-notice event, so offer to cover for them. This is a good way of winning their friendship and you may need a favor in return some day. As my dad says, "You scratch my back, and I'll scratch yours!"

At my bar I waited around for four years to get full-time serving hours before someone quit. I served food, was a shooter girl, and was a beer barrel girl; I was a jack of all trades in the bar industry.

I will tell you one important tidbit ... if a bar has a slow turnover of servers (meaning that some of the girls have been working there for a number of years), it's a good possibility that it is a very good place to work at. The clientele, staff, and money must all be good! That is why I hung in there as long as I did to wait for full-time serving shifts, and I'm glad I did.

Be Known for Your Excellent Service WHILE Playing the Game!

A sociable and friendly server that gets you a drink in record time ... it couldn't get any better than that! How could you not be a customer's favorite?

I have talked to endless customers about what rates high on a customer's list of their favorite server; most say it's a server's personality. They feel *at home* when they are greeted by a cheerful person. They like to receive a smile and be asked how their day is going. Sure, they love a pretty girl to look at, but if the server doesn't enjoy people and it shows through their personality, they won't make much money and they won't last long in the business. This rings true for male servers as well.

I've been told over the years from many of my regulars, if I ever decide to leave the bar, they want to know because they would follow me to the new bar I work at. I couldn't ask for a nicer compliment! I wonder what they would do if I went to work in a non-strip bar environment?

I'm flattered when regulars ask which section I'm serving and they go to the trouble of cramming themselves at the only available table in my area that is too small for their party. They drag chairs over from around the room.

I've had an old manager from many years ago tell me that he was in another bar forty-five minutes away and my name came up within the group. They were talking about "the awesome service from Romana" they get when they come to my bar.

I've even had owners and managers of other bars (one as far as an hour away) offer me a job at their establishment. I'm a firm believer in staying loyal to a company, unless I'm extremely unhappy there or not treated fairly. The grass is *not* always greener on the other side, so don't get in the habit of jumping ship and moving from bar to bar. Every time you start at a new place of work, you start at the bottom of the ladder and must work your way up. Seniority is KING in business.

It's not IF you will get hit on while working in a club or strip bar, but WHEN. It's a fact and you can't get around it. So, if you want to make a lot of money in this industry, it helps if you play the game. *Playing the game* means that you go along and flirt with the guys that hit on you, so they'll give you that tip. Your voice may raise an octave or two and you find yourself giggling over some really bad jokes that don't even make sense. If it makes the customer feel special, then what is the harm in that? Everyone has a different reason for being in the bar. I love my regulars who all know I'm married. We do some harmless flirting, a hug ... and that's as far as it goes. My wedding ring is my security blanket. All I have to do is show some Romeo my left hand and he backs off.

If you get hit on all the time and told you're beautiful, you should feel flattered because guys find you attractive. If you get mad or your boyfriend has a problem with this, maybe you shouldn't be serving in a strip bar or a nightclub. Sex sells, especially in this business, and that is why we make good money in tips. Isn't that the reason why we're there in the first place?

"Ro, how does Rod handle you working in a strip bar?"

This is a common question that most people ask me quite often. On more than one occasion, I've had young shooter girls complain to me about how their boyfriends hate them working in this environment and what should they do about it? Not much, I'm afraid. Either keep fighting with him about it until he figures out that you're there to make money and not going to pick up strange men, quit the job, or dump him.

Some girls have had the problem of their man coming to work and sitting there staring at them through the course of their shift where they have a hard time concentrating on their job because it makes them uneasy.

I'm married to a smart man who understands what it takes to make money in this business.

The Nevers and the Always

The Nevers...

Never tell patrons your problems. Everyone has their own problems to deal with, and customers want to have a good time and forget their own troubles.

Never argue with customers. If there's a problem, settle it. If it's something silly such as the regular saying that the draft beer tastes off, replace it with another. It could be the end of a keg. NEVER argue with a beer drinker! I've been told this piece of advice years ago by a senior server.

Never bad mouth staff. Don't agree with customers if they start telling you that "So and so is a really shitty waitress and needs to get fired." Instead, stick up for her because she may be having a bad day.

28

Never argue with a coworker in the bar. Take it to the staff room and iron out the problem. This is a fun place for customers to hang out and they don't want to see this.

Never discuss memos or problems you have with the bar to customers. It is extremely unprofessional.

Never interrupt your bartender or another server if they're in the middle of talking. I'm embarrassed to admit that I do this now and then.

Never pick and choose serving your customers. Years ago we had a server that would avoid certain tables or customers because the people were too rowdy, were too creepy, had too many women, made her too nervous, so on and so forth. Serve everyone and give them a chance.

Never walk up to a table to take an order while eating. People don't want to see you with a mouthful of chicken wings. It is rude and unprofessional.

Never interrupt people at the bar. One of my coworkers will always ask, "May I speak?" It's a polite habit to have as I will be memorizing a large order of drinks and trying to punch them into the till in order and I can't have anyone talking to me for twenty seconds or more. If I don't respond, I'll hold my hand up or shake my head and she'll wait until I'm done. (Thanks K!)

The Always...

Always stay positive.

Instead of complaining and saying, "Oh man, it's so dead!" it sounds better and more positive if you say, "It's not as busy as we'd like it to be."

Always use your manners! Use "Please," "Thank you," "You're welcome." Use your manners whether you receive a tip or not.

Always say "Have a great weekend," "Enjoy the rest of your day," or "See you next week," when your customers leave for the day.

Always greet customers with a smile when you arrive at their table. Say something like, "Hi everyone! How's your night going? What can I get for you guys?" Say it with enthusiasm.

Always walk over to a table that is flagging you down, even if they're in another server's section. If the room is busy, take the order. Either their server is not paying attention to them or she's busy.

Most important Always ... Every single server is *always replaceable*. There is always another girl or guy standing behind you waiting to take your job!

Your Personal Conduct While Off Duty

My husband said that my job (in a minor sort of way) is in the public eye. I notice it when I have customers comment to me, "I saw you on Sunday afternoon shopping in London Drugs. That must've been your daughter that you were with, right?" Or, "How was your dinner at the Keg last weekend? I presume that was your husband that you were dining with." I feel like my outside life lacks a bit of privacy at times.

So, while you're going on with your daily life, conduct yourself in a mature manner. This reflects on your place of work and yourself. I'm not saying that you have to wear make-up and be all dolled up when you're out shopping for groceries, but be aware of your actions. If you're out drinking at another club, I'm sure you'll hear all about it if you decide to enter the wet t-shirt contest, decide to pee out in the parking lot, or end up puking all over the bar.

Romana's Story... "The Romantic Getaway"

About twelve years ago, Rod had planned a romantic getaway at a fancy hotel for the two of us on a long weekend. It was only an hour drive away from home and our pretty room looked out onto the beautiful lake. The weekend was pretty rainy, so we weren't able to do as much walking as we'd like to around the quaint little town.

Our first evening there, we got all dressed up and went down to the dining hall to have some dinner and do some dancing. The dining room was pretty busy, so they sat us at a table stuck behind a post where we didn't have a very nice view of the dance floor. We understood because they were very busy. What got our panties in a knot was the waiter. He barely uttered a "Hello" and hovered like a vulture over the table of twelve situated next to us. Rod's water glass was empty and I wanted another margarita. We were very disappointed in the service

30

and remarked how we probably would've left him a better tip than the party of twelve would leave him if we got great service because I always tip more than expected. We didn't bother with dancing, as we were upset with the way our evening went anyways.

The next evening, we had left the hotel to go eat and watched a movie at the theatre in town. Coming back late, we decided it would be fun to get dressed up and go hang out in the piano bar to have a few drinks. We strolled into the lounge and saw that the bartender and waitress were playing cards together at the bar. We noticed that we were the only customers in the bar as we sat down and waited for almost five minutes, wondering if the server was going to come over and ask us for our drink order. She didn't even make a move to crawl off her bar stool, so Rod walked up to the bar and bought our drinks. We were absolutely stunned. I guess she didn't want to make any money that night, and we weren't surprised that the place was dead.

Our last day there, we hung around our room all day watching movies and ordering room service. That was the highlight of the weekend.

When we got home, I was tempted to write a letter to the management on how rude the staff was and the service being pathetic. I guess I just didn't want to waste my time, as we had decided then and there that we would never return anyway.

I was told the place had changed ownership and the service and staff is quite good now. Maybe one day we will go back and try again ...

Romana's Story... "I'll Sell You an ID"

I found out some really interesting information from a customer not too long ago. It was a little side scam that probably made someone some pretty good money.

This guy had asked me if I remembered a certain waitress we used to have many years ago.

I told him I did and then I asked him, "Why?"

He said that when he was underage, she had approached him with a driver's license she had found at the bar and told him that if he gave her $50.00, she would give it to him. From what he said, she approached many underage people whenever she found a driver's license.

I guess it is a pretty good way of making some side money, as long as you could live with yourself doing it.

The Essential Aspects of Your Safety at Work as Well as Leaving

You're in the public eye and mingle with many different people when you serve. You listen to your customer's stories and feel like you know their wives or kids after hearing about them a lot. Sometimes you don't even know that they're married, because they have never mentioned a family, and with the subtle ways they hit on you, you've always thought that they were single; there is also no hint of a wedding ring on their finger.

The bar brings out all types of people, so you've got to be able to keep a lookout for the creepers and the stalkers.

To check out one of my creepy stalker stories, please refer to **Chapter #6, Subchapter #2 under "The Creep and the Player."**

Some Basic Safety "Don'ts"

• **Don't** get in the habit of telling too many people exactly where you live, especially customers. It's not safe.

• **Don't** get in the habit of telling customers that you'll be out of town, especially if you've told them where you live.

• **Don't** get into the habit of taking off with customers and partying with them after work. If you're dying to get to know the hot guy in the group, get into your own vehicle and meet them at the destination, preferably another bar or somewhere where there are lots of people. Bring a friend if you can and don't go to a house.

• **Don't** hand out your phone number to people like it's no big deal. I'm not saying that every person that walks into the bar is trouble and out to get you, you just want to stay safe and have some degree of privacy. I have friends and coworkers that met their partners in the bar and they are still happily together.

• **Don't** break up fights. Alcohol and testosterone is a recipe for a fight. Working in the bar, you will witness many of these. Years ago, we had a tiny shooter girl that would jump in and try to break up fights. We would get mad at her for getting involved and try to talk the guys out of the argument, as she stood there in her bikini. Guys will not listen to reason. If they're furious, watch out because fists will fly, and you will get bowled over in the process! If you notice that a couple of guys or a group start yelling at each other or you sense trouble brewing, let the doorman or bartender know immediately. They'll have to diffuse the argument, hopefully before it blows up into a fist fight. If a fight breaks out, get out of the way and yell for the doorman, DJ, and bartender. It'll take a few guys to drag these troublemakers outdoors. Do not leave the room and follow the group outside. There should always be a few staff members that stay indoors to keep an eye on the room and the tills. Keep serving your drinks and try to keep some sort of normalcy in the room. A fight always seems to make people nervous and you'll find that it'll clear out most of the room anyways.

- **Don't** wear flip flops in the bar. You could end up with glass in your foot if a glass or bottle breaks. If a bottle or something else slips off your tray, it could land on your foot. Wear footwear that covers your heel and toes. This is a Worker's Compensation Regulation.
- **Don't** throw or smash empty bottles into cases. Pieces of glass could end up flying out and end up in your eye.
- **Don't** be too trusting and believe all business cards. Anyone can get a business card made up. While people like to network and build their business, be wary about getting involved with people that approach you with their business at your place of work. I've had guys handing out their cards to dancers and staff at my bar saying that he's an agent that could get them modeling work or work in the porn industry.

I knew a guy years ago that had professional-looking business cards made up that said that he was a *Playboy* scout. Of course he wasn't, but it was his way of getting together with many young, gullible girls. I couldn't believe all the screaming girls that came running after our limo one night, as he would crack the windows a bit and hand out the business cards.

Getting to your Car SAFELY

I'm lucky that our parking lot is just outside our front doors and fortunate that I always seem to end up parking near them.

33

Regardless, I am always careful when I walk out to my car. If I feel uneasy or something just isn't right, I return inside and ask a coworker to escort me to my car. It pays to be extra careful and always listen to your gut. You don't want to end up in a bad situation because you're in a rush to get home. If I have items I need to bring home in the evening, I make sure to put them all in one bag so I'm not juggling and struggling with a whole bunch of stuff while trying to make it out safely to my vehicle.

A small tool like a compact flashlight could be used to defend your life. The bright light shuts down the attacker's iris, giving him a blind spot, and this gives you a chance to get away if you were to flash it in the eyes quickly. Although tasers and flashlights may be helpful, they are also tangible items that must be carried and could fail to work if they short-circuit or if the batteries die. Having awareness, knowledge, and a focused mind are most important as the goal is to get away, not fight. Give up any property like your purse or wallet as it's not worth your life.

If you work downtown and have to get to your car after hours in a parkade or parking lot, ALWAYS have someone escort you. You want to keep yourself from becoming a target. Stay off streets that are deserted and have no traffic or people traveling on foot. If your car is quite a ways away, pay for a taxi to drive you there. It's a small price to pay for your safety.

If you have no choice but to walk to your vehicle, before you leave the building, change your clothing into something that doesn't attract attention to yourself and remove or hide costume jewelry. Hide the hot, tight skirt and cute shoes in a bag and put on track pants. Walk in sneakers as they are more comfortable and perfect for running if you need to. Slip on a big coat to hide your figure.

Don't wear your hair in a ponytail as an attacker would have a firm grip on your hair if he were to grab you from behind. Better yet, put on a cap or hat. It's better to look like a bum than a hot bombshell.

Hold an individual key in your hand and have it ready to jab at anyone if they were to jump on you. If you carry a purse, strap it on you under your coat; out of sight, out of mind. If you must carry a bag, hold it in the hand opposite the street. Walk near the curb, away from doorways and shrubbery, unless there are vehicles parked along the road. Never assume that all parked vehicles are empty.

If you suspect that you may be followed, cross the street and do not duck into dark alleys or a building. You want to stay out in the open where you can be seen.

If you think that a vehicle might be following you, turn in the opposite direction and continue walking. Get the license plate number and write it on the back of your hand or even on the sidewalk (a lipstick will work).

Walk with a purpose in your step and keep an eye out for anyone approaching you. If someone were walking towards you, look them in the eye and hold eye contact as they pass. You will look confident and powerful with this attitude, and you are less likely to be messed with.

As you near your car, peek in the front and backseat to make sure nobody is crouched and hiding inside. Slip inside and immediately lock your doors.

If you find a van parked next to your car, enter your car through the passenger side. Serial killers pull women into their vans while their victim is getting into their car. Ted Bundy, the serial killer, was well educated and good looking. He played on the sympathies of unsuspecting women by walking with a limp and a cane, and by asking his victims for help into his car.

What to Do In Case of an Attack

In case of an attack, do everything in your power to get away and out of his grip. Scream, hit, kick, and scratch like a cat. Don't back down and reason, cry, plead, or try to buy yourself out of a situation. Don't let yourself be pulled into a vehicle, into a building, or around a building. Stay where others can see you and drop to the ground if you have to in order to keep him from hauling you away.

If the attacker says to you, "If you scream, I'll kill you," do the opposite and start screaming. You want to create chaos and ruin his plans. I put my daughter into a kid's safety course when she was very young and they taught the youngsters to scream the word "FIRE!" instead of "HELP." I learned that people respond to *fire* more than *help* if anyone were to hear you.

Don't hesitate to use your elbows to defend yourself, as they are the strongest bones in the body. Kick the attacker in the groin or knees, or go for his eyes with your fingers or a car key. You are fighting for your life and you have one chance to do it, so don't panic—aim and hit hard!

If you have a bag or purse in your hand, swing it with all your might and hit him as hard as you can. If your attacker were to choke you out or get your hands tied, it is unlikely that you will make it out of this situation alive. If he asks for your wallet or purse, don't hand it to him. Throw it away from you and then run in the opposite direction. He'll be more interested in your purse or wallet than you.

If you get into your vehicle and find someone pointing a gun at your head, do NOT drive off if he asks you. Slam the gas pedal with your foot and smash the car into anything. Your airbag will protect you and as soon as the car comes to a stop, jump out and run. He will get the worst of it.

If the creep has a gun and doesn't have a hold on you, run in a zig-zag pattern.

Some Self Defense Moves

Although the following are moves that may help if an attacker gets hold of you, do yourself a big favor and invest the time and money to take a self defense course to learn the proper techniques from a professional. Practice of this kind is needed so that you get your body used to how quickly it needs to react in an attack and with what amount of force. One day it may come in handy and could save your life.

• Clap/smack your hands against the attacker's ears hard and quickly! It can cause him enough pain to release you and give you a chance to run!

• Karate-chop him in the throat.

• Gouge his eyes with your fingers. This move can be done if the attacker surprises you from behind. Pull your arms up and over your head and behind you.

• If you're attacked from behind, spin around and strike with your fist into the pelvis (below the stomach and hip bone). If you hit hard enough, it can be fractured as it is a very vulnerable area.

• If you're attacked at close range, like a stairwell, pull the attacker closer to you so that you can reach with your thumb, middle finger, and index finger and squeeze his throat (trachea). This can cause damage, so only do this move in the event of an emergency.

- Look into learning Krav-maga. This is a fighting style that can be picked up very fast. It teaches you to hit an attacker in vulnerable areas whether you are smaller in size than him or you are outnumbered.
- I've heard Bas Rutten, the MMA fighter, comment that if you find yourself in a bad situation where you've got a drunken person who tries swinging at you, bend over quickly and pull his legs out from under him. Alcohol dulls a person's senses where his thinking is slowed down and this will give you time to get away. A woman may have more trouble than a man with this move as she does have less strength.

A note about car alarms...

You can ask to see if it is a possibility to have your car alarm programmed so that when you press the button on your wireless remote once, it will unlock the driver's door only. Pressed twice, it will unlock all four. Rod informed me that the newer Toyota vehicles have this feature, but some of the after-market alarms MAY have it as well. This is a great feature to have when you need to quickly and safely slip into your vehicle at any time of the day without anyone surprising you by hopping into any one of the other doors.

Some alarms have a "Panic" button on the wireless remote. Pressed once, it turns the car alarm on. It is another great feature to have if you want to bring attention upon yourself or your vehicle. If someone were to jump on you by your car, the button is pressed and it startles your attacker and may give you or him a chance to flee. To turn the alarm off, press unlock.

Your Safety While Driving Home After a Shift

Driving home is another thing to be aware of. Always be aware of anyone following you, whether you just finished a day- or nightshift. Some people are mentally unstable as you will find from reading the various stories throughout my book. I have been lucky through all my years of working at the bar; I haven't encountered too many problems, but I am aware of the possibilities every time I drive home. Once someone knows where I live, I would be very uncomfortable for the safety and invasion of privacy for my family and myself.

If you drive home late at night, try to get into the habit of stopping to fill up on gas during daylight instead of late at night. Make sure your vehicle is in good working order by keeping up with regular oil changes and tune ups.

Keep your car in gear as you wait at red lights. If you feel threatened, hit the horn and as soon as it is safe, drive away.

If you know that you are being followed by someone in another vehicle, do not drive home. Write down the license plate number if you can and drive to the police station or an open business where there are people. If you have a cell phone, call the police while you're driving.

If you happen to get into an accident on your drive home late at night, do not get out of your car unless the area is lit up and other people are there! I've heard of stories where a vehicle "bumps" into another one, the victim jumps out to survey the damage to her car, and she gets attacked. Stay in your vehicle with the doors locked and call the police. If your cell phone is dead, crack your window open and ask the other party to call the police. Rather be safe than sorry!

Romana's Story... Follow the Leader

Many years ago, two of our servers called a taxi cab and needed a ride home, which was about forty minutes away. As they got closer to their destination, the cabbie told them that a car had been following them from the bar. They told the cabbie to just keep driving and they were able to lose whoever was following.

Romana's Story... "Don't Ever do that Again!"

Years ago, I had a little red Suzuki Forsa. It was a standard, great on gas, an awesome little car that I could cruise around in, and it went like stink!

One summer day, after I finished my dayshift, I was itching to get the hell out of work and go home. I zipped out onto the main street and passed a couple of cars, my mind focused on wanting to get home. I ended up on the street running parallel to the street my work is on and as I was cruising along, a big, white 4x4 truck sped up past me, swerved into my lane in front of me and slammed his breaks on, basically cutting me off. I was a little startled and figured that obviously this guy was upset at me. I slowed my car down and hung back, letting him go ahead of me.

We drove along for almost seven minutes and as I was nearing my street I slowed down and wanted to make a sharp turn to the right without him noticing. As I whipped the car around the corner, he slammed his breaks on and I noticed the back end of his truck swerving side to side and skidding to a stop. I panicked and drove right past my house as I didn't want this nut knowing where I lived. I grabbed for my cell phone and was ready to dial Rod when I saw the truck come straight towards me in my lane! I slowed down and eventually stopped (I panicked and froze) and then he slowly drove beside me. Both our windows were wide open. He had big dark sunglasses, a moustache, and curly, black, wild-looking hair.

He looked down at me, saw the cell phone in my hand, and said, "Don't EVER f-----g do that again!"

I'm sure my eyes were as big as saucers as I said, "What did I do? I apologize for whatever I did!"

He repeated the phrase and then drove away.

After he left, I broke down in tears and drove home. I was terrified of big, white 4x4 trucks for over a year after that.

Server Sign Language

Why Is Sign Language Important?

I love sign language at work. It saves my voice during a shift and I don't have to interrupt a group while someone is talking. If I know what a group is drinking, it keeps me from walking over to them; therefore, I'm saving time.

Here are a few of my favorites that work great!

Some Basic Sign Language Signals

When walking by a table and you make eye contact with a customer ...

"Another Round?"

Put your finger up and twirl it up in the air, raise your eyebrows and nod your head yes. This signifies, "Would you like another round of drinks at your table?"

Customer means **yes**- if they nod their head yes, or repeat the finger twirl.

Customer means **no**- if they shake their head no, or hands wave almost like a windshield wiper move.

"More Drinks?"

Put two fingers up (three, four, or five), raise your eyebrows and nod your head yes. This signifies, "Would you like two (three, four, or five) more drinks?"

Customer means **yes**- if they nod their head yes or put up the number of fingers noting the number of drinks wanted.

Customer means **no**- if they shake their head no, or hands wave almost like a windshield wiper move.

"Your Usual?"

If a regular customer walks in and sits down, I'll wave at him. He'll wave back as a response. At this point I will raise my eyebrows and hold one finger up. This signifies I will bring your usual.

Customer means **yes**- if he smiles and nods or puts one finger in the air.

Customer means **no**- if he waves you over to him (this is a time when I find that he would like a pop because he's on his way to a meeting, just had dental work, or is on some medication).

If regulars happen to change their drink choice that day, sometimes they will meet me at the till or on the way to their seat as soon as they walk in.

"Pint Please"

If it's one guy and he wants a pint of beer, he'll usually signal this to me by putting his hand in a fist and hold it with the thumb side up, heel end of hand down (like he's holding a make believe pint of beer in his hand).

If it's one guy and he wants more than one pint, he'll signal as above and with the other hand, he'll hold up the number of fingers signifying the number of pints wanted. Perhaps he has a friend or two arriving at any moment.

"The Usual for Everyone?"

If it's a table full of regulars that just sat down, I'll say my "Hello" and I'll make eye contact with everyone and say, "The usual for everyone?" I have everybody's drink memorized and know what to bring without asking.

All customers mean **yes**- if they all smile and nod. Any customer wanting a change of drink will speak up and let me know of their choice.

"A Jug of Beer?"

If a group of guys sit down and want a jug of beer, one person will signal to me by looking like he's putting his hands on the top and bottom of an imaginary cylinder. Then he'll put the number of fingers up signifying the number of empty glasses, and mouth the word "glasses."

Another way customers signal a jug is by pointing at the jug on the table next to them and one guy will put the number of fingers up signifying the number of empty glasses.

"Double it Up"

If someone is drinking a single cocktail, and they want a double on their next round, they will hold their drink up, point to their drink or hold their finger up and mouth the word, "double."

"Thank You!"

When a customer is handing over money for drinks or a tip, I will mouth "Thank you" as long as we have eye contact so I can save my voice.

"Bring the Bill, Please!"

There are a few different ways that a customer will signal to me for their bill. A few are as follows:

• The customer will take their hand and make a big check mark in the air (like when your teacher in grade school would mark your exams with a check or an X).

- The customer will hold one hand out flat and use the other hand to look like they're writing on the flat hand.
- The customer will take their thumb, index (pointing) finger, and middle finger and rub them together in air.

In response, don't just walk away. Make sure you nod and acknowledge them. They may have a taxi waiting for them outside or they're in a rush to leave ASAP.

"Good Bye!"
A smile and a wave, while mouthing "Thank you," is nice to do when your customers are leaving.

Learn to read lips. Customers may want to change their drink order from a single to a double, or a double to a single. They may not be able to yell loudly enough above the music for you to hear.

Romana's Story... "The Blind Man and the Deaf Man"

Sign language is great to know when the music is loud and you have a hard time hearing. If you don't make the effort to understand it, you end up relying on your vocal chords all the time. You'll end up with a hoarse and painful throat.

I had a deaf customer visit our bar at one time. I was actually very lucky as he had a notepad, pencil, and very nice penmanship, so we were able to communicate quite easily. Lip reading works wonders too.

Now, what about a customer that is blind? I know what you're thinking ... Why would a blind person come into a strip bar? Well, he does come in on our UFC nights with a lady friend. He can hear the TV and sometimes they order dinner.

With blind people, I'm obviously more vocal. As I arrive at the table and set his drink down, I will say, "There you go Honey. Your iced tea is $4.25 please."

Years ago, I had an older blind gentleman come into the bar carrying a white cane. I asked if I could be of assistance and he said he was fine on his own. I brought him a drink and a short time later he asked me if someone could escort him to the restroom. He said that with the initial help to the restroom, he was able to memorize and count his steps backwards to find his chair when he returned. It was pretty neat. He enjoyed having a beer and listening to the music.

I think it's pretty cool that all people can come into the bar and find some enjoyment, whether it's just relaxing and listening to the music or watching the entertainment.

"What do you have on tap?"
"Budweiser, Canadian and MGD"
"Ok, we'll get a jug of Kokanee"

Chapter 2 – SELLING

Bar Lingo / Terminology

This is basic bar terminology used by almost everyone in the bar industry. Different bars may have other terms they use, so get to know your own bar's terminology. This makes life easier for all.

Drinks

Cocktail	A liquor and juice mix e.g., Vodka cranberry Screwdriver (vodka orange juice)
Hi Ball	Cheap liquor (usually off the gun) served with a soft drink or water e.g., Vodka water Rum coke Gin tonic
Keg	The beer companies sell big, round, metal containers full of draft beer. Our kegs hold approximately 59 Liters
Mix	The pops and juices available to add to a drink. They can be on the gun or out of a can or tetra pack
On the Gun	Cheap (house) liquor on the gun. This is metered and pours a full ounce at the press of a button

Pint/Mug of beer	A pint of beer poured out of the tap
Premium Liquor	Higher end liquor poured out of the bottle (not put on the gun)
Sleeve	A sleeve of beer poured out of the tap. It is slightly less than a pint
Tap	Draft beer poured into a glass or mug once the handle is pulled to open it

Drink Ordering Terms

Bloody Caesar	A Caesar made with tomato juice, instead of the usual clamato juice
Clam Eye	A pint of beer with clamato juice
Coke Back *Water Back*	The liquor is poured over ice and the mix will be put on the side in a separate glass. The customer adds the amount of mix depending on the strength they like e.g., "Vodka over, coke back" "Rye over, water back"
Cubra Libra *Rum coke with a* *twist*	This means, a rum coke with a twist of lime. I find that the only people that still use this term are men in their late sixties e.g., "Cubra Libra"

Dark and dirty	A dark rum and coke
Double dark and dirty	A double dark rum and coke
Easy Ice	A drink with few ice cubes
Extra Ice	A drink loaded with ice cubes
Extra Old Stock (Molson's Beer)	Customers may ask for this brand by using the term *High-Test* or *Black Label*
Frosty	A mug/pint glass that is kept in the cooler to keep it cold and frosty. (A&W does the same thing to their mugs)
Lime Cordial	Lime juice off the gun that some people add to their beer
Neat *No Ice* *Hold the Ice*	A drink with no ice e.g., "Rum coke neat" "Rum coke, no ice" " Rum coke. Hold the ice"
On the Rocks *Over*	A liquor on ice, with no mix. This is a single shot, unless otherwise specified that the customer wants a double or triple shot e.g., "Vodka on the rocks" "Vodka over"
Press	A drink with a shot of water (the water dilutes the drink) e.g., "Rye coke press"

Wine Spritzer	A glass of red wine poured into a beer glass with half 7-Up and half soda water. Some people prefer ice where others don't. This drink has a stronger, drier taste
Red Eye	A pint of beer with tomato juice
Round	An additional same drink to everyone at the table

                e.g.,   "We'll grab another round"

Set-Up *Mug of Ice* *With*	A mug of ice that is served alongside a cider or cooler

                e.g.,   "Pear cider with a set-up"

                                      "Apple cider with a mug of ice"

                                      "Peach cider with"

Shandy	A pint with half 7-Up or ginger ale and the rest is draft beer
Straight Up	A liquor poured in a short glass with no ice and no mix

                e.g.,   "A double shot of Grey Goose vodka straight up"

With a Twist	A drink served with a piece of lime or lemon (whatever your bar carries)

                e.g.,   "Vodka water with a twist"

Other Bar Terminology

Barred	A person not allowed to enter and be served in the establishment. Usually due to causing trouble such as fighting, harassing staff, etc e.g., "John Doe is barred"
Blue Collar Workers	People that work with their hands e.g., Tradesmen: Mechanics, Landscapers, Roofers, Construction Workers, Plumbers ...
Cash and Carry	When a server collects money for drinks as soon as they're delivered to a table. The opposite of running a tab
Change the Keg *Tap the Keg*	When the keg runs out and a full one needs to be connected
Chiseler *Stiff*	A person who hasn't left a tip for the server or bartender
Colors	A gang's name or emblem on a jacket, vest or t-shirt e.g., Hells Angels
Cut Off	A person that is not to be served any longer, usually due to intoxication e.g., "That guy is cut off"
DD	DD stands for designated driver. This person is responsible for driving his

	group of friends home safely and consumes no alcohol
Float	Money that's borrowed from the bar to use as change given to your customers when you deliver their drinks. It's returned to the bartender once you've earned the money back during your shift
Gratuity	Also known as a Tip
Gyno *Gyno Row* *Stage*	This stands for *gynecology row*. It is seating that is situated at the stage where the guys are close enough to talk to the dancer
Head-Hunting	Stealing employees from another establishment (your competition)
ID	It means *identification*
Padding a Tab	Charging a customer for drinks on his tab that he didn't order and the server pockets the money
Promo	This is short for *promotion*. It is a free drink given to a customer that the bar pays for e.g., "Please promo a pint for Jim"
Regulars	These are the same customers you see every day. You recognize them and you know their names or what they drink

Skimming	An employee stealing money out of the till
Slammed	The bar becomes very busy, very quickly; high energy
Straw Test	This is where you take a straw and slip it into a drink. You cover the end with your finger and bring the straw to your lips with your finger still covering the end. Once you put the straw into your mouth, take your finger off the end and the liquid will fall into your mouth. Voila! An easy way to have a taste without putting your germs into a drink
Tab *Open a Tab* *Start a Tab* *Keep a Tab Running*	You keep track of all drinks ordered by a customer and give them a bill when they're ready to leave. They pay in one lump sum, instead of every time you drop a drink off. Opposite of cash and carry
Waitress Apron	A black apron that a server wears to store pens, visa and interac slips, big bills, etc. This is usually used if there are no waitress boxes available
Waitress Box	A lockable box bolted under the counter and used by a server for dropping any extra money, big bills, or visa or interac slips for safe keeping. The box has the server's name on it and there's a slit to slip money inside

Waitress Section	A section of tables that a waitress is responsible for during her shift
Waitress Station	The area around the bar where the servers' till is located, the servers empty and load their trays, and the servers keep their tabs
White Collar Workers	People that are businessmen
Suits	e.g., Lawyers, Doctors, Stockbrokers, Investors ...

Sales Strategies

A sales strategy is to up-sell a drink. This means to make a bigger sale. Big sales look good to the boss and they could possibly mean a bigger tip.

I will give you a few examples to help you learn the art of up-selling.

Examples of Up-Selling: Scenarios #1–3

#1 "Gin Tonic?"

Patron asks the server, "Could I please have a gin tonic?"

Server replies with, "Would you like Bombay?"
Bombay is premium liquor, therefore more expensive.
Patron will usually answer, "Sure."

Server finishes up with, "Should we double it?"
In my experience, I would say that about half the time, the customer will say "Yes."

#2 "Glass of Beer?"

Patron asks the server, "Could I please have a glass of beer?"

54

Server replies with, "A pint is a better deal today at $5.75. A glass is $4.35."

In my experience, most of the time the patron will change his mind and go for the pint.

#3 "A Round of Shots?"

Patron says to the server, "It's my buddy's birthday and we'd like a round of shots. Any suggestions on a good shooter?"

Server says, "How about jager bombs?"

A jager bomb is a drop shot. It's a shot of Jagermeister and you drop it in a glass with Red Bull (or another brand of energy drink).

Jager bombs in our bar are a little over $2.00 more expensive than a regular shooter. It does take up quite a bit of room on your tray as you carry the shot and a tall glass with the small amount of energy drink. The shooter glass is dropped into the tall glass.

Re-Selling Drinks

During the course of the night, you may have gotten busy and decided to start taking out extra beers just to keep up to the volume of customers entering the room. As drink orders are caught up, you may have ended up with a few open beers that are left unsold on your tray.

I like to swing around the room a few times and, if I haven't sold them by this point, I'll give them to my bartender to put on ice for me because I don't want the beers to be warm when I sell them.

If I gave him three Budweiser bottles, I'll write a reminder for myself, *IN 3 BUD*. I don't want to forget because they were rung into the till under my number, and if I don't sell them, I'll be out that money. As soon as I get an order for Budweiser bottles, I remind my bartender that I have my beers on ice so I don't have to ring them in again.

How to Get Rid of Abandoned Drinks

Sometimes I'll get an order for a mixed drink and the customer disappears. I can either dump the drink (which I never do because then I'm out that money) or try and re-sell it.

I'll ask the other servers if anyone in their section is drinking the drink I need to get rid of. If I'm lucky and they just happen to need that drink, they pay me the money for the drink and take it away.

If a server can't help me out, I'll walk through the bar and ask if anyone wants to buy a crown ginger (or whatever drink it is that I'm trying to get rid of). If it looks like a lot of beer drinkers, I'll be asking the younger customers and all customers drinking mixed drinks.

Sometimes the bartender can help me out and pour it into a drink where a double is needed. This will only happen when a server orders it because he can't do this for a customer at his bar.

Lower the Price
I'll lower the price of the drink by a couple of dollars. It's better to get rid of the drink as quickly as you can because the longer you wait, the ice starts to melt and then you sell a watered down drink to someone who will complain that they can't taste the alcohol in it.

Remove the Ice
If I'm still having a problem getting rid of the drink and there's still plenty of time left in my shift, I'll bring the drink back to the bar. My bartender will strain the ice out and he'll set it aside for the next time someone orders that drink. I write myself a reminder, *IN C/R GING*. The next time a customer orders a crown ginger, he'll fill it with fresh ice and add a shot of ginger ale into it to bubble it up again.

Last Call: Final Chance to Sell All Open Drinks

When it's close to closing time, I'll collect any drinks that are sitting on ice or set aside, and try to re-sell them to customers again.

If the drink is normally $6.25, I'll make a deal just to get rid of it. I'll say, "Hey guys, anyone craving for a crown ginger? Someone just ordered it and left. Now I need to get rid of it. It normally goes for $6.25, but I'll give it to you for ONLY $5.00!" Some of the time, they'll give me the $5.00. And other times, they'll still leave me a tip, so I'm still making back all my money plus tip. I would rather lose out on a couple bucks, than lose out the entire price of the drink.

If it is last call, and you still have those pesky drinks on your tray that you still can't seem to sell, you still have a few options. You can either give them away to some good regulars that would appreciate it, drink them yourself after closing, or dump them down the sink. I have *always* gotten rid of my drinks. If I ever had to give them away, I would give them to either good regulars or the table that has been tipping me like crazy. They will remember this and I will have secured a tip for next time.

Romana's Story... "Take the Taste Test"

One of my regular customers drinks a Bombay gin and tonic in a short glass with a twist. This is his drink of choice and that is what he's been drinking for years.

One night while the bar was slammed, I dropped the drink off, only to be waved at by him to come back.

"Ro, this isn't Bombay," he said.

"Sure it is! That's what I always bring you. That's what I rang in," I assured him.

"Ro, I know the difference between cheap gin and premium gin," he argued back.

"Ok Honey, I'll be right back," I said as I grabbed the drink off the table and ran back to the bar.

I found out from my bartender that he had run out of Bombay gin and didn't have time to run into the back to grab another bottle, so he just poured the cheap stuff off the gun.

The bartender and I were both amazed that our regular could tell the difference between gins. Today, he is still the only person that I've run into that can pretty much tell the difference between the taste of cheap gin and premium gin.

Romana's Story... The $3,000.00 Challenge

It's always been something of a tradition for the servers at our bar to try and beat each others' sales. For years I worked on hitting the $3,000.00 mark as nobody in the history of working the busiest Friday nightshifts has ever done so. There were girls that got as high as $2,700.00, but I wanted to beat that number. I knew it was possible, and a bit of a challenge, but one night I finally did it! In the nine hours I worked, I hit $3,330.00 and I even sold over $200.00 in food. My manager brought out a bottle of wine at the end of the night to celebrate.

I can proudly say that I am the only one in history to hit $3,000.00, three times! I guess the number 3 is my lucky number.

Relevant Tips for Running Tabs

During the course of a shift, you may be asked to run tabs with several customers, so it's up to you as a server to pay for all drinks that were rung in during your shift to the bar. If someone were to leave on their bill, you will be responsible to pay for it.

The information that I'm about to provide for you about tabs relates to working in a bar where it's easy for customers to move around or even leave, such as a nightclub or strip bar environment. The servers who work in pubs or restaurants will also find much of this information is very valuable where possible dine and dashes occur.

Why do Customers Prefer to Run a Tab?

• It's more convenient as they don't have to go through the hassle of pulling out their wallet every time you deliver a drink. They don't want their wallet sitting on the table in plain view either.

• They don't want to be bothered tipping you every single time you make a drink delivery. They would prefer to leave one tip at the end.

• They want good service, knowing that you will be working your tail off to earn that tip.

Advantages of Running Tabs

You could be asked by every type of person to run a tab, so be prepared for the nineteen-year-old to the little old man. It would be the scruffiest of the clientele to the clean-cut businessman in a suit.

NEVER make assumptions on who will tip you. You may get an unexpected bigger tip from the youngest person and receive absolutely nothing from the businessman who wears the fancy suit and expensive gold watch!

Running tabs are great time savers. When a drink is ordered, you can drop it off without interrupting a customer while he's talking, and it also saves you time from standing there waiting for him to dig out money.

Running tabs can save you from losing money. When a drink is ordered and you drop it off, a customer may need to use the ATM machine if they have no cash on them. Other times, you may have to go back to that table for money, as the person who is supposed to pay is in the restroom or outside having a cigarette. When you're busy, you could forget to go back and collect your money, resulting in your ending up paying for that person's drink. Consider yourself lucky when a customer will be honest enough to remind you that he owes you money if you happen to forget.

Running tabs can make you a bigger tip. If the customer loves your service and personality, you may be left with an even more generous tip than if he were to pay for all his drinks separately.

Protect Yourself: Scenarios #1–8

There are several ways to make sure customers don't leave you with their bill. Below are some scenarios that I use to make judgment calls on running tabs with customers. The longer you are a server, you will learn to trust your instinct and make your own decisions on running tabs.

Scenario #1

Jim and Bob come into the bar. They're regulars and I know them by name and what they drink. They always run a tab and pay me cash before they leave for the night. I see them in the bar once every two weeks.

… I will not bother them and waste my time asking for a credit card as they have proved themselves in the past to be trustworthy by paying their tab before leaving.

Scenario #2

My Friday night crew of eight guys comes in and each guy runs a separate tab. I've known them for years. A new guy joins the group that I've never seen before today.

… I will not bother the new guy for a credit card. Someone in the group obviously invited him along. If I'm unsure, I whisper to one of the guys asking who he came with.

Scenario #3

Larry, Sam, and David come in. I've had problems with them taking off on their tabs in the past.

... If they're *bad boys* and tip extremely well, I run them a tab, but try to keep an eye on them in case they happen to leave. If they leave, they'll make it up to me with a big tip the next time they return.

... If they don't leave handsome tips, I tell them they have to leave me a credit card or some cash.

If they complain about it, I explain to them that I have to pay their bill when they leave and then have to wait for them to return to get my money owed to me. I also add that it's an inconvenience to me as I have my own bills to pay.

Scenario #4

Two young guys I don't recognize come in during the dayshift, order a jug, and ask me for food menus. They ask me if they can run a tab.

... I'll ask them if they'll be leaving the room to go outside for a cigarette at some point.

If they say YES, I tell them that I need a credit card to run a tab.

If they say NO, I'll say, "One guy has to sit in the room at all times. If you both need to leave the room, you'll have to give me a credit card to keep your tab open or pay your bill right away." This way they know that I expect one guy to stay in the room at all times.

Scenario #5

A young guy I don't recognize comes in during the nightshift. He orders a pint of beer and wants to run a tab.

... I tell him that I need a credit card to run a tab. I know he'll need to leave the room at some point to use the restroom. Night time can get busy and I don't have time to keep an eye on customers.

Scenario #6

Two older, well-dressed guys come in during the dayshift. They just want to have a few drinks. I ask if they will be leaving the room to have a cigarette at some point.

60

...If they say NO but leave the room anyways, leaving their cell phones and keys on the table, I don't panic. They will be back.

Scenario #7

A couple of guys come in during the dayshift, they order lunch and drinks. They say that they're only having a couple rounds and food and then they'll come up to the bar and pay their bill by debit. One guy runs out of the room answering his cell phone as the other guy gets up a few minutes later to go outside for a cigarette. (There are no coats, keys, or cell phones at the table).

... I stop the smoker and say, "Honey, could I please get a credit card before you leave the room? It's the bar's policy and I have been burned with a $130.00 tab that someone had left me with in the past."

Explanation: *Referring to him as HONEY is endearing; guys love getting called Honey from a girl they don't know. If you explain that it's the bar's policy, it puts the blame on the bar.*
The story about you being left with a $130.00 tab makes him feel sympathetic to your story (If you've never been left with a tab, LIE and tell people it's happened to you).

Scenario #8

A stag comes into the bar and all the guys in the group want to pay separately with cash.

... You tell the driver or the oldest and most responsible looking person, "Because it's a stag, it's the bar's policy that someone in the group must leave a credit card imprint at the bar. This way if there's any trouble or damage, management can contact your party."

Explanation: *The guy handing his credit card over will MAKE SURE that everyone is well behaved and nothing will get damaged in the bar.*

61

Other Important Rules to Running Tabs

There are still a couple ways to protect yourself if your customers are adamant about running tabs but they don't want to hand over their credit card, they forgot it at home, or they claim that they don't own one.

If they hand over a bank card, DO NOT TAKE IT! It doesn't help you if they disappear. This is what happened to me when I got left with that $130.00 tab I keep talking about. I even called the bank and the woman on the other end told me that all she could do was get a hold of the owner to let him know about the bill, and then she asked me why I didn't grab a credit card. The guy probably laughs to this day and got another bank card.

If the person hands you their bank card and driver's license, don't take it either. These don't pay the bill if they forget and leave. I don't take car keys, wallets, or promises to give me their first born. I want to see a credit card or cold, hard cash. This is your money and you're there to make it, not buy other people drinks and work for free.

1.   If the customer pulls out a stack of paper money to prove that they have cash to pay their bill, I respond with, "Honey, I can run you a tab if you give me some cash to hang onto."

I'm usually handed anywhere from $50.00 to $300.00, depending on the amount of drinking the customer and his friends plan on doing.

2.   I point to where the ATM machine is so that they can retrieve cash. If they don't want to get up right away because there's a naked girl on stage, I let them know that I'll collect when her show is over (and I write myself a quick note that he owes me money so I don't forget).

Sometimes, people don't want to use those little ATM machines standing in the corner of a room. They don't trust the security of it, they don't want to pay the high fees, or the machine is down and not working. Customers are very appreciative of the fact that I offer to swipe their debit card and help them take money out of the debit machine at the bar.

3.   Customers ask me if they can get cash back with their credit card. We're not really supposed to do this because of the credit card

fees and for security reasons as the card could be stolen. I do it if it helps out the customer, and as long as I know them. I let them know that I'm not supposed to be doing this, so they will not expect it every time they come into the bar.

If someone you don't know hands you a credit card to run them a tab, it's a good idea to ask them for identification. If the name and signature match, that person should be the rightful owner.

Some customers have commented to me, "Why should I trust you with my credit card?"

I'll respond with, "Why should I trust you not to leave on your tab? I've been working here for fifteen years and I have never lost a credit card. Besides, if you leave, I'm stuck paying your bill."

Many people have this misconception that if a bill were left unpaid, the bar takes it over and pays for it. WRONG! The server is responsible for it. Not everyone is a scammer and leaves you with his bill on purpose. Some people have a little too much to drink and they don't even realize they haven't paid their tab. Patrons run outside for a quiet place to talk on their cell phone, converse a little longer than usual, and then have autopilot kick in as they head to their car and forget their tab. Before you know it, you're stuck with their bill, and would you recognize these people a few weeks or even months later? Servers see hundreds of people a week and it takes me a few times before someone looks remotely familiar.

If I'm working the nightshift and I don't recognize a person who wants to run a tab, I will definitely not run a tab without some sort of collateral. The nightshift crowd drinks a little more, parties harder, and are mostly younger in age.

The dayshift crowd is a little quieter. A lot of guys will come in by themselves, as well as people who are on their lunch break. It's not unusual to see a guy working on his paperwork or a laptop. The energy in the room is a little more subdued and mellow. I still try to keep to my rules on running tabs, as I've been left with plenty of them during the dayshift as well.

Every now and then on the dayshift, I break my own rule about asking a customer for their credit card. I think to myself, "That guy looks like a normal kind of person who won't bolt on his tab. He's by himself and he's eating lunch. He'll probably have a couple beers and then go." Before I know it, he's had six beers and I'm all jumpy because he's leaving to use the restroom. I hate being leery of people. It makes your job easier if you just have that credit card as back up. If you find yourself gambling like this from time to time, you can still save yourself by mentioning to the customer that since their bill is around fifty dollars, they will either have to square up or give you a credit card to continue running the tab. If they question this, I blame it on the bar.

Like I mentioned in a couple of the scenarios above, when I work the dayshift, I find that customers expect to automatically run a tab when they're ordering food from the kitchen. I now always tell customers that if they're planning on leaving the room to go have a cigarette or use the restroom, there always has to be one person sitting at the table at all times. If they all leave, they will either have to pay their bill or hand me a credit card. If they ask me why, this is when I tell them about the stack of unpaid bills we have behind the bar.

When a customer hands you a credit card to run a tab, they may tell you that they will be paying you cash at the end of the night. Make a note of this at the top of the tab in case you forget or if another server ends up taking over the bill.

Customers appreciate it if you avoid any awkward moments. If it looks like a big group is going to run tabs, reply with, "Wow, this is a big group. Are all the tabs separate?"

Keep all credit cards in a safe place at the bar. Don't leave them sitting out in the open. People mingle around the bar and if there is a chance for a scammer to steal an unsecured card, it'll happen. Be aware and look after customers' credit cards as though they were your own. It would be extremely hard and embarrassing to explain to a customer who has put his trust in you to keep his card safe that his credit card was stolen and he has to put a hold on it or cancel it.

I've been told by a fellow server that when she worked at another pub, at the end of every shift, all the servers put one dollar into the *dine and dash kitty*. This way, if a customer leaves on his bill, there's money in the kitty to pay the server, so she's not out that money. It's a great system for new servers, but I would never take advantage of it as I'm on top of all my tabs and I see it as my fault if a customer leaves when I didn't have some insurance (a credit card or cash) to run the tab. I also feel that it allows some servers to have a sense that it's okay not to stay on top of their tabs because the fund will always be there to save them. Some servers will take advantage of this system and everyone else will be left with nothing. I don't want to pay a dollar into a kitty when I know that I will rarely need it. A dollar a shift times the amount of shifts per week; five shifts a week equals $5.00, in a month that is $20.00, in a year it would be $240.00! What if a customer comes back a day later and realizes he left on his tab the previous day? Would you trust the girl to put the money back that she took out of the kitty the day before?

When a customer hands you a credit card, it's extremely important to do a quick inspection of it. Make sure that there's no sticker on it reminding the customer to *call in and validate it*. If they didn't do this when getting the card, they won't be able to use it. Inspect the expiration date because if it's before today's date, it will be declined. Look at the front and back and make sure it hasn't been altered in some way.

When you deliver a tab after a customer asks for it, make sure he's sitting there before you drop it off. You don't want to leave it at his table when he's out having a smoke or in the restroom because the credit card can be stolen.

Check the name on the front. If a guy hands you a credit card, make sure it doesn't read a Mrs. Samantha So and So.

Do not accept Travelers Cheques. They are easy to alter and steal.

When a credit card says "preferred customer" on it, it means that it's a pre-paid credit card and sometimes these cards rarely have a balance left on it. We make it a policy in our bar that we do not accept these cards if a customer wants to run a tab.

If another server's customer is in a rush to leave, I will try to help out if I'm not busy. I'll usually find the bill and run over to the server and ask her if the tab is updated and explain that they need to leave right away. She may ask me to run it through for her and sometimes she'll take the bill, run back to the till, and want to deal with it herself.

Tabs are a big part of serving, so ask your senior server any questions you may have about them. You will want to know all the bar's rules and any policies related to them.

Romana's Rules for Pre-Authorizing and Advising Tabs: Scenarios #1–3

Ok, so you have the credit card in your hand. Now what? You want to make sure that it works.

Do yourself a favor and pre-authorize it. What pre-authorizing does is makes sure the person isn't over their limit and has money available, or ensures that the card is not stolen. You'll know right away if there's a problem with the card when you pre-authorize it. It will come up as *Hold Card, Call Bank* for a stolen or problem card, and, for people that exceeded their credit limit, it will come up as *Declined*. If you've never pre-authorized a credit card, a server or bartender will show you how.

Nowadays, most credit cards have a chip and the machine will not let you pre-authorize a credit card with a chip because a pin number is needed from the customer to put the transaction through. There is a way to pre-authorize a credit card with a chip, by bypassing the chip mechanism. One day while our debit/visa machine at the bar was being serviced, I asked the man working on it if there was a way to bypass the chip mechanism as all the servers were concerned about this and we couldn't pre-authorize any credit cards with the chip. He programmed it, showed me how to pre-authorize a credit card with a chip, and now we're good to go! The only problem that I have run into is if I'm too quick to advise the pre-authorization slip and I accidentally punch in fifteen cents, when I should have advised it for fifteen dollars, for example. There is no way to go back and fix it from the fifteen cents to the fifteen dollars because of that chip. So, be aware of punching in your numbers when you're advising your slips.

There are a couple of rules I like to follow on pre-authorizing credit cards.

Scenario #1

If Johnny B. gives me his card and says, "I'd like to run a tab. Do not let any of my friends put any of their drinks on my bill."

This is a responsible person who is aware of what he puts on his card and I find that there won't be a problem with this guy's credit card declining. I'll pre-authorize it for $20.00 and keep the pre-authorization slip with the card.

If Johnny B. ordered one beer for $5.25 and then wants to sign off the bill, I can do one of two things.

#1. Redo the pre-authorization slip for $5.25. Then once it's approved, I'll rip up the first slip for $20.00 and throw it out.

Or

#2. Scratch out the $20.00 and hand-write $5.25 beside it.

This is faster to do if you're in a rush or slammed. Be prepared though that the customer may ask why you put through $20.00 on his credit card. Then you'll have to explain to him what pre-authorizing actually is, which will waste more time than if you pre-authorized it a second time in the first place. Pre-authorizing the second time looks more professional anyways.

Of course it would be advised for the total of $5.25 plus tip.

Scenario #2

If Billy C. gives me his card and says, "Run me a tab. I'll pay for the first round." I will pre-authorize his card for about $50.00.

If Billy C. wants to sign off his bill and the total amount came to $83.00, I can do one of two things.

#1. Redo the pre-authorization slip for $83.00. Once it goes through as approved, rip up the first slip for $50.00 and throw it out.

If the $83.00 pre-authorization slip is declined, proceed to #2.

#2. Scratch out the $50.00 and hand-write $83.00 beside it.

Don't worry; it will not be declined when you advise it through for the total of $83.00 plus tip.

Scenario #3

If Bruce M. gives me his card and says, "I'm treating the guys tonight. All drinks are on me!" I'll pre-authorize his card for $100.00.

When Bruce M. wants to sign off the bill and his total ends up being $167.00, I can do one of two things.

#1. Redo the pre-authorization slip for $167.00. Once it goes through as approved, rip up the first slip for $100.00 and throw it out.

If the $167.00 pre-authorization slip is declined, proceed to #2.
#2. Scratch out the $100.00 and hand-write $167.00 beside it.

Don't worry; it will not be declined when you advise it through for the total of $167.00 plus tip.

*** A note about pre-authorizing a credit card twice***

Pretend you had pre-authorized John Doe's card for $50.00 earlier in the night, and a couple hours later he wants his bill because he's going home. You pre-authorize it a second time for $38.00 because that ended up being what he owed you.

Now, pretend the second pre-authorization of $38.00 was declined. I have found that this has happened to me now and then. The reason for the decline is he might have been at the end of his limit with the $50.00 pre-authorization that you did the first time. This is why you don't rip up the first slip right away in case the second pre-authorization of $38.00 was declined. This way, you can scratch out the $50.00 and hand-write in $38.00 beside the scratched out $50.00 as backup.

It's a great idea to pre-authorize every single credit card, so you know that all tabs are covered. If I get extremely busy, I will not pre-authorize everyone's cards because I find that most cards don't decline anyways. I'll only pre-authorize the owners of the cards that seem to have a lot of activity, like if they're buying drinks and shooters for their buddies. I like to be on guard and pre-authorize their card, because if they happen to disappear and then I run their card through, resulting in a decline, I'm in trouble!

Authorizing the Pre-Authorization Slip

First thing to check is to make sure the customer signs the bottom. Now, make a quick calculation of the bill amount plus tip. If the bill says $39.00 and the customer wrote a $6.00 tip, the amount should be $45.00. But what if he wrote $35.00 in the total line by mistake? Well, I still authorize it for the correct amount of $45.00. The proof is there of $6.00 on the tip line, as well as a signature. You don't want to be in a rush and not pay attention to your slips. If you were to advise it for the $35.00 and not notice the mistake, you would have been out $10.00. Pay attention to details as it is your money!

Some people sign their name at the bottom and leave the tip line blank. I always say to them, "Honey, you don't want to leave the tip line blank because I'm sure you don't want me to write a hundred dollar tip for myself," and give them a flirty wink.

*** *Authorizing the Credit Card Slip* ***
If the pre-authorized credit card slip has the customer's signature and the total at the bottom, it's time to authorize it. This means that you are running it through as final. You will be shown how to do this by your bartender or another server.

Organizing and Reading Tabs

As I've mentioned before, at our bar we hand-write all our tabs. This is not unusual as I have talked to a few other servers that have the same old system in their bars or pubs.

Sometimes there could be more than a dozen or so credit cards and tabs waiting by the till between all servers. There must be some sort of organization system to keep tabs from getting mixed up. Every server has her own glass that houses all her tabs. As I get a credit card, at the top of the bill I write the customer's first name and last four digits on the credit card, as well as the table that they're sitting at in the room. The reason I use the first name is because it is more personal. If you feel more comfortable writing the person's last name, do that (this would be better to do because it would be more obvious to notice if giving a wrong credit card to a customer).

If your place of work doesn't have waitress boxes, ask your liquor reps to get you a waitress apron. They are great to hold all your credit cards, visa slips, pens, big bills, etc. Usually the liquor reps can get them for you for free.

When you're preparing to sign off someone's tab, **ALWAYS double check the name and digits that match the name on the credit card to the bill**. There could be three tabs with the same first name on them. Many years ago I mixed up a couple of credit cards and they were both regulars. I didn't know until I came to work the next day and was told by the senior waitress at that time about it. I was mortified. She was able to straighten everything out because she also worked in the office. To this day, I am careful to double and triple check all tabs!

Romana's story... The Stolen Travelers Cheques

A few years ago I had a gentleman come into the bar and order a double rum coke and a steak sandwich. I went to the bar and punched the drink order into the till, and then I sauntered into the kitchen to place the food order. Walking back to the bar, I grabbed the drink and any napkins, cutlery, and condiments. I returned to the customer and set down the drink. "$7.50 for the drink please. If you want to pay for the steak now, your total comes to $18.75."

He said, "I'd like to run a tab."

I said, "I need a credit card to run a tab."

He pulled out a $50.00 Travelers Cheque and held it out for me. I said to him, "We don't accept Travelers Cheques."

He said, "This is my only method of payment. I'll be back later with cash." He got up and walked out.

I ran back into the kitchen and told them that I didn't need the steak and explained what happened. Then I went back to the bar and explained the situation to my bartender. He was kind enough to promo the drink, so I didn't have to pay for it.

I was curious about this Travelers Cheque, so I inspected it and found that it had a woman's name on it.

The next day I took the Traveler's Cheque to my bank and explained the scenario to one of the tellers I knew. She told me to leave it with her and she would make some calls inquiring about it.

She called me later and, as I suspected, it was stolen.

Later on that day when I worked the nightshift, the customer returned with cash and said he wanted to pay his bill from yesterday and collect HIS Travelers Cheque. I told him that I took it to the bank and it was reported stolen and if he wanted it back, he had to go to the bank. He didn't argue with me and took off immediately.

I assume he was a drifter, passing through town, because I've never seen him before.

Romana's Story... The Altered Credit Card

Years ago, a young lady came into the bar with a couple friends. She asked me to run the group a tab and handed me her credit card. She seemed a little jumpy and as she handed me the card she said, "Don't be alarmed with my credit card. I damaged it and I'm having some problems with it. You'll have to manually punch the card through."

I didn't know what she meant by this, so I took their order and walked back to the bar. I inspected the card and noticed that the name on it was flattened and there was another name that got punched in on top. When you flipped the card over, on the back at one point it read MR. SO and SO. The female name on the front wasn't even put on straight, it had angled downward. It was obviously stolen and then altered.

I called my manager and left the rest up to him. The group was kicked out and we told them that they weren't getting their stolen card back.

Romana's Story... "I Don't Want to Pay for Your Bill!"

A few years back, I had a lady come into the bar with her boyfriend and sister. She gave me her credit card and asked me to run a tab for all of them. I was very busy, working alone and I meant to pre-authorize the card when I had a spare moment, but I ended up forgetting.

Another server came onto the floor and she took over that side of the room. When the small group was ready to leave, my coworker pre-authorized their bill which was approximately $120.00 and it declined. We tried pre-authorizing the card for $75.00 and that declined as well.

Nobody in the group had any other method of payment, so the boyfriend gave me his driver's license and said that he would return the next day with cash. I had her credit card, his driver's license, and the bill, and I put all three aside.

During the rest of the night, I was unnerved with the whole scenario as I owed about $100.00 on this bill and my coworker owed the rest. I kept thinking that these people may not come back; she could cancel the credit card and he would go get another driver's license. It sure would be cheaper for them to do than to come back and pay the big bill.

When the room calmed down, I pulled out the credit card again and started pre-authorizing it for smaller amounts. I tried for $50.00, it declined. I tried for $25.00, it declined. I tried for $3.00 ... it was accepted! Now I tried advising it for $120.00 (I didn't care about the tip at this point. I just wanted to get our money that we owed the bar on the bill), and guess what? It went through for the $120.00 and we got our money! I stapled the yellow copy of the advise slip to the bill and put it aside with the credit card and driver's license.

The boyfriend did not come back as he had promised.

Story was not over yet.

A little over a month later, the lady and her boyfriend came back and she was irate. She was yelling at me and wanted to see my manager. She had a copy of her visa statement and was upset the $120.00 was on her statement and she was insinuating that I was trying to rip her off!

Calmly (this was hard to do as I wanted to smack her and scream back in her face), I explained what I did to pre-authorize the card for the $3.00. I then proceeded to tell her that I DID NOT add a tip and I wanted the money owed to me for the drinks that they consumed that night. I turned the tables on her by asking why they didn't come back the day after with the money as they had promised. She really couldn't argue with me after that as I had their bill, which I had written the date on. I gave her the bill, advise slip, credit card, and driver's license. I promised myself to be on top of my pre-authorizing!

Stay on top of all your customer's tabs by pre-authorizing all credit cards and then you won't find yourself in a similar predicament. I wouldn't recommend you do what I did as you could get in trouble. I was very lucky that the woman didn't call her credit card company and refuse to pay for that transaction. I consider it a good lesson learned!

Securing a Tip

Every day a customer is faced with the decision of where to spend their money when they want to go out on the town and have a few drinks. There are many good establishments to go to and if a patron ends up walking into your place of work, you'll want to do everything in your power to make their visit as enjoyable as possible and you'll want them to return.

What is an Average Tip?

Many new servers that are starting in the industry may wonder what an average tip is. You must have an idea, as I'm sure many of you tip servers when you go out.

The average tip is between 10 and 20 percent. If you're not sure how to work out what 10 percent is, take the total amount of the bill and move the decimal point one spot to the left.

Examples:

$50.00	10% is $5.00	
$50.00	15% is $7.50	(10% is $5.00 plus 5% is half of $5.00, which is $2.50)
$50.00	20% is $10.00	(10% is $5.00 times 2)

Sniff Out the Tippers and Bend Over Backwards For Them

The main reason why we work in the hospitality industry is to make tips. TIPS stand for *To Insure Prompt Service*. It doesn't mean, "Because I ran up to the bar and grabbed a drink for you, you have to give me a tip." This is often forgotten by many in the serving industry.

As servers, we receive tips more often than we don't receive them. When we do come across that non-tipper, they will stand out from the crowd. The person that looks at his hand and recounts his change as he quickly slips it into his pocket will be lucky if I don't forget his drink next time he orders, while the guy that throws a couple of quarters on my tray gets a "Thank you" as I hurry on to the next customer. The patron that leaves me the big tips gets a little extra attention and smile, and there will sometimes be a customer who leaves that crazy tip that I have to re-count and say, "Are you sure?" hoping that it isn't a mistake—I could kick myself as to why I have to be so honest. I want to jump for joy as they say, "No mistake, keep the change." They are the ones to get the big hug of gratitude, as well as impeccable service.

If customers are not tipping, there is usually a reason for it.
1.   The service is extremely slow. You're stopping to chat with people and taking forever to deliver their drinks.
2.   You have forgotten their order, or keep forgetting about them.

3.   You're grumpy, rude, or seem mad.
4.   They don't believe in tipping (while they don't get tipped at their job, they feel we don't deserve to be tipped).
5.   They don't know what a tip is (this is usually the younger generation).

Customers may want you to get things for them other than drinks and shooters. If you do the little extras, a tip may be rewarded.
• I've been asked to get customers a pack of cigarettes. When I get them, I remove the plastic wrapping and slip a pack of matches to the customer at the same time. They'll appreciate the thought.
• Customers have asked me to get bags of chips out of the vending machine for them.
• Redeeming keno slips and removing pull tabs out of the machine is another way to help out a patron and possibly receive a tip.
• Customers will ask me if I can give them money in exchange for winning pull tabs. I don't mind as long as they're not big winners that I have to pay out more than twenty dollars. We had a problem with a five hundred dollar pull tab a few years ago. Each bar has a barcode on their winning pull tabs and in order to collect the money, the code must belong to the bar. If a customer redeems it at another establishment and gets paid out for it, the bar is out that money which will come back to the server or bartender who paid it out. You don't want to end up with a winning pull tab that you paid someone out on and then find out it's from a bar located three hours away.
• I've been asked for Tums or aspirin by my regulars who have a hangover. I'll ask the person twenty minutes later how they're feeling and the response is usually, "Great! You're a lifesaver!" (I don't make it a habit of giving headache medication to an intoxicated patron as it's not good to mix with alcohol).
• If I'm extremely busy and don't have the time to stand in front of machines and pump in coins, I let customers know. "I'm sorry Honey. During a time that I'm not so busy, I would be happy to get you pull tabs/cigarettes, but right now I need to stay on top of all my drink orders. If you'd like, I can give you change, so you don't have to go and stand in line at the bar for it." Some customers compensate me by throwing a loonie on my tray.

- Calling a cab for customers is another nice gesture to do. My bartender is kind enough to do this for me as he has better access to the phone. The taxi company will want to know the customer's name and whether they'll be waiting at their table or at the door.

- Mentioning the special of the day when customers sit down could earn you more of a tip because of the cheaper price.

- Birthday celebrations and stag parties are great to serve because they keep you busy and reward you with some awesome tips if you show them a good time. For some great information on making extra tips on your stag party or birthday customers, please refer to Chapter #2, Subchapter #5 under "Promotions, Special Events and Parties, Etc."

- Don't be so quick to dump drinks down the drain if people happen to get up and leave. Usually customers let me know that they're going outside for a smoke and are coming back; however, some people walk outside without saying a word, go to the restroom, or end up talking on their cell phone. If fifteen minutes goes by and they haven't returned, I'll take their drinks and set them near the glass washer on the ledge. I'll let another half an hour or so go by, and then dump the drinks if they haven't returned by that point.

If you dump someone's drink out by mistake and they get very upset about it, do the right thing and buy them another. Customers will always remember this kind gesture and you're sure to secure any tip given to you from them in the future. If you argue back and respond with, "Well, I didn't know that you were coming back," they may never want to order from you again. Say good bye to any tips that would have been given to you in the future.

- Over the years, we've heard about jerks dropping date rape drugs into girls' drinks. I have many guy customers worry about someone dropping something into their drink while they use the restroom or go outside for a cigarette, so they'll bring their drink over to my till because they want me to keep an eye on it for them. I pacify them by telling them that I'll leave it right beside my water by the till. This way it shows that the drink won't be tampered with if I'm satisfied with my own water sitting there.

- Customers go to a bar to have a good time or to get away from their own problems. I've had customers in the past that have had a parent or pet pass away and I'll give them a few minutes of my time to tell them how sorry I am and give them a hug. Years later, a few of these people told me how much that meant to them. Be sympathetic to your regulars and show them how much you care. After all, you are in an industry that shows you like people. Daily life is happening around us and as people enter the bar, they long to get away from the pains of broken marriages, deaths of pets or loved ones, financial troubles, and other difficult situations they deal with. Giving someone just a few minutes of your time while they complain about their boss laying them off, troubles with their kids, or wife leaving them will mean the world to them.

- Every time I greet a customer, I always ask how their day is going. Once in a while, the response is, "Not good. I've had such a bad day at work today, it's not even funny." This is a time that I feel is important to ask my bartender if he could please promo me a beer. I love it when I can smile, drop off a beer, and say, "Here Jim, this one is on the house. Hopefully this will make your day a little better!" I walk away while my customer sits there beaming and yelling out a warm, "Thank you Ro!" If there's no room on the promo tab, I'll pay for it.

- When customers order food and they're outside having a smoke, if I'm not busy I like to pop my head outside the door and let them know that their food is ready, so it doesn't get cold. I make an effort to do this especially if it's one guy in a big group who's ordered food because I've seen friends polish off the guy's plate before he has a chance to return to his table.

- One of my bartenders goes that extra mile and offers samples when customers ask him what the difference is between the dark and the white beer we have on tap. They're grateful for the nice gesture and as a result, I always hear the tinkle of change in his tip jar. He gained us a happy customer that will definitely return.

- I have lent my jumper cables a few times to customers in need. It's a bit of an inconvenience, but if I'm not busy I run outside to retrieve them from my truck.

- Once in a while, a regular wants to order another beer and tells me that he's short a couple dollars. I don't make a big deal out of it and tell him to get me next time. These are the customers that will hand me a ten dollar bill and tell me to keep the change, saying that they owed me some money from a couple weeks ago.

76

• Desperate customers craving for a cigarette are more than grateful if I can hunt one down for them and in exchange throw me a buck or two. I take the money they gave me and give it to the staff member or customer that gave me the cigarette in the first place. Years ago when there were a lot more people smoking, if I found a pack of cigarettes and nobody claimed them, I kept them in my waitress box and kept them for customers in need.

The "Art" of Handing Back Change

Always carry change on your tray. I know of servers that don't carry any nickels, and they're asking for trouble.

When I returned to work from a vacation not too long ago, I had a few regulars complain to me about the servers that ripped them off. A couple people threatened to go to management because they weren't given their nickels and, because of this, they told me that they didn't tip that server a penny— these are people that *always* tip me a dollar or more! Absurd, I know, but most people don't like you to assume that you can keep any of their change, no matter how small of an amount. If the customer returns, he may not tip you at all because of that dumb little move you made about not returning some measly little change. Let the customer be in control of keeping what he wants. After all, it is his money and by not handing back that measly little nickel, it is considered stealing.

If you happen to run out of change and you need to run to the bar to exchange a big bill, do it as soon as you can. You don't want to forget and have someone accuse you of stealing, even if you are the most honest person alive.

When a customer hands you a bill and says, "Keep the change," this means the small coin and it doesn't mean all of it unless he waves the bill away as you try handing it over to him.

If a customer mumbles, "Keep ____," where you can't understand what he said, always say, "I'm sorry, I didn't hear you." There's been a time when someone mumbled and actually said "Keep six" and I thought he said "Keep nine." I'm embarrassed when he yells, "Hold on! You still owe me three dollars!" I get flustered and feel like a dolt because I'm sure he thinks I tried ripping him off on purpose.

When dropping off a drink order and the customer tells you to keep the change that ends up being a nickel, I like to pretend I didn't hear him and set the nickel down in front of him anyways.

I've heard of waitresses setting the nickel down and saying, "That's okay. You probably need this more than I do." I don't recommend you do this as you'll easily upset your customer and you may have screwed yourself out of any future tips. I like to put the nickel down so he realizes that that was all it really was. Your customer may not have been paying attention, didn't register the amount in his mind, or didn't hear you properly above the music. Most times I'll find a couple of dollars on the table when he leaves. Don't always think that patrons want to rip you off on purpose. They get sidetracked by the TVs, naked girls on the stage, shooter girls, and their buddies chatting with them.

Sometimes patrons that enter the bar tell you that they don't want anything. The rule of our bar is that everyone must buy at least one drink, whether it's alcoholic or nonalcoholic. I explain to them that it's the bar's policy and since we don't charge cover, this is the way we pay the dancers. Usually people understand once I explain this rule and remember to be nice about it as they will be paying for their bottle of water or pop and you might still get a tip from them. The only exception to this rule is limo drivers for large parties such as stags or birthdays where I give him a free pop or coffee.

People that expect to sit at a table and not order anything because they have no money make me want to give them a little talking to. They have to understand that servers are there to make money for the bar and when those non-drinkers take up chairs in a prime location, this upsets the server that is working that section. Servers want the patrons who are spending their money and tipping like crazy to be sitting at those tables.

As you get to know customers and serve them on a regular basis, some will eventually say, "Ro, every time you bring me a beer from now on, always make it $7.00," or, "Ro, whenever you serve me my pint, always take a dollar for yourself." This is the only time you are allowed to help yourself to the money. The first few times, the customer will usually remind me, "Did you take your dollar?" Always remember your manners and thank them before moving on.

Being a goof can usually work in your favor. During the slow parts of the dayshift, as a dancer walks into the room in her costume ready for her next show, I yell out, "Hey everybody! My friend Sandy Tease is in the house, yahoo!" I start to clap and everyone responds by joining me in the clapping while they whistle and yell, "Yay!" It brings a little pep and energy into the atmosphere and the customers know that a dancer will be on stage momentarily. The girls tell me that they love it when I do this, as it makes them feel a little special.

Pause for the Change

Ok, say a guy buys a beer that costs $5.25. He hands me over a twenty dollar bill. I'll set the bill on my tray and proceed to count his coins first and either hand them or place them in front of him on the table. I would first give back the $4.75 in change. Now, I move to the bills that are locked in my fingers under my tray. As I move my hand to pull out a ten or two fives, I'll watch out of the corner of my eye what the customer's next move is (it's like playing poker!). Does he just sit there staring at the stage or keep conversing with his buddy? Give him a moment to put his hand on the coin and see if he throws some onto your tray. He's making no move now, but there's still a 50 percent chance for him to leave some change on the table when he leaves. Does he scoop up all the change and slip it straight into his pocket or does he slowly fondle it, perhaps counting out what he wants to hand back to you. If he's fondling the change, pause a minute and give the table a quick wipe or pick up empties to give him a chance to give you a tip. Sometimes the fondling means he's counting his change to make sure you didn't rip him off!

If a customer gives you a twenty dollar bill for a few drinks that total $14.75, give back the change in separate bills and coin. This way, he will be inclined to give you a dollar or two. If you handed over a five dollar bill and a quarter, most likely you'll only end up with that quarter back on your tray.

Use your judgment when handing back change. If someone hands you two twenty dollar bills when their total came to $27.00, don't make them mad by handing back all their change in loonies. No one wants the weight of thirteen loonies. Besides, you don't want to run out of loonies before you get back to the bar.

I've heard a story similar to this one a few times ... a customer will enter the bar and pull out a fifty or one-hundred dollar bill. They will take the bill, rip it in half, and give you one half of it, saying to you, "We are celebrating my mother's birthday tonight. If the service is excellent, I will hand you the other piece of the bill at the end of the evening when I pay the bill." If this happens to you, run your tush off for this group and remember to be friendly and outgoing!

"We'll Leave You a Big Tip on the Table When we Leave"

Every server I talk to cringes when they hear that sentence! In chiseler terms they're actually saying, "I acknowledge the fact that I haven't tipped you and I'm not wanting to. You'll just think that I forgot and not hold it against me." If they really wanted to tip the server, they wouldn't make that comment and would tip them then and there instead of making a big deal out of it, or they would just leave the tip on the table when they left. In my experience, the percentage rate of people not leaving a tip on the table after they make that annoying statement is about 98 percent.

Give Away the Extras & Emphasize the Freebies

When I sign off a tab, I put the bill, both copies of the pre-authorization slip, and a pen into an empty glass. If I'm giving away any type of promoting material such as tickets for future events, I like to insert a couple of those into the glass as well. As I drop it off I say, "Thank you guys! Have a great night! I'll see you next time!"

Then you can finish up by saying, "By the way, I slipped you a couple of complimentary tickets to the Jell-O Wrestling Competition we're having here next week." They'll thank you for the tickets and may even ask you for some extras for friends they'd like to bring by as well. This considerate gesture may earn you a bigger tip. If they were nice, fun, and/or good tippers, you'd be delighted to serve them again. Happy customers become repeat customers, who may end up becoming regulars; regulars are your bread and butter in this business.

When customers run a tab, depending on how much money they're spending, I'll give them a coffee or pop for free if they order one. If they bought four beers and a lunch, and finish up by ordering a coffee, I won't charge them for the coffee.

It's important to put the coffee on the bill and put a zero or no charge beside it. This way, when they look over the check, they'll see that it has been counted but not charged. If it wasn't put on the bill, they'll think that you forgot, or they may have forgotten about the freebie themselves. It's obvious that people love things given to them for free. If they aren't charged for something as measly as a coffee, you may end up with a bigger tip.

When there's a group of people out to have a good time, such as celebrating a friend's birthday, give the birthday boy or girl a free shooter or drink. Usually, someone in the group will let you know and say, "It's my friend's birthday today. Does he get a free birthday drink?" I'll respond with, "I'll see what I can do!" When I return and drop off the free shot, I'll say "Happy Birthday!" The buddies think that you pulled some strings and you get all the credit. This may result in you getting better tips from this group.

Oh No... The Dreaded Price Increase!

There'll be times when the bar will increase its prices. This is inevitable and all servers must go through these times where customers complain, and for a few weeks we seem to make less money. Before we know it, everyone gets used to the new price and customers adjust their tipping accordingly.

Sometimes prices go up by a few cents. Don't think that a few cents are not a big deal because it all adds up at the end of a shift. The sooner you let customers know about the increase in price, the sooner they get used to it. Many regulars have said to me, "Ro, every time you drop a beer off for me, make it $7.00." Now, what do I do when the price increases from $6.00 to $6.50? Do I still say something to the regular who is already giving me that dollar tip? Yes, I do. Dropping off the beer, I say, "Jim, just so that you know the bar has increased their prices."

He'll ask, "Oh really, by how much?"

I would respond with, "Well, your Jack Daniels got raised by *only* fifty cents." I like to use the word *only*, so that it doesn't seem like that big of a deal.

Some people find that fifty cents is a big deal and you'll have some customers make the annoying comment, "Well, I guess it comes out of your tip." One of my regulars got mad and made that same remark

81

last price increase and I responded with, "Guess you start going to the bar for your beer from now on Larry." He looked at me in a stunned and funny way, and decided to continue to tip me my usual amount. Of course I was only joking when I said that!

Don't be embarrassed to say something. The first week is hard, but before you know it, things eventually even out and end up working out. If customers moan, groan, and freak out on you, don't get mad or defensive. Don't start cursing the bar and jump on their bandwagon. Calmly explain that unfortunately the bar has to keep up with other local business' prices and inflation always has a way to catch up. Be business-like and professional about it.

Information to Help Put Cash in Your Pocket!

Have Fun as you work the Floor! As I walk around the room, I like to joke around and have fun with my customers. When this happens, a sincere smile ends up on your face. If it's one thing that can grate on a server's nerves, it's a customer making the comment, "Why aren't you smiling?" It can come out of the blue while you're cruising through the bar in a good mood and not expecting it. Try not to get upset as most of us do. If you give someone a dirty look or you say something back like, "Why don't you give me something to smile about?" you might as well say "good bye" to any tips. People don't tip bitchy girls.

I respond with a smile and say, "Oh, I'm just busy and concentrating!" and move on before the guy has a chance to make another irritating remark and gets me even more annoyed.

Keep your bad day at home! If you look mad at the world, neglect to smile, throw drinks down on tables, don't greet your customers, and stomp around, you might as well say good bye to most of your tips that shift. I'm serious! I have had days where I'm in a pissy mood and notice how money is quickly slipped back into customer's pockets. Why should anyone want to tip a sour puss? Don't get in the habit of coming like this to work. Word travels fast between customers that "So and so is a bitch every time we come to the bar." I've heard it from customers about past servers.

People come into the bar for a good time, and they'll pay for it, so if you're in one of your bad moods, snap out of it quick. In your car on the way to work, listen to your favorite tunes. Do whatever it takes to get into your happy place. You're there to make money, so make good use of your time and make as much money as you can!

Working on Your Birthday is not considered a bad thing when you work in the bar. Let all staff know about it and mention it as often as you can to customers! When a coworker works on their birthday, I mention it every time I walk by that person. "Hey guys, it's Laura's birthday today!" is what I'll say as I point at the shooter girl.

When I'm at the bar waiting for my bartender to get my drinks and he's tending to his customers, "Hey guys, it's John's birthday today!" The DJ gets into it on the microphone and it's nice if that person makes a little extra cash on their special day. Helping out your coworkers this way means they'll reciprocate when it's your big day. I find that I make big money on my birthday because customers will put extra money on my tray and tell me to buy a drink after work. I'm asked why I work on my birthday and my response is, "It's not a big deal, it's just another day."

I bet a server would make even better money if she responded with, "I can't afford to take the day off." Maybe I'll try that next year.

Smile a Lot And Make Your Customer Feel Important!

I mention this a few times in the book and as you can tell, it's one of the most important aspects to this job. You want to smile when you're happy, smile when you're sad, smile when you're tired, and smile when you're mad. Happiness is contagious and when you see someone smiling, you feel happy. When customers ask how you're doing, your reply should be "Fantastic!"

Don't reply with, "Actually, my day is shitty because ..." Nobody wants to hear your moaning. Customers come in for a good time and don't care to hear about your problems because they have their own to deal with. People like to tip happy and positive servers.

Make your customers feel important. If your regular tells you that he's taking his wife to the new trendy restaurant downtown for their anniversary, or going on a family trip to Mexico, remember to ask about the restaurant visit or vacation the next time you see him. Your regular will feel important that you cared to remember this little piece of information.

It's a good idea to know the area around where you work. From time to time, out-of-town patrons will ask where a good nearby sushi restaurant, a bank, or even a drug store is located. I've had dancers ask me where to go to have their broken heels on their shoes fixed, or where a nearby tanning salon is located.

When a customer asks me for a suggestion on what is good to order on the food menu, I tell him. I have even steered customers away from certain dishes in the past because of portion size or complaints.

If **customers seem to be in a rush,** I'll ask them, "Do you need to be out of here at a certain time?" Clues to a rushed patron are the questions he'll ask such as, "What is fast to make on the menu?" or "How busy is the kitchen?" Usually they're pressed for time, hungry or perhaps even diabetic and need to eat right away. Once I put their order into the kitchen, I let them know that I explained to the cook to get their meal out ASAP. They appreciate that you made them a priority in the kitchen and you may end up with a bigger tip because of this. I'll even ask them if they'd like to pay their bill before their food arrives, so they can run out the door and get on their way. Halfway through their meal, stop and ask if they'll need a take-out container for any leftovers. Do everything you can to serve them quickly and finish in their time frame.

The high-maintenance customer can be a bit of a pain at times, especially when you're busy. This is the person that almost demands extras from you. Recently I had a customer ask about the steak that was on special that day. He wanted to know what type of steak it was, how much fat was on it, if he can substitute a baked potato instead of the mashed potato and, and if he can get a big mug of water at exactly the same time his meal arrives. You just have to smile and deal with it. If you want a good tip, do everything you can to make him happy.

The complainer is someone you'll have to learn to love. This is the person who will complain about everything. The music is too loud, the fries are too salty, the air conditioning is too cold, and the serving size is too small. Be there for the customer to deal with their complaint because you want them to have an enjoyable experience at your establishment. Happy customers = Tips.

It Sucks to Get Stiffed

We're in this business to make money and while working in this industry, servers put up with a lot, so you need to grow a thick skin and quick. Most of the time, you'll make a tip and then there are the times where you won't. That's the way it is.

It's maddening when you run your butt off for someone; you're friendly and seem to have a great rapport with them, only for them to leave you nothing on the tip line or the table. That's the chance you take. Tip doesn't stand for *you have to tip me now*. But, customers do have to understand that we're there to make money.

Customers want to constantly buy us drinks. That's great and all but 99 percent of us prefer cold hard cash. That really rocks our boat. It's really frustrating for me as a server when a guy is buying himself and his buddy a couple of beers, putting a loonie on my tray, and all the while placing bills on stage for every dancer that walks up there—and this is ongoing for a couple of hours. At times like that I wish I was allowed to say, "Thanks for the loonie. You tipped me exactly 10 percent. If you can afford to tip every dancer $20.00, why can't you tip me a little more than a measly old loonie? You ask ME to give you change for your twenties so you can give them to the dancers, sometimes robbing me of all my fives. You ask me to put your order of food in or bring you nonstop glasses of water. I drag out your nice cold beer, being courteous to put a coaster down for you while I clean up your empties and carry them back to the bar. For that loonie, I have to tip out the DJ, the bartender, the kitchen, and a doorman if he's on shift."

Romana's Story... "You Forgot Your Nickel!"

One of our regulars that come into the bar has this bad habit of pulling his giant wad of bills out into the open and fumbling through it. It's more of a show to show-off to the waitresses and we really couldn't care less because he's just a below-average tipper.

He came in last week with a lady friend and I ran him a tab as I normally do. They were on their way out, so I brought the bill and, as usual, he pulled out his big stack of bills and threw down two $20.00 bills. I thanked him as I put down a fiver and $2.25 in change, thinking that at worst, he'll leave me the coin and retrieve the five. I walked *back to the till to place an order and they passed by and said, "Thanks Ro."*

"Bye guys, have a great day!" I said a second time. I cruised over to their table to give it a quick clean and get my tip and found one nickel. I was insulted!

Later on during shift change, I told the nightshift girl about this regular and said I wanted to throw a nickel at his head next time he comes in. She said she had better idea, "Ro, next time he comes in, tell him that the last time he was here, he forgot his change on the table and that's when you place the nickel down in front of him." Brilliant! Now I have to wait for him to come back in!

Romana's Story... "Thanks for Nothing"

A friend of the family has also been a server for years, working in high-end restaurants.

She told me a story of when a big party of people sat in her section and she spent a few hours serving them. When paying their bill, everyone threw cash into the middle of the table. As some of the customers were leaving, they were thanking her for the great service and she knew that there would be a handsome tip waiting for her.

The last person who was left at the table scooped up all the cash and put the entire bill on his credit card, leaving her a nice big goose egg in the tip line!

Romana's Story... "I'd Like to Rephrase That!"

I have two super awesome regulars who come in quite frequently and always leave me a nice, above-average tip when I bring their bill. I want to bring up this little story as it just happened to me two days ago.

Their bill was $59.50 and, as I dropped it off, I was asking a question to the guy paying the bill. While I took his attention away from the bill with my question, he wasn't paying attention and set down three twenties, then proceeded to fold up the bill and put it in his wallet. I picked up the $60.00 and said, "Bob, did you need your change?"

"Nope, that's good. Thanks Ro."

I was obviously disappointed and very mad at myself. Later on, I thought of how I could've saved this situation. First off, I will not distract customers when they're paying their bill. And second, I should have said, "Bob, did you need your fifty cents back?" He would've realized it at that moment.

Promotions, Special Events, Parties, Etc.

The Dreaded Competition

It's always a good idea to "spy" and see what's going on at other bars. By collecting paper advertising from tables of other establishments, you're able to see what's going on in the business of your competition. This is not just a job for management to do, but staff as well. It's an advantage for the bar to get input from all staff because everyone wants to see the bar busy, as they get to benefit from it.

A few years ago, a big group of us at work rented limos. We went out to dinner and did a *strip bar crawl*. It was a fun night out, socializing together as we ran into dancers and customers we knew along the way. We were able to compare things from other strip bars we liked and disliked and promote ideas to our own bar.

Busy bar = Making money for the bar owner and tips for yourself

Busy bar = Your shift feels like it flies by

Busy bar = You have job security

Busy bar = Happy customers who like the busy energy in the room

Busy bar = Happy staff, happy management, happy owners

When you're out socializing at other bars or pubs, strike up a conversation with new people you meet and tell them where you work. Invite them to your bar and tell them you'll buy them a beer. It's a great way to win new customers. I like to rave about the food we serve in our kitchen. It's fantastic and I mention it frequently as to why new people should come out and visit us if they've never been there before.

The Holidays

Spice things up during all random holidays, no matter how small or insignificant they may seem. Get involved and ask coworkers to do the same if management doesn't make it a priority. You don't have to spend a lot of money. The dollar store is a great place to pick up funky hats, streamers, pens, and other fun knick knacks.

During St. Patrick's Day we like to make green beer (drop of green food coloring in pints), and wear anything green. On Valentine's Day all staff wears red. Halloween is another time we dress up the room and all staff is encouraged to wear a costume.

Around the Christmas holidays, Christmas lights and decorations are put up throughout the room and we get requests for hot buttered rum and hot toddies.

For any holiday, make it special and a little out of the ordinary. People like variety, and it's a nice change for the staff as well.

Sports Events

Hockey, football, UFC ... these are all a big deal for most men and some women. During games, wear your team's logo. UFC (Ultimate Fighting Championship) is a big deal in most bars and pubs nowadays, and especially at my bar. On two separate trips to Las Vegas, I bought UFC t-shirts to wear during the fights while I work. It's a great conversation piece and I love when I can add to my wardrobe and wear something different, especially at work.

It's more of an impact when all staff gets involved.

Fun Clothing

During one of my trips to Las Vegas, I bought a funny tank top that reads, REAL BOOBS. This is another great conversation piece and probably my place of work is the only place that I can get away with sporting it. I wouldn't be caught wandering the street wearing it!

Years ago, a customer of mine who owns a t-shirt shop had t-shirts made up for the girls at my bar that read BIG TIPS while he put the name of his business in small print on the back. I'll say it again ... another great conversation piece.

I LOVE STRIPPERS was made up on t-shirts and tank tops and sold at our bar for a while.

Every now and then, guys ask me if we sell t-shirts with our bar's name on it. They're usually from out of town and I'm told that they collect t-shirts from other strip bars they visit.

Stags and Birthdays

I love stags. The guys are out for a good time and they'll pay for it. Most of the time I'll make awesome tips, my sales are high, and I have almost as much fun as the guys do.

Make it a policy to grab a credit card (and imprint it) from one person in the stag group. This way, the group will be better behaved, knowing that the bar has contact with the group in case of any trouble such as fighting or breakage.

Ask a guy in the group to give you the name of the groom/birthday person and then let the DJ know. He'll shower attention on the poor sap by letting the room full of people know, saying, "It's so and so's birthday! So and so, could you please stand up?!" Sometimes the guy gets dragged on stage, and the guy's friends love any opportunity to embarrass their buddy.

I like to give the stag/birthday guy a free shooter. It costs next to nothing, and it's a great way to win the group. I don't charge him for pop, water, or coffee either, since the rest of the group will be spending lots of money on drinks, shooters, food, and private dances. If there's a limo driver or designated driver, free water, pop, or coffee will be given to him as well. If it wasn't for this responsible and wonderful person, I'd be using up my time babysitting the group and calling for taxis.

I let the dancers know who "the special guy" is, and they'll pay extra attention to him. He'll end up with a poster or some other kind of promo. Of course, I arrange it and I look like the hero = big tips!

Some of the time, the groom will be dressed up in a funny *get up*. I've seen everything from diapers to tacky wedding dresses.

Many guys are on a quest to have every female sign their posters, hats, or t-shirts. This is a reminder of their stag/birthday night, and I'm always asked to join in and sign these mementoes. I'm flattered to be part of these memories, and because of this, I keep a sharpie in my bag and write the same quote. It's dirty, it's funny, and the guys love it. I thank my friend and awesome bartender, Craig, for making it up.

> Guy's Name,
> Hope you enjoyed the *Licker*,
> Thanks for *Cumming*!
> Your waitress, Romana xo

You can use this verse if you'd like, or think of something on your own, but have something prepared. It keeps you from racking your brain while you're busy, and when you have a spare moment, sign away!

If you joke around, flirt, and have a good time with the group, you'll have loads of fun yourself, your shift will fly by, and you'll walk away from your shift with lots of tips. You know you've shown a group a good time when you're tipped handsomely all night and as they leave, they come over to you at the till and gush about the great time they've had. They thank you for the great service and slip you another twenty dollar bill as they shake your hand, pat you on the back, or even hug you. Don't forget, happy customers mean future customers. They are sure to come back, as well as tell all their friends how they had the time of their lives at your bar!

Don't be surprised if random guys walk into your bar and ask, "Are you Romana? Our buddy John was here a few months ago on Larry's stag and he said that they had a great time that night. He wanted us to say hi to you." Even if I don't remember the person, I'll play dumb by responding with, "Oh, I remember John! What a great group of guys. Please say hi back to him for me!" This makes a positive impact on the new guys that came in. If they're new, nice, and tip well, treat them like gold. You want them to tell more friends and return.

Reservations

Offer reservations for special events. These include birthday parties, stags, stagettes, fundraisers, team functions, etc.

Write down the party name, a phone number, number of guests, time they will be arriving, and the date. Find a home for all reservations, like a corkboard in the staff room, and check it before every shift. We like to prepare the tables and put out reservations an hour or two before a party arrives.

I have a group of six to eight regulars who have been visiting our bar every single Friday at about four o'clock for the past ten years. About three years ago, I started placing a reservation sign on their favorite table at the beginning of the day, so that the table is kept reserved for the group. If it was left open and another group took it over for more hours than expected, it would be rude to ask them to move, especially if the room got slammed and there wasn't another decent table to sit at. That's why the table holds a reservation sign until after those regulars are gone, and if they don't arrive by five thirty, the sign is removed.

Contests

Bars host an array of contests: anything from wet t-shirt to hot legs, winning a pair of jeans, and bikini contests. They're fun to work because it's something different for the night.

I find that it all depends on the customers that you end up serving in your section that could make or break your shift. Most of them could end up being power drinkers or they could end up being low key and mellow by sipping on one beer for a few hours.

If your bar holds a contest, start to promote it weeks in advance by personally telling all regulars what's coming up in the weeks ahead. Make an effort to sell tickets so that the bar will be busy and everyone will benefit from it. If all staff help promote the contest, it will be a full house. When it's a full house, the energy in the room is high and people are having a good time. If people are having a good time, they want to stay and that means they will drink and spend money. And when they have a good time and party, you will usually benefit from this and make tips!

Promo the Drinks

There are many occasions that customers will find a reason to go out and celebrate with a night of drinking. There are the obvious celebrations such as a birthday, a stag, the finalization of a divorce, or the birth of a baby. This is a time I like to promo a drink for the person because they picked our bar to celebrate their special occasion. If you give them a free drink, they will appreciate it and feel honored. This is a good way of keeping your regulars happy and perhaps even gain new customers that will return.

50/50 Draws

A 50/50 draw is a way to raise money by going around the room selling tickets. You take all ticket money sold and split it in half. One half of it goes to your charity that you are raising the money for and the other half goes to the ticket winner.

I've done my share of 50/50 draws to help raise money for charities, so I'm pretty good at it. I'll give you some quick pointers on how to make your draw successful.

You'll need to get together a few supplies to make this work. First off you need a jug or a bucket to hold all your ticket stubs. You need a roll of double printed tickets (you keep one part for your draw and the other one goes to your customer). If the tickets are poor quality and hard to tear, I like to grab a pair of scissors (they work great at cutting the long lengths of tickets down the middle instead of fighting with them to try and rip them apart). I put a note at the bottom of my jug or bucket to remind me to remove my float before I get to business and start splitting all the money. Lastly, you need a float. I like to carry two $10 bills, seven $5 bills, and five loonies, which equals sixty dollars. I should have enough bills to keep going for change.

For my draws I sell one ticket for $1.00, seven tickets for $5.00, one arm length for $10.00 and $20.00 for both arm lengths and chest length. If you're trying to raise money for the SPCA, for example, tape the name and pictures of some of the dogs onto your jug. People will want to know what you're raising the money for.

I like to approach people like this:

"Hi guys! How are you tonight? I'm doing a 50/50 draw to raise money for the Westwood SPCA. They're in desperate need of some extra dog supplies this month and I'd like to help them out."

Most people hear the word *dog* and they're dropping cash on the table. For the people who say "No thanks" and are a little reluctant to part with their money, I continue with, "Come on guys! Don't you like dogs and winning money?"

If they give you the "I have no money" speech, then I respond with, "Well, I'm sure you got a loonie or two. All it takes is one measly ticket to win some money."

To my regulars, I tell them that I'm not leaving their table until they help me out and buy at least one ticket. You've got to be slightly forceful and pushy. Get out of your comfort zone and be like a car salesman!

Most of the customers will ask how soon you're drawing. I tell them that as soon as I hit up the rest of the customers on this side of the room, I'm doing the draw as long as there isn't a dancer on stage. You want to do the draw pretty quickly because some people may have decided to leave by the time they finish their next beer. You'll easily sell tickets if you tell people you're planning on doing the draw as soon as possible.

For the draw, I don't like to be the one to pick the winning ticket, so I ask a dancer or a customer to pull it instead. This way, I won't look like the bad guy to the rest of the people who didn't win.

Selling Promo Tickets to Your Customers

Your bar will host a contest or special event at times and all staff will have to buckle down and do in-house promoting to make this event a success. Selling your tickets to customers (especially regulars) is important to do because these patrons are already there on a regular basis, so this is your easiest sell!

Ask anyone who's the shark at selling the most tickets in my bar … ahem, ahem, yours truly, me! I'll give you my take on this subject and my personal secrets.

I was talking to one of the girls I work with and she said she has a hard time selling tickets because she feels as though she's bugging the customers and it sounds like she drones on and on. I told her that you want to be able to word your sales pitch by getting to the point quickly and, more importantly, say it with enthusiasm! If you drone on and on with no energy, you'll just lose people and bore them. If you've got the fire behind your sales pitch, you'll get them excited and they'll be handing you money without thinking about it too much.

Not everyone will buy your ticket no matter how enthusiastic you are and what a great deal it is. Some people will be out of town on business or a vacation, while some guys' wives won't allow them out in the evening. Some people can't buy a ticket because of time restrictions and others can't afford it even if they really wanted to help you out and buy one.

Here's a few Ticket Selling Tactics...

"Hey guys, I've got the 411 on something big-time! You are going to be begging me to buy this ticket!"

"Really, why?"

"Well, we're selling tickets for the week of July ninth for the Miss Nude Canada Championships. With this ticket, you get to come in

Monday through Saturday during the day or night, and you get one free beer or cocktail every day. It even lets you bypass the cover charge at the door if you want to stay for the contest in the evening. That's five beers for the unbelievably low price of ten dollars. Isn't that a screaming deal?"

"Well, I'm not sure if I'll be in town."

"Are you kidding? We're only selling 225 of these tickets and we've already sold over 200. Once they're gone, that's it. It's such a crazy good offer that you really can't pass this up! It's only a measly ten bucks!"

If the bar has only sold ten tickets at this point, lie and tell him that a lot of people took advantage of this offer and most are sold already. You want to add urgency so that he hands his ten dollars over to you now! You don't want him to come back a few days later and while you're trying to sell him the ticket again, he says, "Oh, I actually thought about it and ended up buying a ticket from Jane who works the dayshift."

Another good selling tactic is walking up to a table and saying, "Ok, who likes free beer?" Of course everyone is going to say they do and then you slip in your sales pitch about the ticket.

Always keep in mind that you're doing them a favor by saving them money if they purchase your ticket.

"Guys, you should be thankful that I'm doing you a favor and want you to save money!"

"Guys, between you and me, I think that management is nuts in selling these tickets for so cheap. I don't want the bar to go bankrupt!"

Ok, ok, now I'm getting silly, but that's my point. You want to have fun with this as well. Usually the ticket sales are a contest between staff where the staff member who sells the most amounts of tickets wins some cash or a gift certificate. Not only will the boss be happy you're doing everything in your power to help make this event a success, you might even win some extra cash or a prize.

Selling tickets for a Charity Event...

Every December, one Sunday in the month, our bar hosts a charity event to raise money for the less fortunate around the Christmas holidays, where all the staff and dancers work for free. Throughout this long day there are auctions, 50/50 draws every hour, prizes given away, and the servers auction off their bras. Yup, you heard me right; I auction off my bra every year. The highest it has sold for is $2,500.00 and I don't keep a penny of that money. While this is a very popular and busy event, we sell tickets to customers so that they gain entry. I have a couple of different ticket selling strategies ...

"Hey guys, you coming out for our *Christmas is for Kids Charity Event?*"

"What's that?"

"Well, we host it every year and this year it's held on December 14. It's on a Sunday. If you've never been before, you've just got to come out and check it out! All the staff and dancers work for free all day long. There are thirty-three dancers throughout the day. We auction off beer fridges, hockey game tickets, jackets, tools, barbeques, and beer tubs to name a few items. There are 50/50 draws and the waitresses auction off their bras too!"

If this doesn't get them fired up and they still hum and haw, I throw in, "Guys, even if you don't make it, the money still goes to charity anyways."

"Well, I'm not sure."

"Can you help me out and buy one of my measly little tickets? It's only twelve dollars. Please? ..."

If you grovel, plead and give them the puppy dog eyes, usually you'll make a sale! Don't get too upset if you walk away with the ticket still on your tray and no money; you've tried your best. Try again with the next group. Before you know it, someone will surprise you with, "That sounds like a lot of fun! Ok, I'll buy a dozen tickets."

"But the drink is only $11.75"
"Keep the change, Beautiful"

Chapter 3 – ORGANIZATION IN THE SERVER'S WORLD

What's in a Waitress Tool Kit and Why Does Every Server Need One?

While you're at your job, take it seriously, have your tools, and BE PREPARED! I'm annoyed at coworkers that come to work forgetting their pens, calculators, aspirin, or tampons and think it's not a big deal. They think that someone is always there to save them and lend them tools that they didn't bother to remember to bring to work. Please don't be one of these annoying coworkers and always bring your tools to work.

I like to have a "work" emergency kit at all times. I like to refer to it more as a tool box or a tool kit. Mishaps can happen and if you live quite a distance away, hopping in your car to make a quick jaunt home is not always an option. I've had soles on boots rip open, skirts' zippers break, and headaches, to name a few inconveniences.

If you don't want to lug a bag back and forth from home to work, ask if there's a locker that can be used, or at least leave it in your car. I like to keep my stuff locked away, as coworkers aren't afraid to help themselves to "borrow" something. Before you know it, your gum is gone, your tape has been used up, and your pens have all disappeared.

I'll give you a list of items, which have become extremely useful to me over the years.

Clothing and Footwear

Footwear

In a corner on the floor in the staff room, I keep an extra pair of shoes and boots. Zippers on boots can break and soles can fall apart. If your shift is long, a change of footwear is refreshing as pressure points will be relieved and you're able to finish off the rest of your shift in comfort. I keep a couple extra pairs of socks in my locker in case I arrive at work in flip flops.

I like to do my feet a favor and invest in some good insoles; the gel style is my favorite. I refer to the comfort of my boots as most valuable, so I don't skimp on paying good money for a costly pair to wear at work. I make a living working on my feet, so I like to treat them better than good. If I'm in pain, uncomfortable, or I can't walk, I won't be able to work and make money.

Skirts and Pants

I always keep one spare clean skirt in my locker at work. You never know when it could come in handy.

Tops and Blouses

My locker also contains a tank top and spare blouse.

Accidents such as spills can happen. At the first bar I worked at, I had a girl throw her hands up in the air and she knocked my entire tray of shooters onto me and a customer, and back then I had no spare clothing. Try explaining this story all night long when customers ask you what happened. The story got tiring to explain, and it was pretty uncomfortable wandering around in sticky, stained clothing for the rest of my shift.

Some Basic Locker Necessities

Shoe Polish

I have a baggie containing shoe polish for my boots. It keeps them shiny and moisturizes the leather as it keeps the boots looking new. You'd be amazed at how many guys have made comments about how nice my boots look. Yes, they look down, even in the dark.

Energy Drink

I have a couple of bottles of *5 hour Energy*, which is an energy drink. For times I can't seem to stop yawning and need an extra boost of energy, I down a bottle of this stuff because I don't drink coffee and too much pop is hard on my stomach.

THE BAG And Its Essentials

I was wandering around Wal-Mart and found a cheap $7.00 men's shaving bag. It's not very attractive so someone will not be tempted to run off with it. I put into my locker at the end of my shift before I go home.

It contains:

Gum

Gum is great to keep your breath fresh. Be aware of your breath after you eat, especially garlic or spicy foods. If you have a cold, this is another reason you should be aware of stinky breath.

Note: If you're the type of person that chews gum like a cow, stay away from the gum and pop mints instead. Nothing looks more unattractive than a server smacking their gum like a truck driver!

Nail File and Nail Clippers

A snagged nail hurts like hell and drives a person crazy. I've even saved the day for a few bartenders.

Nail Glue

If you have fake nails, do yourself a big favor and keep nail glue on hand as it has comes in handy quite frequently for yourself and coworkers. In the past I've been caught without it and I hate feeling self conscious of my hand when I'm setting a drink down on a table or handing over change while a nail is missing. It looks so tacky and I can't wait to get home so I can glue the thing back on!

Keep a few spare nails on hand too, in case one pops off and you can't find it on the floor.

Mini Flashlight

I got one of these at the Dollar store for $1.00 ... big spender! I've had coins bounce to the floor, and the flashlight helps me find them quickly. The flashlight has been used to scan the floor for missing wallets and cell phones, and customers with bad eye sight will borrow it to look at a food menu in the dark.

Roll of Tape

When bills rip apart, you want to marry the two pieces back together before you lose either one. "Out of Order" signs have needed to be put up on our vending machine, cigarette machine, and bathroom stalls. "Kick me" signs can be taped to someone's back ... just kidding!

Pens

I have six ... yes, six. One gets lost, someone borrows one, another runs out of ink, a tab or two is being signed off. I always keep at least one clipped on the inside of my skirt beside my hip. This is my main tool to keep on hand.

Calculator

A calculator is used to add up bills, add credit card totals, do your cash-out at the end of your shift, and work out tips split between servers. I have a small one with a cover on it that can be closed up when not in use, so others can't spill booze on it and get it ruined. I keep mine hidden until I need it and have *Romana's – DON'T TOUCH!* taped to the front. In the past, others would use my calculator and then leave it in the open to get sticky shooters spilled over it or leave it sitting in spilled alcohol on the counter.

Mini Stapler

When our main stapler at the bar disappears or jams up, and we're slamming busy, the last thing I have time for is to start pulling it apart and turn into the stapler-mechanic.

The stapler is usually used to staple together kitchen bills and the advise slip to its pre-authorization credit card slip. It has also been used in an emergency to staple ripped bills back together when the tape has mysteriously disappeared. You can even staple a hem back onto a skirt when you're in a rush as this holds until you have a chance to get it repaired.

Mini Kleenex Pack

This is great to have on hand for blowing your nose or blotting your lipstick when you don't have time to run to the restroom.

Mini Mirror

Having a tiny mirror nearby saves you time from running off to the bathroom when you need to re-apply lipstick or doing that quick check for boogers after blowing your nose.

Sharpie (felt marker)

This is handy to have on hand for writing out reservation signs, and I've used it to sign hats and t-shirts for grooms on their stag nights. I lend it out to dancers needing to sign a poster for a customer.

102

"SHOUT" Individual Wipes
These are great to take out spots and stains. If you don't have these on hand, soda water with a clean rag works well too.

Hand Cream
I keep a small container of hand cream to cream hands and legs.

Tums
Great thing to have on hand for gas and tummy upsets. I've been the hero and saved the day for staff, dancers, and customers when they ask me for Tums or aspirin; I don't give headache medication out to intoxicated patrons.

Aspirin
Used for relieving pain of headaches and menstrual cramps.

Lipstick or Lip Gloss
Keep nearby for those quick touch ups.

Crystal Light Packages
One of the girls at work got me hooked onto these, which slip easily into a purse and are great for flavoring a bottle of water.

Scissors
This is a very valuable tool that is useful for cutting up paper, reservation signs, loose threads, tags, etc. When they're not around, that's when you seem to need them the most.

Sample Bottle of Perfume
A quick freshen up.

Safety Pins
These are always handy to use for pinning bra straps or loose hems. I seem to get customers and dancers ask me for this little item quite regularly.

Travel Size Sewing Kit
During break time or after a shift, you can hand-sew that loose hem or button back on. This saves me from dragging it home during

the week when it's not time to launder it yet. If I would take it home, the item would sit for a month in my way and I'd never repair it anyways.

Tampons and Pads
I'm sure you can figure it out!

Pit Stick
Convenient to have on hand for that mini freshen up. There might be that ONE DAY that you get to work on the busiest night of the week and you realized you forgot to apply your pit stick. It's happened to almost all of us!

Bandages
Keep a few of these on the side as the bar's stash can be used up quickly.

Small Antibacterial Lotion
I like to keep this beside the till and clean my hands periodically, especially if I'm munching on something. Not too long ago, I bought a larger bottle with a pump that now sits on our staff table where we eat.

Hair Elastics and Hair Clip
I like to keep a few hair elastics and a hair clip on hand. During really hot weather where you feel like you'll die of heat exhaustion if you don't get your hair up off your neck, this is a life saver! It's handy to have around when I need a massage from the massage girl and need to pin my hair up and out of the way.

- The bag is great for keeping together any promoting cards or tickets that you need to give away or sell.
- Every Saturday night, I pack up any clothing used during the week and take it home to launder it.

Hang Onto Coworkers Phone Numbers

At home and in your cell phone, keep a list of all staff phone numbers. If you're sick or an emergency comes up, you can phone your manager to call in a replacement for you. If you can't get a hold of your manager, take initiative and call a replacement yourself. This way you can call your manager back and leave him a message saying that because he didn't answer his phone and you wanted to make sure that your shift was covered, you got a hold of Lynne and she'll be covering your shift today because you're sick.

It's a good idea to keep all staff phone numbers. Keep numbers of servers, bartenders, DJs, kitchen staff, doormen, and all management. You just never know who you need to contact, or you may be asked by a fellow coworker for someone's number.

Romana's Story... The Ripped Skirt

Years ago, I had a zipper get stuck and after numerous attempts for help from my bartender and shooter girl, I had no choice but to rip it open to get out of it. It was either ripping it open or pee myself. Thank goodness I had a back-up skirt to change into.

The Ways You Can Protect Yourself From Losing Money

The reason why you're working in the first place is to make money, so keeping it safe and not losing any of that money can be a challenge at times.

You look forward to doing your cash-out as you were busy all night and the majority of your customers were being more than generous with the tips! As the end of your shift nears, you do your last call, finish your clean up, and lock up behind the last customer. You just want to grab your tip money and go home.

Unlocking your waitress box, you pull out all cash, credit card, and interac slips, grab a cash-out sheet, and start all your calculations. Counting up what you owe as a tip for your bartender, DJ, doorman, and kitchen, it's set aside. Adding up all your interac and credit card slips, you subtract this total from your sales ... that can't be right, thirty dollars? You re-calculate everything again and that's what you're left with. You killed yourself tonight for thirty bucks? You feel like crying! What happened?

At some point, every server has had that sinking feeling of lost money. It's happened to us all, and it's one of the worst feelings in the world. I'm going to give you some tips on how to keep yourself from losing that money you've worked so hard to make.

Ask for a Credit Card to Run a Tab

As I've already mentioned, I will always ask a patron I don't know for their credit card if they want to run a tab. People get drunk, leave the room to answer their phone, use the restroom, go outside for a cigarette, and then get sidetracked by forgetting about their bill and leaving. I see many faces every day and I wouldn't recognize them the next time they returned anyways. I've been stuck once with a big bill for $130.00, and cried when I got home. It's bad enough when regulars take off without paying their bill, but a complete stranger that I would never recognize again, no thanks! I don't need the unnecessary headache of eyeballing strangers and with the credit card in my hand, I can lower my stress level.

I don't ask regulars for a credit card if they have a proven track record, but the ones who are known for leaving without paying their tab, I won't start them one unless I have their card in my possession. For the regular that does happen to leave on his bill, I let all servers know about it and leave a note by the till for the other girls because he may come in while another server is on shift. On the tab I write my name, the date, and then staple the bill behind the note. If the customer comes in while another girl is working, she'll collect the money for me, staple the cash to the bill, and drop it in my box.

Don't let any customers bully you into running them a tab without some sort of collateral. It's completely up to the server to call the shots, and while it is convenient for the server and patron, it's definitely not mandatory.

Having customers leave you with their unpaid tabs is one way of losing money, especially strangers that you will never recognize again.

Claim All Credit Card and Interac Slips

When you pre-authorize a credit card, put your initials or your name at the top of the pre-authorization slip. Working in a fast-paced environment, the advise slip could accidentally be misplaced instead of dropped in your waitress box or placed in your cash caddy. With your name or initials on it, it stops dishonest coworkers from submitting it into their own cash.

While helping a customer retrieve money on their interac card at the debit machine by your till, don't walk away while the transaction is in motion and resist the urge to hand over any cash or let the customer leave until you see *Approved* on the final slip. See that slip in your mind's eye as cold hard cash, because if you misplace it and it's for $50.00, that's $50.00 cash you've lost. Jotting your initials or name on your interac slips is a good habit to start as well.

Don't leave your slips in a glass by the till or out in the open where someone could grab them or mistakenly throw them out. Advise your pre-authorization slip right away and slip it into your box for safe keeping. You don't want someone running off with an important piece of paper as a visa or interac slip, as customers have helped themselves to random pieces of paper around my till so they could jot down a phone number.

If there is a wind storm brewing outdoors and you notice the lights flickering, you may want to pre-authorize all your credit cards right away. Years ago, our power went out and I had a few tabs on the go. Since these guys had no other method of payment, we had no choice but to do a manual swipe and it was put through the next day. One of the cards was declined and I was out that money.

With the older machines, when you pre-authorize a credit card and it doesn't get read, you'll have to manually punch in all the numbers. When you do this, your bar will want you to take a manual imprint of the card to prove that the customer was physically in the bar. In the past, I've forgotten to do a manual imprint and had to pay the bar for the credit card purchase until the transaction cleared at the bank. (I didn't worry as they were regulars whom I saw every single Friday afternoon for the past ten years). Most bars have the newer machines by now anyways and the cards seem to get read without any problems, no matter how beat up the magnetic strip on the back is. If you're ever in a jam and can't find the manual imprint slips and the little machine, there is a faster way to do it without all that stuff. A quick way to do a manual imprint is to take the customer's credit card and place it behind and at the bottom of the pre-authorization slip. Take a pencil (keep a few Keno pencils by the till) and scrub lightly over the name, card number, and expiration date. This proves that the customer was physically in the bar and his signature is there to prove it.

So, if you have a credit card or interac slip go missing, you just lost that money. Treat all interac and credit card slips as cash.

Keep On Top of All Tabs

I know of a few bars that still run with an old till system, and to run tabs, you need to handwrite all drinks and food on a guest check. Our bar's till can let you keep track of tabs in it, but you can't have more than one server add to a tab, table numbers can't be changed if a customer moves, food can't be included, drinks can't be voided off, the tab can't be separated if customers need you to, and there are too many steps to take in bringing up a bill on the screen that it's just too confusing and time consuming. During busy times when three or more servers are working the till at the same time, it's just not practical to use so we all end up handwriting all bills anyways because it's just easier and quicker.

If your bar has a modern till system, consider yourself lucky that you can keep track of all customers' drinks on it. Make it a mission to learn that till and be quick about it as the newer systems are very user friendly and easy to operate.

If you handwrite your tabs and you feel as though you'll forget to write drinks down, do yourself a favor and ask your customers to pay you every time you bring them a drink in cash. If you explain that you're new and still training, customers are quite understanding.

I like tabs because it saves me time, and saving time means that I can use that time to make more money. I can drop off a round of drinks and not have to stop and wait for the group to stop talking or pull out their wallets, and if a big group orders and they like to pay individually, this takes up even more of my valuable time.

When a new group sits down and asks you to run them a tab, find out if they're all on the same bill or separate. You don't want to try and separate four different tabs while you're busy and hold up other servers at the waitress station. When you start reorganizing bills and end up rushing, you get flustered and make mistakes, which could cost you money. Other customers will be waiting longer than necessary for their drinks, and as a result you get confused and

108

forgetful. Save yourself the time and aggravation by asking if all bills are kept separate in the first place.

I find that forgetting to write drinks or food on tabs is the number one money loser! Stay on top of your tabs or just do cash and carry.

Guard All Big Bills

When you're given a fifty or one-hundred dollar bill, inspect it carefully to make sure it's real, then immediately stash it away. While working, don't fold big bills and slide them in between your fingers with your other bills as I once did because it was almost given away for change as a five dollar bill. I've known of girls stuffing their big bills into their boot or bra to keep from losing it and immediately dropping it into their box as soon as they get to the till.

Never leave loose bills lying on your tray because as you start to walk or air conditioning in the room blows at you, while you're looking in another direction, the bill may fly to the floor. I had a guy waving a five dollar bill while he chased me across the room once because he said it flew off my tray. I like to slip my bills into the side of the ashtrays stacked on my tray, place an empty bottle on them, or clamp the loose bills in my fingers under my tray. If you feel uncomfortable doing either of these methods, set the bills on your tray and stack empties on top (never garbage). The bills may get wet from spillage on the tray, but you can always cram them in your waitress box while wet, and by the end of the night they'll be dry as a bone. A wet bill is better than a lost bill. The reason you don't want to set garbage on top of any bills is because you'll scoop all the garbage and throw it into the trash can without realizing there may be money hidden underneath. I witnessed a waitress years ago do this.

Big bills handed to a customer as change without realizing and money dropped onto the floor are a couple different ways of losing money.

Other Random Ways of Losing Money

• During a shift, you may have started taking extra drinks out on your tray when the bar starts to get busy, or sometimes a customer orders a drink and then disappears. You'll try to sell these drinks to other people and if you can't seem to get rid of them, you take

109

them back to the bar and give them back to the bartender. He'll put the opened bottles on ice to keep them cold, and any mixed drinks will have the ice strained out to keep them from getting watered down. Make sure to write yourself a reminder of the drinks that were put behind the bar because you'll be paying the bar for these drinks if you don't resell them during your shift. As an example, if I gave the bartender five Coors Lights, I'll write myself a note that reads, IN 5 COORS and keep the note in a glass by the till. As my shift progresses, I may need these drinks, so I reclaim them from the bar, deliver them to my customers, and collect my money. If other servers order these drinks, the bartender will give them the opened beers and they can either pay me for the drinks and not ring them in or if they do ring them in, I'll void them later. This way, they're all sold by the end of the night and all I have to do is void them at the end of my shift if I need to.

Relying on your memory to re-sell drinks or not voiding the ones that coworkers sold for you are other ways of losing money, so keep organized and jot down your random reminders.

• *Another way that a server can lose money is by not paying attention to how she's ringing drinks into the till and the bartender not catching the mistake.* Let's say that Budweiser bottles are on sale today at $5.35 and you must ring it in the till under the *special beer of the day* button (this depends on your till system). So, as you punch your order into the till, out of habit you're ringing the Budweiser beers under the regular button, regular price of $5.75. You proceed to your customers and ask for the special price of $5.35. If they tip you $.25, you're still out 15 cents. Doing this periodically throughout a shift, you're ripping yourself off way too much money, so pay attention to how you're ringing drinks into the till, especially the daily specials!

• *Remember to get paid out on any tab from the server taking it over if you're changing sections, the customer moves tables, or you go off shift.* I like to write the table number, the amount of the tab owed to me, and which server took it over. I'll either throw the note into my waitress box or keep a running list of all tabs taken over on a scrap sheet of paper in a glass. This way, if I forget to collect on any tabs during my shift, I have a reminder in my box when I do my cash at the end of my shift.

• Another important point to remember when getting paid

out on tabs is to remember to get paid out on the drinks and not just the tip. If you're not paid out for the drinks that you rang in, you'll owe it to the bar in your cash-out at the end of the night.

Sometimes we concentrate too much on the tip, forgetting about the drink money owed to us.

- Be careful and slow when sliding bills out from between your fingers while your hand is underneath your tray.

If you pull too quickly, you may remove more than one bill and not realize as it falls to the floor.

- When a customer wants their tab, into a glass I put: the bill, pre-authorization slip, and a pen. I like to keep each tab contained in its own separate glass because at times I'll have more than one tab to drop off at different tables. I don't want to juggle separate slips, credit cards, and bills and then give a customer the wrong bill or slip, or even another person's credit card.

How would you explain to a customer that you gave his credit card to a stranger, and charged him for someone else's bill?

- Another example of mixing up tabs is if you charged the first party at table #6 for two jugs and then they leave after signing off their bill. A short time later, the other tab at table #33 informs you that they ordered two jugs and not five you just charged them for.

If the first party wasn't honest and had quickly paid you for the two jugs and then left, you'll be stuck paying for the three remaining jugs that you obviously can't charge the wrong party for.

- When dropping off a tab with a customer, I make sure that I swing by their table and grab the pre-authorization slip before they leave. I have had customers slip both copies into their wallet without realizing and sometimes this is a person's first credit card where they don't know that they're to leave me a copy. Also, if another server happens to grab my slip for me and decides to do me a favor and advises it, out of sheer habit she may drop it in her own box instead of mine.

Keep on top of those credit card slips and remember to retrieve them from your customers.

- Check the customer's total. If the bill was for $72.00 and he wrote $13.00 in the tip line, the total should be $85.00. What if the customer miscalculated and wrote $75.00 instead? I advise it through for the right amount of $85.00 as the proof is in the amount written in the tip line and the signature.

Get in the habit of making sure the tally is correct as this is a common mistake that occurs.

• *Do not accept old bills.* Apologize and say that this is bar policy or that you've had trouble with them in the past. See my story of how I ended up with a fake hundred dollar bill and how I was lucky enough to get rid of it under the **Bonus Chapter of 100 of Romana's Unforgettable Customers, Story #38 titled "Fake Hundred."**

• *Do not accept bills from out of the country if you don't know how to inspect them for a counterfeit.*

I don't mind smaller American money, but I do not accept the fifties or hundreds anymore as I do not deal with them very often and I'm not experienced in identifying the fakes anyways.

• *If your bar has a pull tab machine, be aware of what's in it and don't pay out large sums of money to big winners.*

Let the customer go up to the bartender to collect his money. All winning pull tabs must be redeemed at the bar that they are won at, as each bar's pull tabs have a code on them and if you pay out on a pull tab that didn't come out of your machine, you'll be responsible for paying it back to the bar. What if that pull tab came from five hours away? The only time I'll take any pull tabs is if a customer throws them on my tray as a tip.

• Our bar is busy most of the time, so to keep myself organized when staff or dancers order food or drinks from me, I start a sheet of paper with their names and amounts owing. I like to start collecting on any outstanding bills from staff and dancers when I'm not busy or close to the end of my shift.

By forgetting to collect any money owing to you on food or drinks from staff or dancers is another way to lose money.

• During the nightshift, ask customers to pre-pay for all kitchen orders. The easiest time to do this is when you drop off cutlery, napkins, and drinks before the food arrives.

It's too easy for someone to wolf down their food and run out the door without paying while you're busy and not paying attention.

• *Pay attention to all change you're handing back a customer.*

When a customer hands you a ten, place it on top of your tray and hand back the change, counting it out loud. This way if the person says that they handed you a twenty, show them that the ten is sitting right here on top of the tray. While pulling money out from your fingers under your tray, look at the bills and register in your mind what you are handing over to your customer.

- *Don't let new coworkers use your server number for the till while training.*

If there's a new person working, ask management to give her a distinct number or key right away. You don't want a new person using your number and getting used to it because if both girls end up working on the same shift, all drinks will be rung up under the same name and it could be quite the nightmare to try and figure out who owes what to the bar.

- If you start at a new bar or your bar has a price increase, when you punch in a drink order, most tills can let you print off a copy of the receipt with all the drinks and their prices that you just punched in. Use this as your cheat sheet for a few weeks until you get accustomed to all the prices.

Not knowing prices of drinks by undercharging customers is another way of losing money.

- *Pay close attention when handing the bartender money to buy small change or rolls of coin.*

A server is always thinking of numerous things at the same time and trying to stay a step ahead. Many times I have given the bartender forty dollars to buy a roll of loonies and three fives, only to grab my tray of drinks and run back onto the floor, forgetting about my money back at the bar.

When you give money to the bartender to buy small change, always double-check what you're handing over. Sometimes he's in a rush where he slips the money into the till only to say, "Did you give me $25 or $60?"

- *Forgetting to sign out on your shift is another way of losing money.*

My shift is always the same, so I sign out part way through my shift or even at the beginning. If I know that I might be leaving early or end up working overtime, I'll write myself a note and pop it into my box as a reminder to adjust the sign out sheet before I go home.

- *Not knowing how to add up drinks properly in your head and shorting yourself frequently is another way of losing money.* If you do this repeatedly, it will add up quickly. For more on this subject, please refer to **Chapter #3, Subchapter #3 under "The Fundamentals of Counting Money."**

- If you're going off shift, don't assume that the customer wants to continue his tab with the other server. Many of my customers prefer to square up with me by making sure that I am paid out on my tip and then they start a new tab with the new girl. I find that some of my regulars leave me a bigger tip when I sign out with them than if I were to leave it to continue running with another server.

Give the customer a choice whether he wants to continue his tab with another server or to finish it up with you as you could end up with a bigger tip this way.

- Don't leave any loose paper money sitting on your tray as you run off to place an order in the kitchen, use the restroom, or deliver drinks to a table. If a scammer feels like they can get away with it without being noticed, they will make the move and take your money.

Don't trust anyone! Keep all paper money on you and your cash caddy full of coin clipped closed or a cloth sitting on your ashtray of coin to hide it.

Romana's Story... The Tip Jar Scammer

Years ago while I was working the nightshift, my bartender at the time had a patron standing around his bar talking to him for a couple of hours.

I had come up to the bar in tears because I had a problem with a customer. I was visibly upset, so my bartender came over to my till and leaned over the bar to talk to me. When he went back over to his till, his tip jar was gone and so was the customer!

He ran outside with me in tow and we saw a dirty white van speeding out of the parking lot.

Romana's Story... Pay Attention!

I had a regular run a tab with me one evening and at the end of the night he came up to pay his $300.00 bill by debit. I ran his card through and wasn't paying attention the whole time as we were busy chatting away with one another. As I gave him his copy of the slip, I asked him what he was up to for the rest of the night and he said that he was going to the nightclub next door.

114

About an hour later, I was cashing out and noticed his slip which screamed "declined." I ran to the club next door and found him. He was nice enough to come back and redo the transaction so I could get my money.

The Fundamentals of Counting Money

The one thing that scared me the most when I looked into waitressing as a job many years ago was adding up prices of drinks in my head. I'm going to give you some useful tips to help you get over the same hurdle that has freaked out so many servers.

Practice Those Times Tables

Now is the time to learn your times tables if you didn't do it back in grade school. I'm not kidding! Practice counting while driving, watching TV, showering, etc. By learning to count quickly and accurately, you'll know how to calculate drinks efficiently in your head. Saving time means making more money! If you've never been good at math, now is the time to get better at it and it'll even keep you from losing money.

If you'll be working in a bar, it will be "cash and carry" most of the time and this is why you want to be good at adding up random prices of drinks in your head.

Add Your Drinks Up Properly

Over the years, I've been told by girls that when they add up drinks, they round up prices and tack on a couple of dollars, just so that they don't risk ripping themselves off. Don't get in the habit of this, as customers will eventually figure it out when another server charges them a lesser amount on the same round of drinks. You'll be looked at as the waitress that rips off customers and they'll never sit in your section or want to be served by you again. I assure you that no waitress wants this kind of a reputation. Some customers will tell management, and you can end up with a written warning or possibly even be fired because this is considered stealing.

It's Really Very Simple... Remember the Fundamentals

Here are some scenarios:

- Two guys sit down and order two bottles of Kokanee at $5.90 each.
  $5.90 + $5.90. Look at it as ... Round up the price to $6.00.
  $6.00 + $6.00 = $12.00. $12.00- $.10 from each beer.
  $12-$.20=$11.80

- A double Crown coke is $10.25 and a Kokanee is $5.95.
  Look at it as $10.25 + $6.00 = $16.25 - $.05 = $16.20

- A round of 8 Kokanne beers at $5.90 each.
  8 times $6.00 = $48.00
  $48.00 - $.80 ($.10 times 8 beer) = $47.20

- Three beers at $5.75 each.
  Look at it as $6.00 times 3 = $18.00
  $18.00 - $.75 ($.25 times 3 beer) = $17.25

- Four beers at $5.50 each, Caesar at $6.50, and a Crown coke at $6.75
  $22.00 + $6.50 + $6.75 =
  $35.25

- Corona $6.50, coffee $4.00, pop $3.25, bottle water $4.00, Double Rum $10.25, Basket of Wings $10.00
  Add up big numbers - $10.25 + $10.00 = $20.25
  Then add up the same two numbers, then Corona and then the water. $8.00 + $6.50 + $3.25 = $17.75
  Then add up the two totals - $20.25 + $17.75 = $38.00

It's just an easier method of counting. It saves your time and brain power, as well as makes sense in your head.

Adding Up Large Orders with Random Prices

If a large group comes in and orders several different drinks at different prices, write the full total on the back of your hand or a

116

scrap sheet of paper. I could kick myself when I drop off twelve drinks and one person slaps down a hundred dollar bill and says, "I'll pay the first round." For large groups, you can even grab a small calculator and take it out onto the floor with you in case you need to quickly add up large amounts of random drinks.

I have dropped off large orders where a guy will say to me, "Ok, I'll pay for his drink, that guy's last three drinks, my food and the stag guy's food, and the thirteen shots. Oh, and by the way, I need to do it immediately because my ride is here and I have to leave right away."

I always have a pen or two clipped on the inside of my skirt so that I can scribble down a few prices if I'm really stuck. Our bar has promo material lying around the bar on tables throughout the room, and I'll grab a sheet and do my number scribbling on this if I'm stuck.

The most important advice I can give on this subject is that you should memorize those times tables and practice your counting. It does take time and the more you do it, the easier and faster it comes. Don't let this be your one hurdle that keeps you from doing this job.

Romana's Story... Romana's First Day on the Job

My first serving job was selling shooters in a nightclub. I was terrified on my first day, thinking that I'd look stupid by not knowing how to add up drinks or even end up losing money.

For the first two weeks, I carried a little security blanket on my tray; a tiny cheat sheet that gave me some confidence. As I think back, it's a little funny because it was only adding up multiples of $3.75! My tiny cheat sheet read:

1 shooter	*=*	*$3.75*
2"	*=*	*$7.50*
3"	*=*	*$11.25*
4"	*=*	*$15.00*
5"	*=*	*$18.75*
6"	*=*	*$22.50*
7"	*=*	*$26.25*
8"	*=*	*$30.00*

Fifteen years later, I'm pretty quick at counting odd prices in my head, thanks to my husband Rod! He taught me the art of fundamentals and how easy counting in your head can actually be.

Learn to Memorize All Orders

The Memorizing Secret

I'm always being asked by customers how I manage to remember so many drinks at one time in my head. There really isn't any magic to it as I just do it and I'm good at it because I've been doing it for many years. That's my secret: just lots of practice.

I was trained over fifteen years ago to memorize all of my food and drink orders, and I'm glad that I was forced to learn this way because it has made me more efficient over the years. For example, when a customer is talking to me, instead of stopping to write an order down, I'm grabbing for empties at the same time or wiping their table while listening to them. I'm able to point at drinks and do the "thumbs up" signal if I am being waved at for another round and if my free hand is full, I'm still able to nod or mouth "Okay" when needing to communicate with someone while I'm passing by. I'm doing all this at the same time while registering all these drinks in my head. A good server definitely has to be good at multi-tasking.

The Advantages of Memorization

My tray is *stuck* to my left arm. What I mean by stuck is that my tray does not leave my arm. It does not get set down on a table until I loop around the room and end up back at the waitress station.

I don't like to set my tray down on a table because people can accidentally kick into the table, resulting in drinks sloshing and spilling on or off my tray. I can accidentally tip my tray over by setting it down and the bottom side can get sticky and wet. The drinks are exposed to customers who can slip something in there while my head is turned and I'm not paying attention. My change is visible for anyone to help themselves to if I remove my rag to turn around and give a table a wipe. By hoisting my tray up and then setting it down constantly, I'm wasting valuable time. Time is money. With that tray

118

stuck on my arm, my right hand is free to grab empties and garbage, wipe tables, push in chairs, deal with money, or touch people on their back if I'm passing by so they know I'm there (this way they won't get up or move back, knocking into my tray). I can fly around the room pointing at drinks, using hand signals or even waving at customers as they enter or leave the room. I'm extremely talented at giving one-arm hugs with a full tray of drinks without spilling a drop!

When I loop around the room and end up back at the till, the first thing I do is start punching my drinks into the till. Then, I spin around and take a look at my room to see if there's anyone that I've forgotten. I like to backtrack and think about all the drink orders I've taken. If I'm really busy, I'll add four to six extra drinks that are on special to my order. This way, if there's anyone I forgot or some new bodies that entered the room, I have extra beer to sell.

I have coworkers that would rather jot down drinks as they move through the room. If you're new or haven't used the memorizing system before and you'd prefer to write down your orders, then write them down. You want to use whatever is easier and less stressful for you, especially during the busy times. I suggest that during the slower times, you get into the habit of stretching your mind and work on your memorization. Make it a mission to work a full shift while memorizing everything. Yup, all drinks and food orders! It will make you a stronger server.

Write Down the Random Information

Many times I'll drop off drinks and a customer tells me that he has no money on him because he needs to grab some out of the debit machine. I'll point to where the ATM machine is and mention that I'll collect money next time I walk by. This way it puts the pressure on him to have my money ready for me the next time I'm by. I make sure to jot down a quick note to myself on a scrap piece of paper. *JUG, TBL 32* seems to do the trick for me. Many times I would try and rely on my memory to collect, but I get busy and side tracked with other things. When I drive home at night or lay in bed, IT pops into my head ... that guy who owed me for the Stoli coke at table nine or the guys who owe me money for the two cheeseburgers at table thirty-two. Of course, some people don't stop and remind you, "I owe you money." The honest people do, but there are those that won't or they may have forgotten as well. It's my responsibility to collect my money, so I can only blame myself if I forget.

Try to stay organized so you don't have to concentrate on remembering every random thing. Anything that you should know for a later time, such as staff meeting dates, schedule changes, and supplies you've run out of, write it down on a piece of paper and pop it into your waitress box so you don't have to memorize it.

For coworkers and dancers who owe you money for food or drinks during your shift, put their name on one small sheet of paper as a reminder and keep it in a glass near the till. I put it in list form with the name and amount due and I cross off the people as they pay me. This way, I can put away any unnecessary paperwork, such as food bills, and get them out of my way, and it keeps the till area rather clutter-free. By writing down random information, it saves your brain power to remember drink and food orders, and even to learn customer's names!

At the beginning of the week, get in the habit of rechecking the schedule. Even if you've worked the same shift for years, people go on holidays, quit, or get fired unexpectedly, or there's some other last-minute emergency change. If you were scheduled and didn't show up for your scheduled shift, you will be to blame. You know what they say ... never assume—It makes an ass out of u and me. By writing stuff down, you don't have to rely on your memory all the time.

If you don't carry a day timer, you can get a small one at the dollar store or use your cell phone. It's extremely handy to keep track of your personal life as well as anything to do with work (staff meetings, promoting trips, special functions, change of shifts, etc).

Many years ago, I had four jobs going at one time. My day timer was my best friend at that time, and it kept my life organized so I didn't have to think too much about where I was supposed to be and when. I just had to remember to check it the night before.

Master the Till and Store the Popular PLUs in Your Mind

When you're new to a job and familiarizing yourself with a new till, you'll struggle with it in the beginning. By using it regularly, you gain speed in finding your items in the till quickly. During slow times, play with it to become knowledgeable about it. The faster you ring in your drink orders, the quicker you get them from the bartender and deliver them to your customers. By learning to punch in your orders quickly and in proper sequence, you make your bartender's job easier and you don't hold up the other servers who are in line behind you.

In order to save time, memorize as many PLUs as you can. A PLU is a code number for an item in some tills. If I want to ring in a Crown Royal, I would look for it under the rye button. All the rye that we sell would be listed there with their own code numbers under alphabetical order. I have many PLUs memorized for the most popular premium drinks we sell, as well as local bottles of beer.

It's a great idea to memorize food prices as well. This way it saves you time when you add up bills or you can help out a customer when they ask you how much an item costs. It comes in extremely handy when you want to get a customer to prepay for a food item when you work the nightshift.

Some Memorization Tips

If you've never memorized drink or food orders, all it really takes is practice. The more you do it, the easier it gets. To this day, customers are absolutely amazed that I can remember an entire tray of drinks and know one cocktail from another.

- If you want to try memorizing food, start easy on yourself. Try with one customer first. Move onto two, three, and then a whole table of people. It really is not that hard when you practice and do it a lot. Take your orders and file them in your mind. In the beginning, have a pen and scrap paper as a security blanket just in case you start to lose control and start to forget.

- If you work on the art of memorizing drink orders, you'll be more successful at this job and make more money. There's nothing wrong with writing down orders, but when a server does, she spends much of her time writing when she could be doing other tasks at the same time.

- As I head towards the bar, I'm thinking about the loop around the room I just did. I'm starting to rearrange all the drinks I have stored in my head. I'm doing a calculation of how many bottles of Kokanee I need or how many Coronas that are needed. If I have an estimate of needing seven pints of beer, I take out a couple extra in case I forgot anyone. I will pack out nine as I can always sell a couple extra pints to new people if they happen to enter the bar.

- You want to figure out an easy system for yourself. Remember when you were in school and you had to memorize stuff for an exam? I thought of the craziest things to get something to stick in my mind. I still use this system to this day. Here are a few examples of memorizing I use:

1. A customer orders a clubhouse on brown with a salad and ranch dressing. I don't repeat to myself in my head, clubhouse on brown with a salad and ranch dressing. I shorten it and say to myself ... *club, brown, ranch*. I know it's a clubhouse on brown with salad.

2. A customer orders a steak sandwich, medium rare with Caesar salad. I just think to myself, *MY steak*. This is exactly the way I would order a steak for myself. If a steak is ordered well done, I picture the guy's face almost blackened. I use visualization when I can.

3. When a guy orders a bacon cheeseburger with fries, I just think *burger*. This is the most common way customers order their burgers. If he were to order, no tomato, just think *burger, no tomato*. If a plain burger is ordered, I think naked burger.

4. A customer orders a pulled pork sandwich. I visualize him pulling my hair!

5. An order of hot wings, I imagine his head blowing up from the hot sauce.

- It can get a little hairy when a table of customers ask for specifics such as a side of mayo, extra guacamole, no onions, and so forth.

- If you forget a customer's food order by the time you get to your till, just run back and ask him again. People understand that you are busy, so don't sweat it and move on. If you dwell on it, you'll end up getting yourself flustered and go into a pattern of forgetting more orders.

- If a large table of people wants to order food, I let them know that I will be back in a moment as I need to grab my food pad. If I'm busy, I know I won't be able to remember twelve different meals on top of a head full of drinks. I'm good at my job, but I'm also not Superwoman!

Romana's Story... "Who Are You?"

A few years ago, Rod and I were in the lobby of a restaurant waiting to be seated to have brunch. There was a girl there who started talking to me and asking how I was and what I was up to. Then she asked me if I was still working at the bar and such.

Finally, the hostess took us to our table and when we were seated, Rod smiled at me and said, "You have absolutely no idea who that was, do you?"

"None. Could you tell?" I asked him.

"She couldn't tell, but I could." He said.

He knows me too well ...

This has happened to me more times than I can count. It usually ends up being someone that I've served at one time or another at the bar anyhow, so I usually just go along with pretending that I know them. It's just politer that way.

"Can you take this away?"

Chapter 4 – DIFFERENT STRATEGIES OF SPEED

Gettin' Slammed

A Typical Slammed Night

Picture this … It's a pretty mellow night as you're cruising along serving your customers. You've got a moment or two to chat with regulars, gossip a bit with your bartender, and even cruise into the kitchen to help out by scraping old food off the dirty dishes and running them through the dishwasher.

Six new customers walk in, they ask for menus and a round of drinks. You saunter to the bar and grab their order. After dropping it off, you pass by a small group of young men that just sat down at the next table over. After asking them for their identification and waiting patiently while they pull out their wallets, you take their order. Continuing around the room, a few more tables want rounds, Andy asks you for more ketchup and napkins, Jim would like a glass of ice water, and all the while you're grabbing empties, pushing in chairs, and wiping tables. Stopping at table thirty-three, you scoop the large amount of change onto your tray that was left for you as a tip and pick up the last empties. While wiping the table, you notice the amount of bodies entering the bar is starting to increase rather quickly and you feel the energy level in the room start to rise.

Back at the bar you ring up your order, and then unload the empties and garbage off your tray. You decide to add six extra beers that are on sale to your tray because the number of people entering the bar is steadily increasing and you know you'll easily sell them. Quickly, you load your tray and then heave your full tray onto your arm and off you go. Oops! You forgot that mug of water and menus, so you backtrack towards the bartender.

Heading back out onto the floor with your full tray, water, and menus, you notice a new group hooting and hollering while strolling into the room. The guy dressed in a tacky dirty wedding dress is looking rather sheepish—a stag. You glance at the large party heading down to the stage while you pick up your speed and drop off your drinks, grabbing empties and pushing in chairs that are scattered in your way, while staying on the map of the room so you don't miss anyone.

Table five now wants their bill and is asking if you could please call them a taxi. A punk at table seven has his feet propped up on his table while busy texting on his cell phone and you abruptly push his feet off while walking by. He yells, "What the hell?!" before you ask him if he'd mind you coming to his house and sticking your feet up on his kitchen table. He gives you a dumb vacant look as you shake your head and continue towards gyno, noticing the neighborhood drunk falling asleep. Shaking him awake, you warn him that you'll be asking him to leave if you have to wake him a second time.

As you walk around gyno, Mike hands you thirty dollars and says, "Here Ro. I owe you for three beers. Keep the change!" You smile and wave at him as he runs out the door.

A new group of young people now sit at table twelve and bicker with you as to why you're asking them for ID. You tell them you don't have time to argue and demand that they either pull out two pieces of identification or leave. As your tray arm starts to shake from the weight, they further waste your time by asking what the cheapest alcoholic drink being sold is, and then ask you to name all the specials. Two kids tell you they have no money and you let them know that they all have to order a drink or they have to take off. They decide to get up and exit, leaving all their chairs strewn about. While pushing in the chairs that are in your way, you feel your blood start to boil while thinking of the valuable time they just wasted. Your arm feels like it's going to fall off now.

Glancing at the bar, you notice the party from table five is standing at the bar, patiently waiting for you so they can square up and pay their bill. You haven't made it to the stag party yet sitting at gyno who seem to be getting rowdier by the minute. You scream, "Stop!" as you suddenly freeze and hold your foot out to stop a drunken girl from backing into your tray because both hands are unavailable to block her.

Wayne waves you over and tells you that he has just got to tell you this great joke he heard yesterday. You try to keep calm as you politely tell him you're really busy right now and you'd love to hear it when you've got a spare moment.

You make it to the stag guys and they order every different drink under the sun that seems to range from a Miller, Stella, Rum coke with three cubes of ice and two lime twists, a Bombay tonic, coke neat, coffee with three sacks of sugar, a double Crown ginger short, Smirnoff Ice with a set up, Grey Goose water with a shot of cranberry juice, and what was that last drink ordered? You've got a guy in the group asking you how much a private dance costs and another guy informs you that the group is starving and wants to order food right away. The big shot in the group wearing the sunglasses mentions, "Could you bring out a dozen shots of Cuervo right away?" As you listen to him order, you wonder if he's stoned, in hiding, trying to look cool, or is just stupid. You decide on all of the above.

As you make it back to the bar, your arm is singing with the pain of dragging your tray of empties around the room. You wonder where that party at table five went to. Hopefully, just to the restroom or out for a smoke. You don't panic because you remembered to pre-authorize the credit card they gave you two hours ago. You remind yourself that you've served this group many times in the past and they always leave a handsome tip. As you head to the bar, you notice a twenty dollar bill lying on the floor. With a shaky arm, you set your full tray down on the empty table beside it and retrieve it off the floor. Picking up your heavy tray of drinks and balancing it on your arm, you finally make it back to the till.

Glancing at your bartender, you notice he's pouring and serving his line as quickly as possible, and you hate to tell him that the glass washer is full and you have no room to add any more dirty glasses to it unless he starts to unload it.

Punching in your next orders, you realize you won't be able to carry it all out. You run out the three jugs and glasswear and quickly mumble to the group that you'll be right back for money. As you stand there punching in your order, a few regulars are leaving for the night and have brought their empty bottles up to the bar for you. You thank them as they put the empty bottles in the proper beer case.

You try to keep your cool as you feel the panic rise. More people are walking in the room, a group of regulars are asking which section of the room you're working, and if you could please bring out their usual drinks right away. A group of your regular bad boys come in right after, hug you, and ask if there's an available table for them. You tell them that they can sit at the staff table with the staff sign on it and you'll be out with their usual drinks right away. You know it's turning into a great night for making tips, even though you'll be dealing with a sore back, shoulder, and feet later.

Glancing at your watch, you realize another server won't be on for another hour and the doorman who checks identification at the door won't start for another hour as well.

You feel like you're losing control. You start to sweat and shake and ... STOP!! You've been slammed! You're only human and there's only so much you can do.

First, punch in all the drinks you remember. Look back at the room, retrace your steps, and punch in any drinks that were not thought of. As the bartender starts loading the counter with all drinks, grab another tray and run out drinks to regulars that are on tabs and close by (this saves room on your tray). While running back to the bar, only gather empties from deserted tables because people will continue to order from you and you definitely won't have any room on your tray to add more drinks. If customers try stopping you, respond with "I'll be with you in a moment!"

When taking out your full tray, while waiting for customers to pull out money, ask people at the next table if they need another round and grab their empties—use those precious moments.

When you get slammed, carry as many extra drinks as you can, as you'll always get rid of them and the bottles don't take up too much room on your tray. Depending on the crowd, I carry extra pints as well and bottles that are on special, as they're a hot seller because of the cheap price. This way, if someone who just came into the bar asks you for a Canadian, you can say, "I have an extra Budweiser on my tray you can have right now if you don't want to wait for me to run to the bar." Nine times out of ten, he'll buy it just so he doesn't have to wait for you to come back or he has to go to the bar and stand in the line up. Believe me, you'll have a table buy all the extra beer you have on your tray because some people are power drinking and they get caught up in the moment and love to show off.

Full Tray OUT / Full Tray IN

When you're busy, the rule is FULL TRAY OUT/ FULL TRAY IN. When you take a bottle of beer off your tray, replace the spot with an empty. Turning the bottle around so you can't see the label symbolizes an empty. By stacking empty glasses into one another, or empty bottles into pint mugs or jugs, this saves room on your tray for more empties.

If you really feel out of control, your room is beginning to look like a mess, and you're starting to run out of clean glassware, ask the DJ for help. Ask someone (if there's a shooter girl or food girl working) if they have a moment to grab a bus pan and fly through the room to grab empties. Make sure you remember to slip them some money, as no one likes to work for free. They'll be more than happy to help you out the next time you need it.

During times that I'm not slammed and if I have a free hand, I like to help out our food girl (if there's one on shift) when she's busy. If she's running her tail off, I'll grab that empty plate out of the customer's way. It only takes a moment and it keeps the room from looking messier than it could. If you help her out when she needs it, she'll do the same for you.

I could bang my head against the wall when I see servers walk past a table littered with empties and run to the till to ring in orders with a bare tray. This is where I take a look at her section and see how many empties are laying around on tables and around the stage area. Servers need to stay on top of cleanliness because when there are numerous amounts of empties down at the stage, there's more of a chance that a dancer can kick into them. They'll break and shoot out into the audience when she swings around the pole while doing her pole tricks. Keep empties from accumulating on tables because it looks messy and they get in a customer's way. There won't be room on a table if the guys ordered meals as tables in bars are not that big to begin with.

Stay Focused and Do Not Panic

If you stay focused and move quickly, you'll do just fine. When you panic, you feel like throwing down your tray and running from the room. Before you know it, help arrives, your room gets back to being orderly, and your heart rate comes back down to normal from panic mode.

Customers are usually pretty understanding, so if someone asks you why it's taking so long for drinks or looks like they're getting annoyed with the amount of time it's taking for you to deliver their order, open your mouth and tell them that you're the only waitress on the floor right now. Usually they'll understand and feel empathy for you. On the other hand, if someone is rude, tell them you're doing the best you can and maybe they should go to the bar for their drinks. Remember, you can't please everyone.

Ask a Coworker for Help

If you're working with another server and the bar gets overly busy where you can't keep up, you can always ask her to take over some of your tables. I'm usually pretty happy to help out a fellow server when asked because its extra money that I can make and I love being busy to the point of where my shift feels like it's flying by.

People will get up and go to the bar to buy a drink if they see that you're too busy and not coming around fast enough. If you can't keep up any longer to drink orders, tell customers nearest the bar that you're extremely busy right now and that it would be a lot quicker for them to get their first round of drinks at the bar, and apologize for this. They'll appreciate your honesty, and it will relieve some of the pressure off you.

Most Important... Sell the Alcohol First!

"Selling booze pays the bills" is what I always hear in my head from my first manager, Mary, who hired and trained me. If you get slammed, leave the wiping and move the chairs that are in your way. Grab empties as you run along, cramming garbage into empty jugs or pint mugs. Hang a couple of empty jugs from the fingers under your tray if you run out of room on your tray or in your free hand. If there's no food girl on shift, leave dishes; you can always run out next time around and stack a pile on top of each other and take them away in one swoop, or you can even ask the DJ or shooter girl to do you a favor and clear them away. Pick up your speed, stay focused, keep organized, and you'll manage just fine.

When you're remembering all drinks, flying through the room dropping off cocktails and beer, collecting money, staying on top of your empties, wiping tables, and pushing in chairs, it's an exhilarating feeling! You know you're doing a great job when customers are tipping you like crazy (you can't wait to count your tips at the end of the shift) and patrons are commenting on what a great job you're doing.

132

Romana's Story... A Crazy Night at the Contest!

A few years ago we were holding a contest for the dancers at our bar on a Wednesday night.

Since we held this contest in the past and it was usually pretty mellow, management didn't plan on scheduling any extra staff on for that night. The night of the contest, the room was packed and there was only my poor bartender, a very inexperienced server, and myself. We didn't even have a shooter girl on, and since it was in the middle of summer, we were short staffed as some of the servers were on vacation. There were people everywhere and the lineup didn't seem to shorten at the bar for a few hours. My bartender worked like a mad man and did an incredible job!

I worked my section and took over some of the other server's side as she couldn't keep up. At one point, she looked at me with big eyes and said, "Ro, I don't know what to do! I can't remember anyone's drinks and I'm so behind!"

I said to her, "Load your tray full of bottle specials and when you take one off, replace it with an empty. Grab empty jugs or pint mugs and stack empty bottles into them. If people complain about you forgetting their beer, just tell them you're sorry and ask if they would they like a Budweiser bottle instead as they are on sale today anyways."

I was doing the "Oktoberfest Moves" all night (waddling but moving as fast as I could with a FULL tray and my right hand was carrying three jugs or five mugs at one time). I was starting to lose my concentration by the end of the night myself and started loading out the Budweiser bottles as well.

At the end of the shift, I was tired like you wouldn't believe with my shoulders and feet screaming in pain. But we made it through the night and I went home with an amount of money that would knock your socks off!

Hustle... Kick it up to the Next Gear!

Every server will encounter times when she gets slammed and you feel the panic starting to rise. You get so bombarded with drink orders that you wonder if you'll be able to fit them all on your tray and carry them all out. Will the customers still be there by the time you come back around? You feel like you need to almost break into a run but you need to keep your cool and stay focused. You'll get there when you get there. If the customers disappear, you'll resell the drinks to someone else; "no big deal," you tell yourself.

Manage Your Time and Stay Two Steps Ahead

When the bartender starts making your drinks, help him out by putting straws and lime twists into them, then arrange the drinks on your tray very tightly together. If there are tables nearby that just ordered (and these customers have open tabs), grab those drinks and run them over to the table in your hands or a separate tray (leave your original tray at the bar). I'll interrupt with a "Sorry to interrupt guys!" as I drop off the drinks and leave. By the time you return to the bar, place more drinks on your tray. Running out drinks to nearby tables saves room on your tray, it's less weight to carry, and the drinks are delivered quicker, which equal more tips.

Don't Forget to Collect Your Money

If you have a jug or two for a table, run out the jugs and empty glasses. I will stack glasses into one another and carry them all in one hand. Tell the group, "Guys, I'll be back in a couple of minutes for money." If you think you'll forget to collect money as you pass by their table, jot down a quick note for yourself. I'll write JUG, TBL 39. This reminds me to collect money for a jug at table 39. If a patron has left the table to go smoke, use the restroom, answer his phone, or use the ATM machine, and you dropped off a drink without payment, make a quick note to collect money the next time you pass by. Don't always rely on your memory for random things when you're busy.

On my drive home after work on a Friday night, I remembered the girl at table twenty-three who owed me for a Caesar, but I forgot to collect from her because she went to use the ATM. I don't know about you, but if I'm going to pay for anyone's drink, I'd prefer to pay for a friend's and not a stranger's.

134

Carry Extra Drinks On Your Tray

If you notice new people coming into the bar, carry extra drinks. If bottles of Canadian are on sale, carry an extra four to six extras on your tray. If you don't sell them during this trip around the bar, then maybe you'll get rid of them on the next. If they still haven't sold, give them to the bartender to put on ice. Make sure you write yourself a note that you are in/up those beers.

Customers love it when they sit down and you tell them you have extra bottles on your tray they can purchase now, instead of waiting for you to go all the way to the bar. They'll usually buy the beer on your tray, instead of waiting for that Kokanee or Corona.

I like to joke around and say that I knew that they were coming in the door, and I purposely planned for them to get the beer right away. If you joke around and make it fun, you'll put them in an even better mood than what they were in, and usually receive a very nice tip!

Friday afternoons are really busy. Not just for my bar, but for most pubs. The blue collar workers get off of work for the week and like to go out for a couple beers with their buddies, and some will only have a certain amount of time to kill before they have to go home to their families. Some of these guys are on a drinking frenzy, so the quicker you serve them, the more drinks are bought. Higher sales means you look good to the boss and you make more tips!

Pick Up Your Speed When Necessary

Speed is important in this industry. Customers don't want to see you sauntering around the room at a slow pace when the room is buzzing. When the lunch or dinner rush starts to pick up, I increase the pace of my walk and everything I do is with speed and consistency. My walk has a purpose and I don't mosey around or wander aimlessly as I want to get around the room or my section quickly. This way, customers see my face more often and know that the drink they ordered will arrive quickly, so they won't be as inclined to get up and go to the bartender or move to another server's section for better service. If they go to the bar for the rest of the night, it's bad for you because it's a table you aren't making

135

any money off of and you're stuck picking up all the empties and cleaning up after them. After all, I'm there to make money, so I want people to keep me busy and order their drinks from me.

During a lunch rush, the blue collar workers only have an hour for a lunch break and I'm usually told by certain people that they're in a rush as the first aid course across the street starts in forty-five minutes or a customer lets me know that they're killing half an hour before an appointment. The quicker you serve your customers, the quicker they drink, and the quicker they'll leave. This means that new customers will replace the previous and you continue making more money in tips.

Stay on top of your efficiency because this is the time to make some money. Before you know it, the room empties and you can go back to slowing down your pace. Keep this in mind for any rush that occurs during your shift at any time of day or night.

It may happen that a party will sit at one of your tables for a longer time than usual and sip on their one drink. This is a waiting game with this type of customer, and you have to wait for them to leave. Before you know it, they'll be gone and a new group will be there keeping you busy and making you money.

Romana's Story... Colliding With the Shooter Girl

Many years ago, I was working the nightshift with our shooter girl. For the majority of the evening, it wasn't very busy. But at one point, I got a small rush, so I picked up my speed and was zipping around the till. I turned around in a hurry and ended up colliding with her as she was just coming up to the till with a tray of shooters. She was quiet, so I didn't hear her and she wasn't expecting me to fly around and collide into her.

We called the manager at the time and he told us that we had to split the cost and pay for the whole tray as he wasn't going to promo anything. We both felt like crying, and probably did when we counted our tips later that night.

Saving Time

I always keep my mind open to new ways on saving time. Any time saved is used to sell drinks, which means more money for the bar (higher sales—you look good in the boss's eyes), and tips for yourself (the main reason why you're there in the first place).

Know About All the Daily Specials

Before starting your shift, check on all the drink and food specials. Take a walk into the kitchen and find out the special of the day. During this time, the cook will let you know if the kitchen is out of wings or that there are only ten steaks left until the afternoon delivery order comes in.

It drives me crazy when I'm busy and a customer asks me what the soup of the day is and I have no idea. I have to walk into the kitchen and make an unnecessary trip to find out, and then dash back out to the customer. Then I'm running back into the kitchen a third time to put the order in.

Our bar's system for putting food orders into the kitchen is to write them out on a guest check. We pay our money separately to the kitchen, so knowing many of the food prices off by heart is a big time saver. At my bar, we don't have the luxury of putting the food orders into a till and having the price come up. If your bar's system calls for you to program all your food into the till, consider yourself lucky, and learn to use that till quickly.

Take Initiative

When the room is humming, all staff is busy doing something. As your bartender puts all the bottles on the counter, start popping the caps open yourself and place them on your tray. Try to stay one step ahead of him to help him out. Put limes in your Corona bottles and drinks and place your straws in as well. Not only are you helping him out, you're helping yourself out by getting drinks ready to go on your tray quicker. This gets you in and out of the bar immediately.

Pull Your Weight

The rule is when you fill a beer case up, don't leave it there for someone else to get rid of; move it! It's annoying when you come up to the bar with a full tray of empties and you've got to start moving full cases of empties out of the way.

When unloading empty bottles from your tray, quickly tip them upside down over the sink, to get whatever liquid is in out, before placing them into the case. If you put bottles into the case with liquid inside, when someone goes to move the case and it drops slightly, they get splashed in the face with stale beer. It's not a good feeling!

Don't slam empty bottles in the case. It's easy to start hurrying when you get busy and rush by slamming bottles. In turn, they chip at the mouth area and glass can fly. I've almost been shot in the eye this way a couple times. When you put the bottles into the case, stack them neatly from the beginning because when it gets busy, you don't want to waste time re-stacking and organizing them.

If the glass washer is full, turn it on and run the dirty glasses through. On busy nights, the glass washer will be kept turned on most of the time anyways.

Make Good Use of Your Spare Time

If you write out all food bills, when you have a spare moment, grab the slips from your glass and put them all in numbered order. Add them all up, putting the total on the back bill, and then staple them all together. As the night goes on, organize the rest of the slips, stapling them behind the original stack and add up the new ones to the last total on the back bill. By the end of your shift, you may only have a few bills to add to the last total and you'll have your cash-out done quicker so you can go home. Before you use the final tally, recalculate the whole lot and make sure the total matches up to the original. If it doesn't, add up all bills one more time.

As you walk the floor, get in the habit of organizing your coin, folding loose bills into your fingers, and reorganizing the bottles or glasses on your tray to make room for more empties.

I work with some great girls. When I arrive at the till and one of my girls isn't that busy, she'll start unloading my tray for me while I ring up my orders. When I have a packed tray, girls will offer to run out drinks for me if I need to. It's great working with such an awesome team of people. We love to help each other out when we can.

Romana's Story... Madam X

I'd like to tell the interesting story about Madam X, a dancer from many years ago. This dancer stands out from the rest as she had a very unusual show, compared to all the other girls.

138

Madam X was really very quiet and had an Eastern bloc European accent when I heard her speak to the DJs. In between her shows, she would stay in the dancer room to watch TV and she really didn't mingle a whole lot with the other dancers.

By Friday and Saturday during her shows, the room was packed with guys who brought in their wives or girlfriends. I'll tell you why, and I will tone down the story for the book.

Madam X took her bag of goodies onto the stage. During her show she would lie on her bed of nails and pulled out a big dildo and sat on it. She buried beer bottles into her "cookie" and I removed the offending bottle off the stage with a handful of napkins and threw it into the garbage. She put four big candles in her "cookie" and one in her "bum," flipped upside down and lit them all, like a birthday cake.

On Friday she was told that she was not allowed to do any more of her crazy stunts because we were warned by the Liquor Inspector that they would be keeping an eye on us and we would get fined if she continued doing them. All week, the other dancers complained that they didn't want their shows to go on after hers and I don't blame them. I don't remember Madam X coming back to dance at our bar again, but I do remember how busy she got our bar within a matter of a few days because customers wanted to see her perverted show!

What To Do if You Forget a Drink

"Sorry, I AM human, and I WILL forget a drink or two!" I catch myself reminding an upset customer about this once in a while.

When You Just Can't Remember Drink Orders

If you find that you have a hard time memorizing drink orders, do yourself a favor and get yourself a cash caddy and notepad so you can write down your orders. It'll prevent you from becoming more stressed out when you get busy, and you can stay focused and concentrate on getting your job done without any customer complaints.

I use an ashtray as my coin holder, so I don't have a place to set a notepad. No matter how busy I get, I will memorize until my brain is at the point of almost exploding. Fifteen years ago I was trained

139

to memorize all drinks because all servers weren't allowed to write anything down, so this is what I'm used to. I like this method because it's challenging and my hands are free to wipe tables, push in chairs, and move drinks and empties on and off my tray as I cruise around the room.

Charm Your Way Through a Forgotten Drink Order

I have a few remarks that I use on guys if I happen to forget their drinks. It keeps them from getting too upset with me and it keeps the mood light and fun.

First off, I apologize profusely and then I throw in, "I always seem to forget all the good looking guys!" This makes them smile and if I'm busy, usually the returned comment is, "That's ok. We can see you're really busy."

I respond with "Oh good! Then I can forget you guys again?" as I wink at them. At this point, if I have all empties on my tray, I quickly run back to the bar to grab their drinks, and then run them back out right away. If my tray still has full drinks, I keep on my map of the room and deliver them. As soon as I return to the bar, I grab the drinks that slipped my mind and run them out to the forgotten ones. Then I zip back to the bar for the rest of my order, and get back on track.

A word of advice ... when I forget someone's drink, I try not to panic and dwell on it because, if I do, I'll end up forgetting other people and it turns into this vicious cycle of forgetting more and more drinks. I'll get myself so stressed out and start to feel like I'm out of control and falling apart.

If I forget a customer's drink and they're extremely rude about it and I can tell by their attitude that they just won't let it go, I say to them, "Sorry, but I'm only human and I do forget a drink now and then. I suggest that next time you go get your drink at the bar."

I'm not mean about it and I don't wait for a response. I walk away and continue doing my job. He'll be able to tell by my reaction that I'm busy and have plenty of other people to serve.

Sometimes customers joke back at me when I ask if they want another drink. They'll usually tease me and say, "Should I order now in case you forget my drink again?" or, "Are you going to forget me again?"

I usually just smile and respond with, "Guess we'll have to wait and see!"

Another comment the guys make is, "Ok, if you forget me again, you're paying for my next beer, right?"

I respond with, "Ok, It's a deal!"

I make sure to remember the next drink because I obviously don't want to pay for it.

Save the Moment

Another way to save the moment with a customer if you keep forgetting their drink is to buy them one. I've gotten so busy that my poor regular sits there patiently as I run by him two times, only to forget him yet again. I'll leave my tray at the bar, run the beer out, and drop it off saying, "Jim, I'm so sorry! Your first one is on me!"

Sometimes, the patron will stop me as I run by and he'll try to pay for that drink. I refuse and the bill is usually thrown onto my tray as he says, "Ro, then please keep it as a tip!" Other times, the money is left under their empty glass when they leave.

During the dayshift, we do a lunch draw during our lunch rush. If I forget a drink or if it's someone's birthday, I give them an extra lunch draw ticket or two, to up their chance of winning the draw.

Some Forgotten Drink Excuses

Many years ago, I was at a nightclub and I ordered a sambuca paralyzer. I waited almost twenty minutes until the server finally returned. She was extremely busy and said, "I'm sorry. I'll have to go get you another drink. Yours tipped off my tray and fell onto the floor." I will never know if that drink was spilled or was forgotten. I know I would have been more upset if she said she had forgotten it. I'll have to remember to try this excuse when I get slammed and forget a drink for someone.

If you forget a pint or jug of beer, you can say that the bartender is tapping the keg. If a coffee drink is forgotten, tell the customer that the bartender is making a fresh pot. If you forget a cocktail, you can say that the pop is out on the gun and the bartender is changing it. If you forget a bottle of beer, you can mention that the bar ran out and it'll be a moment until the bartender goes to the cooler to retrieve another case. You don't want to get in the habit of telling customers little white lies, but in a pinch use these to keep a customer from getting upset and to keep yourself sane.

If you forget a drink or forget to put a food order into the kitchen, spill a drink on someone, or any other mistake, always over-apologize. If you try your best to save the moment and the customer is just being plain rude, remember that you can't please everyone and personalities do clash. If you just can't save the situation, this is a time where you can ask another server to switch tables with you as a last resort.

Ask For Help

If you find that you're having a hard time keeping up to your section, ask another server if she would like to take over some of your tables. Many times the new girls ask me to do this and I'm glad to make the extra, unexpected money. It keeps the other server from getting too frazzled and the customers are happy, especially if they're on a drinking binge.

Romana's Story... Watch the Medication You Take on Shift!

Many years ago when I was still quite new to serving, I had a really bad cold and felt quite lousy. I didn't want to call in sick because I wanted the money. Feeling stuffed up, headachy, and sore, I decided that I would drink some Neocitran.

That was a real dumb move on my part. Wow, was I ever a mess at work! I couldn't remember anything and I can't believe that I didn't crawl into a corner and pass out. I dropped an empty beer bottle five times in a row and had customers and myself howling so hard that I swear someone might have peed themselves from the laughter. I spent the night explaining that I was sick and made the dumb mistake of taking Neocitran. I didn't have anyone upset at me for forgetting their drinks that night. They said that it was quite comical to watch me struggle through my shift.

To this day, I am reminded of this story from a few regulars every now and then.

"$11.90 please"
Here's $12.00. Keep the change!"

Chapter 5 – DOWNTIME

Helping Coworkers

When Your Section is Dead

Any server can get antsy and frustrated during the periods when she sees her coworkers loading their trays and running back out to their sections, while she strolls through hers barely making a sale. Your sleepy section seems to contain customers that want to take it easy and nurse their drink and others are just killing time with one beer before the nightclub opens next door. Any customers that you talk to seem to wave you away and say, "We're leaving after this drink, thanks." As you scan and look over at the other server's section, it looks like it's busy and humming.

This is discouraging for any server who ends up with mellow non-drinkers in their section, especially when the rest of the room is so alive and busy. The only thing I can suggest is to keep any unoccupied tables clean and inviting to newcomers that enter, think positive, and hopefully the non-drinkers will get tired of hanging around and leave. A turnover in new people will transpire and then you'll start humming along again too.

Keep Yourself Busy During the Slow Times

During any slow periods, I like to keep busy because it makes the time go by quicker. I like to take a walk into the kitchen and see if dirty plates need food scraped off of them and then put onto the dish rack. Then I rinse them off and run them through the dishwasher. On a busy night, I will take a walk into the restroom to pick up any dirty glasses that happen to make their way in there.

Never neglect your section for more than three minutes at a time. As you walk through your section, keep an eye out for new customers, customers wanting another drink, and others wanting their tabs.

Don't walk into another server's section and stand there gabbing with people. It doesn't look very professional and you just end up getting in her way.

Help Out Your Fellow Server

I'll ask the other servers if they want me to walk through their section and pick up any empties that are starting to accumulate. I'll pick up any dirty dishes, condiments, used napkins, and cutlery. I grab my wet rag and give the table a quick wipe, especially if there is spilled food or drink. The customer will appreciate it and so will the server. If customers want to order from me, I let them know that their server will be with them momentarily as I'm only there helping out by picking up empties. Push in all chairs and straighten tables if they're out of position.

Many years ago, I used to work with a server who, when she came onto the floor to start her shift, always started by walking through my section first by collecting all my empties, and then walked over to her side, starting to take orders. In the history of my serving career, she was the only server that ever did this and I can't express how thoughtful and helpful this was! She was one hell of an awesome server with an infectious laugh and so fun to work with! Thank you May!

If you're standing around at the bar while waiting for drinks and a server comes up with a full tray of empties, unload it for her so that she can punch in her next order into the till.

If a fellow server has an extremely large order, offer to carry any drinks out for her and drop them off. Mention to the customer that their server will be around in a moment to collect money from them. Adding up, pre-authorizing, or dropping off a tab for a coworker is helpful as well.

Help Out the Bartender

I'll jump behind the bar and help out my bartender if he's getting behind. Some bars don't allow other staff behind the bar, so find out your bar rules about this.

The glass washer always needs unloading. Check if the ice well needs refilling and if any beer or coolers need restocking. Look at the sugar and coffee supplies if they need refilling as well. Check to see if the straws need topping up or if he's low on lime wedges or other garnishes. There is always something that can be done.

146

Helping out all coworkers is important as you may need the favor returned one day.

Romana's Story... "All Staff on Deck! Big Fight in Progress!"

Last year while I was working a Friday nightshift, we had one of the craziest fights that I've ever seen in our bar. It involved two groups and the fight ended up outside with our doorman and both bartenders. We had to call the doormen from the nightclub next door for help.

The good guys had the troublemakers that started the fight pinned down while waiting for the authorities. As all the guys were outside dealing with the fight and waiting for the cops, we had no bartender. I jumped behind the bar and told the other server to start working the whole room while I started helping the line up at the bar. We worked like this until I had another bartender sent over from the bar next door to relieve me so that I could get back to my own customers.

It's always good to know how to bartend and do other jobs in the bar in the case of an emergency.

Get Ready for the Busy Shifts

For many of us, the slow periods during some of our shifts may get to the point of being so inactive and mundane that they become the boredom blues.

During my daily lunch rushes, I enjoy having a purpose and being busy while running out drinks and serving food. Before long, it slows down to the point of where the room empties out; the blue collar workers take off back to work, the students taking the first aid course that were on a lunch break return to school across the street, and the random single guys have disappeared as well. It's these slow, inactive periods when I like to make good use of time and get random tasks done around the room, so I don't end up dealing with the annoying boredom blues.

Clean Up the Room

When the rush ends, the first thing on the agenda is to clean my room and put things back to normal. Empties are picked up and put away while dirty glasses are run through the glass washer. All condiments are put away, dirty dishes are taken to the kitchen where all leftover food is scraped into the trash can, and then the plates are stacked onto the wash rack and rinsed off. The tables are straightened if moved out of position and then given a thorough wipe while all chairs are pushed in and any promotional material is reset on top.

As new customers enter the room and sit down, I stop what I'm doing and walk over to serve them immediately. After they have a drink on the table and maybe a menu in hand, I return to where I left off. If they're looking at a menu, I don't forget to check on them in a couple of minutes to take their food order.

Random Chores You Should Do to Keep Busy

There is never a time when a server should be standing around yawning and complaining, "I'm bored." If you're all caught up with tidying the room, look around and you'll always find chores to keep you busy.

Speed up your cash-out...
At our bar, we handwrite all food orders on guest cheques. Once the bill is paid, I put the slip into a glass so that I can get it out of my way. When its time to do my cash, the bills are arranged in numerical order and stapled together. They are put into an envelope along with whatever cash is owed and my cash-out sheet.

During my slow times, I like to put whatever food bills I have accumulated in order by number, staple them together, and add them all up. The total is marked down on the bottom left hand side, on the last bill. This way when I add more bills a couple hours later, I add the new bill totals to the previous and mark the new total on the very last bill, then staple the lot together. This saves time at the end of my shift, because instead of adding up all the food bills at the end of my shift, most of it is already calculated and all I need to do is tally up my tip for the kitchen and put money aside owed for the food. I always double check my calculations, and if the numbers don't add up, I do a third tally. Watch your numbers carefully as you punch them into your calculator because I find that with calculators in bars, over time the buttons get sticky from spills or sticky fingers. When this starts to happen, it's time for me to get a new calculator.

As long as I'm by myself at the till and there are no customers milling around me, I like to unlock my waitress box and organize all my paper bills. I stack all the bills in the same direction with the same side up, separating all denominations. If I have a large stack, I'll count up my twenties and slip a rubber band around every five hundred or thousand dollars.

I check all my visa slips to make sure that they have all been advised and for the right amount. On a scrap sheet of paper, the totals of my visa and interac slips are written down, as well as any promo drinks or pull tab totals. All the slips, pull tabs, and my scrap paper with the totals are clipped together with a paper clip and then this little stack is popped back into my waitress box. When the time comes to do my cash at the end of my shift, I just need to add any other interac, visa, or other totals to my last totals and this saves me time so I can go home that much earlier because I've done most of the grunt work earlier on in the shift.

When a customer runs a tab, he might move to the other side of the room to see a friend, order shooters from the shooter girl, or order food from the food girl. This means that other servers are putting drinks or food on his bill and when he pays his tab and leaves a tip, it's only fair to split the tip amongst the servers that served him. The slow period is the time where I like to work out any tips owed to other servers on all of my closed tabs. It's really quite easy and not hard at all to figure out. Please refer to **Chapter #5, Subchapter #3 under "Tipping out Fellow Servers"** to see how we work out splitting up tips at our bar. By working out tips on tabs during the slow parts of your shift, you don't have to do it at the end of your shift when you're itching to get your cash done and go home.

Other jobs...
• Periodically, I like to go through all glasswear. Taking a clean, wet rag, I re-wipe all glasswear, beer glasses, beer mugs, shooter glasses, martini glasses, and wine glasses. I'll hold them up to the light and inspect them for greasy finger prints, lipstick on rims, coffee rings, dark foggy type of discoloration from cola, and reddish tinge from clamato or tomato juice that's added to beer or Caesars.

It's not unusual to find a coating of cinnamon inside some of the shooter glasses from the China White shooters. About once a month I take all our plastic beer jugs into the kitchen, pour some bleach and hot water into them, let them sit for 20 minutes, and then run them through the dishwasher in the kitchen. This gets rid of any discoloration that scrubbing by hand doesn't help. The glass washer does a pretty good job cleaning and disinfecting, but it takes some elbow grease to get rid of the hard stuff.

• As most servers are in a rush to leave at the end of their shift, the only attention that trays are usually given is a quick wipe with a dirty cloth, so it's a good idea to give them a thorough clean every day. Sprinkling baking soda and pouring hot water on trays with a cork liner helps to neutralize the foul odor that accumulates from alcohol spilling on them during a shift. Grab a glass, flip it upside down, and scrub the soda into the cork. Finish up by rinsing it away with warm water and dry with a clean cloth. The baking soda is great to use on any tray.

• Our shooter girls have plastic, glow-in-the-dark trays with a removable rubber tray liner. They take it apart and run both pieces through the glass washer. Over time the rubber liner starts to crinkle up and harden and doesn't sit flat against the tray any longer. When this occurs, the shooter glass won't sit flat and it can tip and spill when the girl walks with it. Not too long ago, my bartender decided to take the tray and its rubber liner into the kitchen. He held it under the salamander (this is the heating element that melts cheese quickly on nachos) to heat up the liner for a minute and this is what flattened it to the point of functioning like new again ... ingenious!

• Trays that hold random glasswear are sprayed and wiped with a cleaner, while the rubber mats are run through the glass washer.

• We have spray bottles that contain glass cleaner, deodorizer, and the sanitizer that is used at the end of the night to spray down all tables. I like to fill up all bottles when I have some time to kill.

• Mirrors or glass in the room that looks foggy, dirty, or contains fingerprints are cleaned during slow periods as well.

• Cleaning and de-cluttering once a week around the till is a good idea because by Saturday night there are too many lipsticks, perfume bottles, and odds and ends that have collected in a glass.

Every Tuesday I collect it all up and put it into the staff room and then I wipe down the till, the phone, visa machine, and any other machinery that may have dust, dirt, or spills on it. The sink is given a good scrub every couple of days with a handy little brush I picked up at the dollar store and sanitizer. The soap dispenser is filled when low.

- I refill the stapler if needed and check stock on any guest cheques, till tape, or coasters that may be running low.
- Going through the laminated kitchen menus, I check if they're sticky or covered in ketchup or other food. They're given a good wipe with a clean wet cloth and then dried with a dry one. Do not use a spray cleaner as that makes the menus stick together and they feel tacky to the touch.
- Take a look at the chairs in your bar and see if they need a wash down or the crumbs and dirt wiped out from the grooves. Look at the foot rests on the bar stools as many get caked with mud and grime from dirty work boots. Cleaning with a bucket filled with warm water and soap and a clean cloth works wonders. Don't forget to dry with a clean cloth as you don't want new customers sitting in wet chairs.
- I like everyday chores to be effortless and tools to be easily accessible around the bar. So to accomplish this, many times I take initiative myself to organize items and get things done. Many years ago when our bar did renovating, they put in new lights with a nice big section of twenty-five light switches. When lights around the room needed to be dimmed or brightened quickly, you didn't know which switches controlled certain lights because there were too many of them. I brought my label maker into work one afternoon and labeled them all during some downtime I had. It makes daily life easier around there, especially when you're in a rush.
- Other than helping pass the time, another good reason to clean and organize during slow times is you'll be able to tell if you're low or missing supplies. This is important as you may still have time to order supplies before a busy event.

Look After Your Staff Room

Every Tuesday I clean up our staff room as it's always kept locked and we don't have a cleaning person that goes in there. I empty the trash can and pick up any garbage that litters the floor. While staff goes in there for their breaks and eats food or drink while doing their cash-out, I take cleaner and wipe the table with it to get rid of any glass rings, crumbs, or spilled make-up. For shoes or boots that are in the way, I put them in the old milk crate that houses the random footwear. Any clothing that litters the floor is put into an unlocked locker that I labeled *lost clothing*.

If there are any reservations for the end of the week, during slow times is the time to write out any reservation signs and organize them so that they're ready to go.

It's a good idea to check stock every week. You should always have an extra box or case of all the glasswear you carry at the bar. When big events happen and the bar is filled to almost over capacity, you can pull out the extra stock when needed. When the event is over, all glasswear is washed and put away for next time. If there seems to be a lot of breakage, you have back up, but remember to order another case right away if you get low. Organization is the key to running an efficient and busy bar smoothly.

If you have a big event planned for a night, have all your weapons ready to go before the army comes rushing in. You should have a stack of rags ready to go, extra pens sitting in a glass, extra calculators, and whatever other tools are needed. All reservation signs should be out and make sure everyone is clear on their duties and sections that they're responsible for. You don't want any miscommunication as there won't be any time for mistakes. We like to move any tables that are in high traffic areas for the servers and food runners.

Why You Should NEVER Sit Down on Shift

I've heard of servers who would grab a coffee and sit down at a table with friends or regulars when the room is slow. This is an extreme no-no and I'll explain the reasons why.

1. You neglect the customers sitting in the room.
2. New people that walk in and sit down think there may not be a server on the floor.
3. You get too comfortable sitting down and may lose track of time.
4. It looks extremely unprofessional to all those in the room.

5.   It looks very bad to the owner or the manager if they happen to come into the room unannounced. During slow periods, the only girl allowed to sit with customers is the shooter girl.

Whatever you do, NEVER sit down on a shift!

Romana's Story... The Corona Bottle Joke

I remember when I was a rookie waitress. I got flustered easily and didn't know the system.

I was told by a senior waitress that my job at the end of the night was to pull out all the limes from the empty Corona bottles. I must've spent half an hour wondering and worrying how the hell I was going to accomplish that while I served my section.

She told me that it was just a joke close to the end of our shift.

Tipping out Fellow Servers

Working at most establishments, the server keeps her tips earned, but she will be expected to tip-out (share) with coworkers like bartenders, doormen, DJs, kitchen staff, busers, and hostesses at the end of her shift. Starting at a new place, you will be told by your manager or coworkers how much will be expected for you to put aside for these people that may have a hand in helping you make tips.

I have also heard of places in the serving industry where all servers and bartenders throw all their tips together and then split it among themselves and everyone else.

The following information shows how to share a gratuity between several servers who had served a customer on a tab.

How to Split-up a Tip

There are times when a customer who is running a tab with you may have another server add a drink or food to his bill. This happens when a shooter girl delivers shooters, a food girl comes on shift, the customer may move to another server's section, or the original server goes on a break or leaves to go home. When the customer signs off and leaves a gratuity, the tip will have to be split evenly among all servers who served him.

To make working out a tab easy at our bar, we like to use the multiple of five. Keep in mind that it's not to the penny, just a rough estimate.

Examples of Splitting a Gratuity

Example 1: Total of a bill is $44.00. Tip left was $5.00
Mary had $19.00 worth of drinks on the bill.
Sandy had $25.00 worth of drinks on the bill.

Round Mary's total to $20.00. Divide 20 by 5 = 4
Sandy's total is $25.00. Divide 25 by 5 = 5

Add up 4 and 5 = 9.
$5.00 tip divide by 9 = $.55
$.55 x 4 = $2.20 tip to Mary
$.55 x 5 = $2.75 tip to Sandy
If Sandy is keeping the credit card slip, she will pay Mary $22.20. $20.00 Mary owes the bar for her drinks and the $2.20 tip.

Example 2: Total of a bill is $163.00. Tip left was $15.00
Mary had $4.00 worth of drinks.
Sandy had $31.00 worth of drinks.
Patty had $94.00 worth of drinks.
Cindy had $34.00 worth of drinks.

Round Mary's total to $5.00. Divide 5 by 5 = 1
Round Sandy's total to $30.00. Divide 30 by 5 = 6
Round Patty's total to $95.00. Divide 95 by 5 = 19
Round Cindy's total to $35.00. Divide 35 by 5 = 7

Add up 1, 6, 19, and 7 = 33.
$15 tip divide by 33 = $.45
$.45 x 1 = $.45 tip to Mary

$.45 x 6 = $2.70 tip to Sandy
$.45 x 19 = $8.55 tip to Patty
$.45 x 7 = $3.15 tip to Cindy

The server who takes over the bill has to make sure that she doesn't forget to pay out the other servers, not just on the tip owed to them, but the drinks the other girls owe the bar money for. I find that forgetting to pay out a server on her drinks is quite common since everyone is so concerned with getting their portion of a tip.

Pay attention to your bills. Some may be extremely quick to work out. If I serve two beers and you serve two beers and the customer leaves a $5.00 tip, split the 5 in half = $2.50 tip each. There, done!

Share the Wealth

You don't want to rip off other servers from their tip. We're all there for the same reason and nobody likes to work for free. We all have to tip out the bartender, DJ, doorman, etc, so we are relying on that money. Don't be cheap; share the wealth. This means that if a customer leaves a large tip, be honest and split it up. Don't sneak around and cheat anyone out of their portion of money. If you start ripping off servers and they find out, they'll settle all tabs in the future before they leave and you won't be trusted. You don't want this type of reputation.

One of my biggest pet peeves is if I sell a tab to another server before I go home and I find nothing in my box the next day; especially when I know of regulars that always leave me a tip. Please don't be one of these annoying coworkers where I have to grovel and ask for my gratuity! I already feel stupid asking for it once, but if I have to remind you a second or third time, I am now upset. Drop it in my box in the first place. Believe me, I will not forget about it.

Same goes for bartenders and doormen. If they're done with their shift and standing there in their coat ready to go home, give them their tip without having them ask you for it.

Romana's Story...The Most Miserable Waitress Ever

When Kelsey was about six years old, we made a road trip to Kelowna. On the way there, we decided to stop for lunch at a little restaurant in

155

a small town. Once seated and given menus by the hostess, we decided on what we wanted to order and waited for our server.

An older, heavy-set woman with a dirty apron came over, stood at our table with pen and pad poised, and shook her head at us with widened eyes, indicating for us to give her our order. As she didn't smile at us or say hello, I instinctively knew right away that she was not happy. We told her what we wanted, then she grabbed our menus, spun on her heel, and left.

The next time she came near us was to dump off our plates of food and she didn't return to ask Rod if he wanted more water or even ask if everything was ok with our meals.

Dumping our bill on the table as she scooted by, we didn't hear a "Thank you" or "Have a nice day."

I took the bill to the bar as I was paying by debit and I decided that this server wasn't going to get a tip from us as she was the rudest waitress we've ever encountered! She was standing behind the counter as I approached, so I handed her my bill and debit card. She took it from me, swiped my card, and then handed the card back as she seemed to soften her attitude and I actually heard her voice for the first time as she said, "Here's your card back."

"Thank you" I said, as I decided at the last second to actually leave her a tip, thinking to myself that she was probably just having a bad day.

Boy was I mad at myself! She grabbed my copy of the slip and slapped it in my hand and didn't even thank me. We walked out of there amazed that she still had that job with her crappy attitude and manners!

Cleanliness

In this economy and market, it's challenging to persuade new customers to come and try out your bar, restaurant, pub, etc.

Therefore, you should treat your regulars like gold as they're your bread and butter and there's a reason why they're coming into your place of work on a regular basis in the first place. I've been told that the main reason why many people return to our bar frequently is because of our friendly staff that gives some of the best service around.

156

Look at It as Your Business Too

You don't own the business, but you do work and make money there, so take pride in your room and look after it as if it were your own.

Be anal about cleanliness. When new customers decide to try out your bar for the first time, you may give great service and have hot dancers, but if the place has sticky menus, dirty chairs, or garbage on the floor, it's a bad first impression and it's unlikely the customer will return. Working in a bar, the black lights highlight any white debris on the floor, so pick up any tiny pieces of paper, dirty napkins, promo material, ATM receipts, bottle caps, and toilet paper that you notice. It's especially important during the daytime as the crowd is older and usually not drunk. Business men and women may come in for lunch with clients, as well as customers that like to work on their paperwork and laptops. During the dayshift, it's rare if anyone wants to really rip it up and get drunk, unless it's some crazy people that are celebrating a birthday or a stag party early that day.

Don't neglect chairs with a sticky arm rest or spills on chair seats. Nobody wants to sit in a wet, sticky chair and get their clothes ruined.

Before handing the hand-held debit machine to a patron, give it a quick wipe with your damp cloth if you notice that it's sticky or wet.

When picking up garbage off the table, inspect cigarette packs before removing them. If it feels light, open it and peek inside. I can't count how many times I've grabbed a cigarette pack, thinking it was empty, and threw it in the trash, only to have the owner ask me if I took it. I have to dig it back out because he tells me there are joints or a cigarette hidden inside.

If your coworkers get in the habit of throwing dirty rags on the floor by the till because it's easy and fast, place a small pail there so it looks neater or hand all dirty rags to the bartender to hide behind the bar.

Don't let staff, dancers, or customers throw any food into your garbage can by the waitress till. Give it a few hours and you'll start to smell it and this makes concentrating at the till almost unbearable. Take it from someone who knows ... prawn tails are brutally offensive in smell by the end of the night and you're usually gagging by the time you're ready to go home! Maybe a little more important: all servers have had to dig through the garbage at one time or another, looking for a hundred-dollar pull tab that was thrown out by mistake, a customer's bill, or a pen that falls in by accident!

Why You Should Keep Your Section Spotless at all Times

When a customer walks in and scans the room, they'll be attracted to the cleanest looking table. Keep those chairs pushed in, as it makes the room look neater and those chairs won't be in your way when you come by with a full set of drinks next time around. I've bruised my legs by kicking into chairs that are sitting in my way in the aisle.

When I'm working the floor with other servers, I make sure that I'm even more on top of keeping my side of the room clean. The reason for this is because when new patrons walk in, they'll always steer towards a clean table positioned straight with pushed in chairs, and neatly arranged promo material on it. If all my tables are full of customers, I am maximizing my sales and tips.

Keep the stage area clear of empty bottles and glasses. This is important as girls are dancing, kicking their legs, and whipping around the pole. They can kick into glasswear or bottles and this is dangerous for customers. Full drinks and jugs are kicked over at times too, but you can minimize accidents by keeping empties from stacking up at the stage.

If I notice girls sitting on guys' laps at the stage area, I'll let them know that it's safer for her to sit in her own chair because with her sitting in someone's lap, it's easy for her to get kicked by a dancer.

Remove All Broken Furniture

As you move chairs and reorganize tables day in and night out, sometimes you'll find broken tables or a tabletop that has popped off. Do yourself a favor and pull that broken piece of furniture out of the room and let the maintenance man know to repair it.

Recently, I had a customer pull on his stool and he ripped his finger on a nail from under the seat. As he sat there bleeding profusely, I apologized like crazy while I ran off to get him clean napkins and

158

bandages. Sometimes you don't notice the broken chair until it's too late but when you do, remove it from the room.

My husband and I like to eat out now and then, as I'm sure you do as well. Once in a while, we end up with a server who's wearing a very dirty apron. It's hard not to notice this as it hovers above our table top while the server stands there asking for our order; not appetizing! I'm sure that we're not the only customers that notice this. If you wear an apron, change it every day or when it starts to look dirty. Same for your top; keep a back up at work in case of accidents and spills.

The Sanitizer Isn't Just for End of Shift Clean-up

Our staff room is the place where we change our clothes, go on any breaks, find a quiet place to make a phone call, and do our cash at the end of a shift.

We keep our jackets, purses, food, clothing, etc. in there all the time and since some coworkers don't use the lockers, stuff is usually scattered around the room. This room is under lock and key, therefore the janitor can't let himself in to do any cleaning.

Technically, my Tuesday dayshift is probably my slowest day out of the week, so this is the day that I like to do *house cleaning*. Entering the staff room with a spray cleaner and clean cloth, I spend five to ten minutes in there tidying and doing a quick clean up.

Romana's Story... The Jell-O Wrestling Contest

Many years ago, our bar decided to hold a Jell-O Wrestling contest. It was basically a wrestling match between the dancers while they wrestled in a kiddy pool filled with Jell-O on the stage.

I remember coming in that night for my shift and it was already busy. I was thrown a beer shirt to put on and the bartender told me to start right away. During the matches, customers would get their hands on the Jell-O and throw it back at the dancers, at other guys across the stage, and even at the servers (Jell-O in hair is disgusting). By the end of the evening, we had high sales and made fistfuls of cash, but there was Jell-O everywhere; it was all over the chairs, tables, carpet, mirrors, and ceiling.

To end the night, we were told that we couldn't leave this aftermath of a tornado for our poor cleaning lady. We all grabbed buckets of hot soapy water and clean rags, and got to work. Have you ever tried cleaning dried up Jell-O that had already set?! Not fun and not easy to clean, I can assure you. We needed a scraper to speed up the job and make it easier but didn't have access to one. We cleaned for almost two and a half hours and prayed that we'd never do another contest like this again. I don't think I could handle cleaning Jell-O for almost three hours after slugging drinks all night for customers again. So far, my wish has come true ...

"What can I get for you guys?"
"What's the cheapest drink you sell?"
"Nothing…I don't have any money"
"I just want some tap water"

Chapter 6 – THE DIFFERENT TYPES OF CUSTOMERS

The "Regular" Customer

Regulars are the same people you see visit the bar most of the time and you get to know their name and/or what they drink.

I read a very fascinating and interesting book called *How to Win Friends and Influence People* by Dale Carnegie. This seventy-year-old book contains intriguing information that helps the reader understand the psychology of people, and it can definitely help you deal with the public in this line of work. I highly recommend you hunt down this book and read it.

When a Regular Shows Up

If you're busy or on the opposite side of the room and you notice a regular walk in and sit down, a smile with eye contact and a quick wave works well. He knows that I've seen him and I'm on the way with his drinks, so this keeps him from getting up and going to the bar, which means a possible tip for me. If he sits in another server's section, let that waitress know what he drinks. Your coworker will appreciate it and so will your regular.

During slow times, spend a minute or two chatting up with customers by asking how their cruise was, or how their wife enjoyed the spa gift certificates you suggested when you were asked for advice on what they should get for their wife's birthday. Customers are thrilled when you remember the little things that seem so insignificant and they'll be amazed at your memory. You may even gain the position as their "favorite waitress!"

Listen to your customer's needs. If you're always being asked for a certain new beer or liquor, ask management if there's a chance they may be able to bring it in. It may end up being a hot seller, which would make management happy, your customers happy, and you'll be happy counting your tips!

On a regular's birthday, ask the bartender to promo them a drink. If the bar's promo tab is full, pay for it yourself. Your customer will appreciate the nice gesture. After all, these are the people that tip you on a consistent basis and buying one drink isn't going to make you bankrupt.

Memorizing Names

To memorize names, I have found myself writing the person's name down and what they drink. Then I visualize their face and keep the little cheat sheet by my till for a few hours and look at it repeatedly throughout the shift. At the end of my shift, I will pop it into my box where I will come across it a few more times in the next few days. Pretty soon, I've got the name and face memorized and this is when I throw the sheet out. I have also caught myself learning names of regulars as I compare them to people I know with the same name as theirs.

I try to learn as many regular customers' names as I can. It's important to know in not only greeting them properly, but it can help when you discuss certain customers with other servers regarding tabs.

In Dale Carnegie's book he says, "Remember that a person's name is to that person the sweetest and most important sound in the language." Not only is it important to know their name, but to pronounce it properly and spell it correctly. In my opinion, this is one out of many important pieces of advice that you will find in Dale Carnegie's book.

Throughout my life I've had people call me Ramona, and it makes me cringe. Not because I dislike the name, but because it's not my name. When a stranger reads my name out loud and says it correctly, I'm thrilled and touched because they cared enough to make an effort and pronounce it correctly.

Make it a game to learn as many customers' names as you can. When I'm given a credit card to start or sign off a tab, I'll look at the name on the card and use that name as often as I can.

Another way to learn customers' names is to ask their friend when the person leaves the room to use the restroom or to have a smoke.

Asking the other servers if they know the customer's name is another way of finding out a name.

The easiest way to learn a person's name is by simply asking them. You'd be astonished at how touched people are that you want to make the effort of remembering their name and they're thrilled when you greet them by using it on their next visit. You'll feel like an old friend and in return you may be pleasantly surprised to see your tips increase!

Humor Your Customer

Working in the service industry, you have to be ready for the wise cracks and jokes. If dumb comments make you mad or you break down crying, this job will be hard for you to deal with.

When my regular Jimmy visits the bar, he loves to joke around with me, "So Ro, when are you on stage?"

I smile and reply, "I'm on at three AM, Jimmy." The bar is closed by one in the morning and this is some fun we play between the two of us.

Coworkers in the past have admitted to me how this infuriates them when customers ask when they will be dancing on stage. I could never understand why a comment like that would bother them because it's just a guy's way of saying how he finds you attractive. Frankly, I find it quite flattering.

Turn it into a game of amusement. Sometimes guys ask me, "Why aren't you up on stage?"

I reply with, "Who's going to serve you drinks if I'm on stage getting naked? I don't want you guys to die of thirst!"

The guys love the comeback and laugh, but sometimes the game continues. "We'll wait to order a drink until you finish your show and get off stage."

I continue with, "I'm really very shy. But I do have some interesting news for you guys."

They ask, "What?"

I finish off the conversation with, "I have the exact same parts as she does!" as I point at the girl on stage, smile, and walk away before they have a chance to respond. I leave them in a joking and happy mood which means that I'm still in their good books to still get a tip. If you act like a grouch and get mad at them, most likely you've lost the tip.

165

Dealing with Death

I have come to know many wonderful people in this industry over the many years. Considering the length of time that I've been there, I've known many regulars that have passed away. Some have died from heart attacks, another died from a stroke, one of a suicide, a few have died from emphysema, one from a motorcycle accident, and my most recent was from a boating accident.

At the time of writing this book, a regular who was my age, and whom I've known for the entire time I've been working at my bar, died in a tragic boating accident. He was part of our bar family as he was friends with all the staff and he visited our bar on a daily basis as it was considered his second home.

The week of his death, we kept his usual table unoccupied and friends would buy his usual double Stoli water cranberry drink and leave it on his table. At the funeral, I was amazed at the amount of people that appeared to pay their respects as the church was jammed full and there were still at least one hundred of us stuck outside. He was loved by all and had many friends. My friend and bartender said to me, "Isn't it funny how all these people we see at the bar every night, acting like complete idiots, act like civilized human beings at a funeral." He couldn't be further from the truth. Death is usually unforeseen and is to be expected as it's a part of life. It's funny how it brings people together.

The night of the funeral, the bar was packed, and again we didn't let anyone sit at Ty's table. At one point in the evening, someone had set a couple of tea lights beside the drinks and a short time later, there was a picture of him (placed in a plastic baggie) standing against one of the cocktails. Periodically I wiped up the condensation that dripped from the glasses off the table and this was the last table cleaned up at the end of the night.

Sunday morning, Rod and I were talking about the funeral and I said, "For years, every single time that Ty came into the bar, he always gave me that flirty little smile of his and he never forgot to say to me, *"Romansky, you look spectacular!"* Who's going to inflate my ego like that anymore?" All of the staff miss him and still wait for him to come sauntering in at any time. I was told from many of his friends that they still wait for him to call them on their cell phones. It's a weird feeling. We will always miss you, dear friend.

Death is something you'll eventually have to deal with because you do get attached to people in this industry. How could you not? If you are in the service industry and enjoy it, you must love people.

Other Important Random Information

During the nightshift, the lighting is more subdued. The volume of the music is kept a little lower during the day because some customers come in to converse with friends and enjoy a lunch. Business associates are brought in to talk business and the energy level is a bit more unobtrusive as the majority of clientele is older and a more mature crowd. The times that I do notice the young come in frequently during the dayshift is during spring break and summer when school is out.

If customers complain about the music being too loud or ask you to change the channel on the big screen to the World Championship Soccer Game in Scotland or the monster trucks finals, don't tell them to go tell the DJ themselves. Provide good customer service and walk over and ask the DJ yourself.

As for the temperature in the room, keep it at a moderate level. If you crank up the heat because you are cold and you notice customers sweating and complaining of the temperature, turn it down and slip on a sweater. Make the room's ambiance comfortable so your customers want to stay and enjoy themselves. Many years ago during the hot summer when our air conditioning was broken for a couple weeks, the temperature was sweltering and our room was emptying by the minute. Some of my regulars told me that even though they wanted to stay, they couldn't stand the heat any longer. I didn't blame them because I was in the washroom every half an hour dumping my black shirt under the sink in cold water and then putting it back on again.

Get to know your regulars and what they like. Every Thursday afternoon, two of my regulars order bottles of Budweiser. I know that they want me to bring frosty mugs and coasters to set the pints on. They always want a menu with their drinks and to run a tab. When they enter, I bring the bottles, frosty glasses, coasters, and menus. As I set it all down, I'm greeting them with, "Hi Andy and Michael! How's your day going?" I wait to hear their response and then I let them know about the lunch special. I don't ask them for money as they always run a tab separately.

A couple of other regulars always drink the pints that are on special. When they pay me with a twenty and some change, all change given back is in five dollar bills as this is what they like to put on the stage to tip the dancers. I will never hand over a ten dollar bill unless I ran out of fives. This is the routine with these guys and it doesn't change.

Romana's Story... My Embarrassing Moment!

I have a favorite skort that I love to wear at work. It's short and black with little pinstripes and it's extremely comfortable. One day at work, a few of my regulars were bugging me about if I had anything on underneath my skirt.

"Of course I do!" I said and while I said it, I pulled the skirt up exposing the shorts.

"Holy shit Ro! You've got a big hole in the ass of your shorts!"

I pulled the skirt down and felt around to the back for the hole. They were right. I had a nice big hole where the seam split apart. I felt like the biggest dork alive.

A few months later, the servers were being goofy and silly at the bar. I ended up parading around at the bar with the skirt part hiked up around my waist again. Do you think I remembered that stupid hole in my ass? Of course I didn't! As the girls were laughing their heads off, I made a note to myself to repair the stupid skort. Yes, I took it home and sewed it up. I also don't act immature and dance around with my skirt part hiked up around my waist anymore!

Romana's Story... Another Embarrassing Moment!

I remember starting my shift many years ago. I looped around the room three times before a customer asked me, "Ro, is your skirt inside out?" I dropped my tray at the bar and ran into the restroom. Looking in the mirror I saw that I did have my skirt on inside out. After putting myself back together, I wondered how stupid I looked with the white tags and seams glowing in the black light!

168

The "Creep" and the "Player"

The Creep

I have dealt with my share of creeps and it can be rather unnerving. I start to feel out of control because in the beginning, while I'm nice and polite to this person, I'll have to turn the tables and act mean to get him off my back.

The next story I'm about to tell you about, is my "Biggest Creep" story. It upset me enough that I was contemplating on looking for another job just to get away from him.

Romana's Story... Pineapple

Many years ago, I had a customer that visited the bar periodically and I saw him on my nightshift every few weeks. He barely spoke a word and was always very quiet and kept to himself.

Months went by and he started coming into the bar more frequently. I didn't think too much of it as many guys are in the bar on a regular basis. We started calling him Pineapple, because all he drank was pineapple juice and I was super nice to him because I felt sorry for him as he always visited the bar alone.

One afternoon while I was walking through the room, Pineapple was sitting in the corner of the room at a table by himself. As I walked by, he waved me over. I leaned in to hear what he had to say and to this day I remember the exact words he said to me. The hairs on the back of my neck stood up as I heard him say, "I just want to let you know that I really, really, really like you and I can't stop thinking about you." I was stunned.

I looked at him and said, "I'm married and have a daughter, and I don't go out with customers!" I walked away and was taken aback. I made a mental note to myself that when he comes in from now on, I would bring him a drink and not lead him on with any small talk or smiles anymore.

As the weeks went by, when he would enter the bar and sit down, I would walk straight over with his pineapple juice. He would say, "Keep $.50 for yourself," and I would abruptly respond with a "Thanks" and scoot away. I was aware of my body language and conversation because I wanted him to see that I was all business and not interested in him in the least.

169

I knew that things were getting a little weird when customers and staff commented to me, "Ro, whenever that Pineapple juice guy comes in, he stares at you all the time. Everywhere you walk in the room, he would swivel around in his chair to keep his eyes on you ... even when there's a naked girl on stage!" I quickly became aware of his presence when he entered the room. When he did, I would slip my sweater on and zip it up and then I had a hard time concentrating on my job because I started to feel uneasy and anxious. At times, I felt his eyes on me and when I would look over to see if he was staring at me, I would always meet them. Glaring back at him with a mean look, he continued to stare and just didn't get it!

I stopped delivering his drink when he came in and I would ask another server to take it out. If I was the only server on the floor, he would eventually go to the bar and get his drink himself as I would ignore him.

One afternoon a group of guys came into the bar and as Pineapple was leaving, he stopped at the table to chat with them for a few minutes. After he left, I went over to the group and asked them if they knew him. They told me his name and that he has a wife and four children! They said that they worked with him and he is absolutely harmless. I was amazed when I thought of this sucker who lay for three or four hours in a bar by himself a few times a week hitting on waitresses and stalking me!

I asked the manager at the time if we could just bar him from coming in anymore. He said, "We can't just bar him for looking at you, Ro. It's a strip club." I understood his point.

One afternoon while Pineapple was sitting there gawking away at me as I'm starting to sweat like a hog in my sweater, I felt the anger arise in my body. I was mad at him for making my job unbearable and unpleasant. As I walked behind him, I saw him start to swivel his chair, repositioning himself to check my butt out when I would walk away. I didn't think; I reacted. I stopped behind him and dug my long fake nails into his right shoulder, then I said to him, "I'd really appreciate you stop staring at me, cause you're really making my job f-n uncomfortable! Got it?" I walked away, dropped my tray down at the till and walked into the restroom to compose myself because I started to shake.

170

The next time I walked by him, he had his head bent down looking at his lap. The time after that, he was gone. He disappeared for almost three months and it was heaven! I enjoyed my job again.

One day, he started showing up at the bar again and he went back to his old ways, staring at me during my shift. I was seriously contemplating whether I should find another job, as this was really starting to upset me again and I just couldn't put myself through this stress again. I also wondered if he would follow me to a new bar and continue his stalking.

It was getting annoying to hear people tell me, "Don't worry about it! What do you expect? You work in a strip bar. You're just another pretty girl that he's checking out. He's quiet and doesn't cause any problems, so who cares!"

I CARE! And it's those quiet types that you have to keep a look-out for. I was more aware of going home at night as I didn't need this sucker following me home and knowing where I lived! My gut was telling me that this was not normal.

One evening while the bar was busy, our kitchen lady was running by Pineapple with a plate of food for another customer. Pineapple was sitting at the corner of a table and he had a habit of leaning back, with his arms hugging the back of his neck. As the kitchen lady ran by, he brought his arms down and grazed the side of her body with his left hand, by accident. She started freaking out and yelling that he touched her on purpose. It was perfect timing and in his defense, I know it wasn't on purpose. The manager used this as an excuse to bar him for a month.

A month later, as I ran by the hallway from the kitchen, I noticed Pineapple standing in the hall talking to my manager. His month was up and he needed permission to start coming back into the bar. I got a coworker to interrupt and grab my boss.

I said to him, "If you let him start coming back into the bar, I'm looking for another job. I can't work with him in the room anymore. It's too stressful on me."

He was barred for life!

It IS a Big Deal!

I often wonder what would happen if that little accident didn't happen with our food lady ... Would I still be working there with

171

him tormenting me with his stalking? I let it go way too long where it was starting to affect my job and my sanity. If this kind of thing happens again, I would approach my manager and find a way to get it dealt with and solved. I like where I work, but if nobody would be willing to help me deal with this kind of a problem, I would have to find another place to work. Fortunately, I can say that my manager and the owners wouldn't put up with this and I know for a fact that they would be on my side and tell this person he's not welcome to come back.

What would you say is more important? To have happy, content staff that feel safe and enjoy coming to work or to make a few extra dollars a month for a few pineapple juices?

I don't want girls reading this book thinking that any guy who has a little crush on them can be barred or kicked out of the bar as it's not that way at all. I felt that the situation was starting to get out of hand. I know guys check me out and some have a crush on me as I'm often told by their friends and get asked out frequently. This happens to most servers and I'm flattered in these cases and respond with, "Oh, that's really very sweet. I'm really flattered, but I'm married."

Most guys respond with, "He's a very lucky guy," while some will usually push a little further and ask, "Happily?"

"Yes, very happily!"

Use the Other Guys in the Room as Your Security Blanket

In the past, I have had problems with guys in regards to being hit on. Some won't take no for an answer and sometimes they get rather rude or vulgar. At this point I say, "Buddy, my husband is at the back of the room right now!" That always diffuses any other comments.

As I approach the bar, I'll tell a regular, a guy friend, or one of my bad boys, "Dave, I'm using you as my husband today, so just go along with it." Many of my guys find it funny, because they know I have lots of husbands. Rod is grateful because I always have my big brothers looking out for me and helping me out when he's not there to do it.

Working as a server in a bar, my coworkers and I are always receiving gifts from customers, whether it's a red rose for Valentine's Day, a box of chocolates at Christmas, or a gift certificate for our birthday. It starts to get a little creepy when a server is given a box of lingerie for a gift. Yes, this has happened to others, not to me; that is the advantage of being married. I've heard of servers wearing a fake wedding ring on their finger, even if they're single, to use as a diversion.

At times, guys ask me about my coworkers and whether they're single or not. It's our number one rule to say that they have a boyfriend. Even if my friend is single, we all say that we're taken off the market because it's easier and the girls tell me that they would never date a guy that hangs out in a strip bar anyways. You may want to discuss this little rule with the servers you work with.

The Player

Some guys I wouldn't necessarily call creeps, I would call them players. The player is the guy who is always on the make. He's the guy who will ask you out for dinner, a date, or swing by with flowers or a gift.

It's kind of funny when another server comments to the rest of us about a certain customer in the room who just told her that she is extremely beautiful and he would like to take her out some time. Comparing notes, we all chime in telling each other that he said the exact same thing to us as well. To this guy, it's a numbers game. He knows that by asking every girl that he comes in contact with, there's always the chance that one will say yes.

The Friend

I have a lot of friends and sometimes I have a very hard time making time for them in my busy schedule. This is what I tell people in the bar that want to hang out with me outside my job. I have met friends at work that are my coworkers and then I still have customers that became friends of mine who I have gone to concerts with, girls' nights out, meet at barbeques and parties, or have even gone boating with. They've met my husband, and some have met my daughter.

There are customers that want to weave their way into your life. You'll get invited to birthday parties and they'll give you their phone

173

number and want you to call them up so that you can go for coffee. I think you've got to be careful handing out your phone number to everyone in the bar. I'm not saying that everyone that hangs out and wants to be your friend at the bar is out to get you, you just have to be careful. Don't be naïve and think, "Oh, that guy seems so nice and sweet." That's exactly what I thought about Pineapple!

Romana's Story... "You're Too Nice of a Girl to be Working Here!"

Years ago when I worked the nightshift, I had a group of regulars who would come into the bar and hang out for a few hours. One of them was in the habit of always asking me if I wanted to go out for lunch or coffee.

"I really don't have time and my husband wouldn't appreciate me going out for dinner with random men." I would tell him.

"What's wrong with going out for dinner with a friend? That's all you have to tell him, Ro." was his response.

This was another episode that I was on guard with because his entourage of friends made comments to me like, "Ro, throughout the day, John has been talking about coming out to the bar to see if you were working tonight."

"Ro, John talks about you all the time. He really likes you."

I got a little freaked out when John was talking to me one day and said that I was too nice of a girl to be working in a place like this and he talked to his parents and I had a job waiting for me at a neighboring hospital with his mom, one hour away.

"You know what? I like where I work and I'm not going anywhere. My HUSBAND is the only person I would change jobs for, if it bothered him at all," I told him.

This was another person that I stopped being so friendly with.

Romana's Story... "It's Not Out of the Goodness of his Heart!"

I just wanted to make a little comment about guys in general. Guys are motivated by sex, food, and sleep, with sex being at the top.

It drives me crazy when I hear girls say stuff like, "Oh, Bob is just a friend and he's taking me to Vegas out of the goodness of his heart. You know, because he's so nice."

Please girls, remember that even though he seems really nice, he's hoping that you'll take it to the next level and go to bed with him! That's just the way it is. Always keep this in mind when your "guy friend" wants to take you on a trip or buy you something.

Women

Were Women Always Patrons of Strip Bars?

When I started working in this industry over fifteen years ago, the only females you would find in the strip bar were servers and dancers. Once in a while I'd notice some poor guy's wife stomp into the bar and yell at him to get his ass home, or start hitting him in the parking lot because she was mad at him for hanging out in the strip bar (I've witnessed the parking lot beatings three times).

Then the movie industry came onto the scene and starting making movies like Striptease and Showgirls. Soon after, women were noticed visiting the strip bars more often.

Years ago, many of my older regulars periodically commented to me, "Ro, why are there so many women coming in here now? This is a men's club! It makes us feel uncomfortable."

The strip bar used to be a gentleman's club where guys would meet their buddies after work for a beer and relax before going home. Now it's not unusual to find a couple hanging out, having drinks and dinner together. I know of "swinger couples" that come in for some drinks and swap partners before leaving. Stagette parties and girlfriends like to come in and party for a few hours before taking off to go dancing at a nightclub for the rest of the evening.

The Girls Are Out for a Good Time

The main women I deal with are staff, dancers, and some female customers. Quite a few of my women regulars visit our bar and hang out with their husband, boyfriend, or buddies. They're very open to the whole strip bar thing, they're easy to talk to, and fun to hang around and serve. They're the girls that don't mind their man hugging you good bye and encourage him to leave you a generous tip. These are the women that comment on my perfume or the cute top I'm wearing and they're a pleasure to serve.

Women customers that like to hang out in the strip bar may also be lesbian and you'll be able to tell pretty quick with most of them when they do come in as a group. Some of them will appear to dress pretty *butch* and have their girlfriends with them. I've had the pleasure of getting to know and serve many lesbians over the years and they're really very nice. Some of them like to hit on the servers too, so be prepared as they're no different than a male hitting on you. Take it as a compliment!

Groups of Stagette parties are fun as they interact with the dancers on the stage while they whoop it up and like to have a great time.

Women are Another Sort of Creature to Deal With

There's a reason why I like working in the strip bar and the majority of people I serve are men because *some* of the women that come in are not very pleasant. The servers and dancers often wonder why they're in the strip bar in the first place; we imagine it's to keep an eye on their guy. You'll come across the woman who doesn't want to be there in the first place and is there to either humor her man or keep an eye on him. I can usually tell within a few minutes if she'll have a problem with me as she may be rude, uptight, or seem very standoffish when ordering a drink. This is a great time to try and win her over and make a compliment about how pretty her necklace or purse is. I'll usually fish around for something to say so that I can make a comment about my husband, which always seems to put her at ease and relax. If the boyfriend orders a Jack Daniels and coke, I'll say, "Exactly what my husband would order." She'll know that I'm not a threat and not after her man, which in turn may help in the tip department.

Romana's Story... The Five Dollar Tipper

I had a young guy and girl sitting at gyno one evening. Every time they ordered a drink, he would tip me five dollars. The girl looked to be upset and seemed to be quite restless and fidgety. I thought it had to do with her boyfriend checking out the dancers on stage.

After half a dozen drink orders, she yelled at him, "Why the hell do you keep tipping her so much?!"

He yelled back, "Because my mom used to be a waitress in a strip bar too!"

Hats off to his mom for raising a good son!

The Kids

We use the term *kids* or *babies* for young people that recently turned of legal drinking age.

Doing a little research, I learned that the legal drinking age is 18 in the provinces of Alberta, Manitoba, and Quebec. The rest of Canada is 19. In our bar, we encounter many young customers who cross the border and come from the Washington State into Canada as the legal drinking age in the United States is 21.

For more information on checking identification, please refer to **Chapter #9, Subchapter #2 under "The Legalities."**

Give the Young a Break

I know what you're thinking. You're probably groaning and thinking that all kids are cheap and don't tip. You're also thinking that they have an attitude problem and are more of a pain in the butt and you're hoping that they don't sit in your section. Let me tell you my friend, you'd better give these young people a chance and don't make any quick assumptions about anyone.

Yes, I've had groups of young people sit on my side and not tip me a dime, but I've also had kids tip me more than generously every single time I bring them a drink, so that I have actually felt guilty for taking money from them.

Treat the kids with respect whether they tip or not because these patrons are your future customers who will eventually learn the art of tipping. If you're rude, you'll leave a bad taste in their mouth, which would be a real shame when they learn to tip and you won't be able to benefit from it.

Clues to Look Out For in the Underage Patron

The following are some tips to look out for that may suggest that your patrons might possibly be underage.

- Kids avoid eye contact with you while ordering. They look down in their lap, at the promo material on the table, or at a menu.
- When ordering they say, "We'll have a jug of beer with three cups" (using the word cups, instead of glasses).
- When ordering, they say "I'll have a high ball."
They use the term high ball and when I ask what kind, they don't know how to respond.
- When handing me money, they say "Do you have change for a ten or a twenty dollar bill?"
- When you hand them their change, they automatically slip it into their pocket. Some will recount it and then slip it into their purse or pocket.
- Some people throw around their attitude while trying to intimidate you, or even become defensive. They may say, "Do you have any idea who I know?!" They may even throw around another server's name like, "Is Patty working tonight? She knows who I am."
- You may have a large group of kids come in together, and most of them in the group will look of age. Some servers only ID the people they *think* are underage, but I suggest ID'ing the entire group. In most cases, same age people hang out together and there may be someone in the group that forgot their ID or has an underage friend or sibling with them. In these cases, I've caught people using a friend's ID in the same group.
- Young looking girls who wear running shoes is another clue to underage patrons. Some girls are better at faking their age by dolling themselves up to try and make themselves look older. As a rule, I always ID every girl that looks under the age of thirty.
- Girls that look like they are learning to walk in high heels, or look very uncomfortable in them, is another clue that she may be underage.
- Usually (not always), the kids do not wear wedding rings or wedding bands.
- Most of the time (not always), the kids do not have a large amount of tattoos.
- Just because you work in the bar during the dayshift when kids should be in school, it doesn't mean that they won't try coming in at this time of the day.

178

During the shifts when there is no doorman, I need to stay in control of my room and ID all the young people that enter the bar. This is one part of my job I dislike, but it *must* be done. Some kids get defensive and upset because they feel that since they've been asked for ID every single time they come in after they turn of age, you should automatically recognize them. This is when I tell them that even though I know they're of age, I'm making sure that they didn't forget their ID at home. No matter what age a person is, they should always have some form of identification on themselves.

The most common line I hear is, "Don't you recognize me? I'm in here all the time!"

A friendly way to smooth over the situation is by making a comment such as, "I ID all the good looking guys!" This puts a smile on their face and the mood is lighter. You really don't want to upset them as this could affect your tip, if they happen to be good tippers.

If the person is being rude with a bad attitude, my famous line is, "Nope. You know who's in here all the time? Me. I've been here for over fifteen years!"

Catching the Underage Patrons: Scenarios #1–3

Below are some examples of scenarios that I occasionally deal with by staying on top of catching any underage patrons.

Scenario #1

A group of kids sit in my section, so I ask everyone to please pull out two pieces of ID. Sometimes there is one person who says that he has forgotten his identification at home (I'm guessing that he's underage) and I inform him he has to leave.

- There may be someone in the group who will offer you a one hundred dollar tip to let his buddy stay. As tempting as this sounds, don't do it because they may be working for the liquor control board. There may also be an under-cover liquor inspector sitting in the room, or the cops or liquor inspector could do an unexpected walk-through as well. Having cops come in and do a walk-through has happened numerous times on my shift, and let me tell you how unnerving this can be when you're second guessing yourself if you remembered to ID everyone.

•   The person with no ID leaves the room, usually with another buddy. A few minutes later, he returns and gives you two pieces after telling you that he lost it or forgot it at home. I ask everyone in the group to pull out their IDs *one more time*. In my experience, seven times out of ten, the ID has already been shown by someone else in the group and by asking everyone to show me their ID a second time, this is a second chance to see who in the group does not have it in the first place or passed it onto the friend.

•   If you get lazy by not checking IDs regularly or never make an effort to catch the fakes, or catch the people that use another person's ID, these people will tell all their underage friends. Before you know it, you'll have tons of underage kids trying everything in the book to get into your bar. You don't want or even need the headache.

Scenario #2

When you ask someone for ID and they hand it to you, make sure you're paying attention to detail. Sometimes I'll be looking at the date and it's not sounding right in my brain until I realize that the person is only 18 years old, or a month shy of turning legal drinking age.

Many times I've said, "Buddy, you're only 18 years old."

The main response is, "Oh, I'm from Alberta."

I say, "Then why do you have a B.C. driver's license?" No response. I remember when I was that age, so I don't blame them for trying as I was in the bar with my girlfriends two years before we were of legal drinking age.

Legally, a patron is to be of legal drinking age the day of their birthday, not a day before or a couple hours before midnight.

A nice way to gain a customer is by saying, "Honey, I'm sorry you can't stay, but how about you come back tomorrow when you turn 19 and I'll even buy you your first beer." If you end it on a good note, you have a happy customer willing to come back and, who knows, he could end up as one of your best customers!

Scenario #3

This one is tricky and requires some memorization, especially if the group is large. I feel triumphant when I can catch these guys in their game!

When looking at a group of IDs, first check the birthday and make sure it jives with today's date. Then get in the habit of reading and memorizing the photo, as well as the first and last name. As you go through the group, you may come across the exact same person's ID (in different form such as a passport or other ID), or the person with no ID says to you that he'll be right back with it because it's in the car. While you're not looking, a friend will slip him his ID that you had already looked at.

If you notice the same name or photo, don't be shy of asking everyone to pull all their IDs out of their wallets again. You'll hear groaning, so tell them what you're looking for. I'll tell the two people with the same ID to leave, and let them know that if they return and pull this stunt again, next time I'll take the IDs away from them. This keeps them from doing this another time or at least in our bar. You're just looking out for the bar's liquor license and doing your job. It's nothing personal.

Stand Your Ground... What to Do if a Customer Won't Leave When You Ask Him To

Yes, there will be times where you'll have problems with the young, just as you'll have problems with everyone else.

An upset customer who is told he's not allowed to stay sometimes demands to see the manager so he can explain why he has no ID on himself and to try convincing the manager to let him stay. Depending on how busy I am, I sympathize with him and tell him that it's nothing personal as I'm just doing my job. I also point to the sign on the wall and mention that the laws regarding identification have gotten stricter. Some staff members have even told people that if they go home and come back later with their ID, we'll buy them their first beer.

Sometimes you'll end up with a patron whom you can't reason with as he continues to explain a fourth time why it's not his fault that he doesn't have his ID. At this point, I'm very annoyed because I don't like the drama and the scene he's making, and he's wasting my time when I could be serving my customers and making money. This is when I've spent too much of my valuable time arguing and respond by saying, "Okay, time to go!"

If he keeps arguing, I respond with, "Buddy, I've got a lot of power in this room. I can cut you off, kick you out, or even bar you! I'm the person whom you should be making friends with, not making mad!"

If he refuses to calm down at this point, I'll say, "You know what? I have an excellent memory for remembering faces! Next time I won't even allow you to set foot in this bar even if you *do* have your ID with you!"

This usually shuts his trap because his friends are yelling at him to be quiet, and apologizing to me for their friend's rude behavior as they push him out the door. Most people don't behave this badly but I have had many episodes exactly like this one.

You don't want to be a bitch about it, but don't let people walk all over you or intimidate you. You need to stay in control and hold the upper hand. After all, you're there to do your job and make some money.

Another way that the underage kids or kids with no ID try to fly under the radar is have a friend go buy drinks at the bar while they sit down. They're hoping that you won't be fast enough to come and ask them for ID. Once their friend arrives at their table with the jug, he thinks that by pouring himself a glass and starting to drink, he's now allowed to stay.

"Buddy, you got your ID on you?" I'll ask.

"We already bought the jug." he'll respond.

I'll try again. "Do you have your ID? If you don't, you can't stay."

"This is bull! We already paid for the jug. We'll finish drinking it and then we'll go."

"No you won't. If you don't leave, I'll take the jug away and your friend won't even get to finish it and I'll call someone over to physically remove you." I'll respond as I smile innocently.

Usually, the person with no ID will leave and the guy who paid for the jug will stay and finish drinking it.

Romana's Story... The Young Group that Intimidated Me

Years ago when I still worked the nightshift, I had a big group of young people come into the bar. There were about fifteen of them, a mixture of girls and guys. I recognized a few of them and realized that they were bad boys. Please refer to **Chapter #6, Subchapter #5 on "The Bad Boys."**

182

I asked everyone to please pull out two pieces of ID and they all sat there looking at me as if I was from another planet. I repeated myself as they continued to sit there while some of them fiddled with the promo material on the table or fooled around with their cell phones. I felt very uncomfortable and a little intimidated because it was a large group and I was on the opposite side of the room from the bartender and the DJ.

One of the guys started freaking on me. "This is bullshit. All we want is a f___n drink around here!"

I had to stay in control of the situation. "No one gets served until I see at least two pieces of ID." I turned around and returned to the bar to tell the bartender what happened. The group cursed and yelled obscenities at me as they left the bar.

When a group of young people come into the bar and they end up with drinks that you haven't served, ask your bartender if the youngsters drinking at table five all had their IDs checked at the bar. If the room is busy, ask the group to show their identification again, even if they complain that they showed it to the bartender already. Most of my shooter girls are great because they help me out in this department as well.

Romana's Story... "Stop Crying. Take your ID Back!"

Years ago, our bar was dealing with a lot of kids that would come in and use a fake or a friend's ID. I had dealt with one too many of these scenarios and decided to take a little more action. I was getting tired of it so I decided to start taking the IDs away. If kids found it not a big deal to lend their IDs out to their friends, then maybe they didn't need them that bad after all.

Well, one night I took a driver's license up to the bar and hid it in a glass with my credit cards and the young guy came up and asked me for it back.

I said, "Nope. I dropped it in the safe. It's going to the RCMP and they'll notify your parents that you've been lending your ID out to your friends at a strip bar." He apologized and told me that he needed his driver's license because he was driving home that night. I still refused to give it back to him.

He started to cry and said his dad was going to kill him. I felt bad, so I gave the ID back to him after making him promise not to do something stupid like that again. Not at our bar, anyways.

Romana's Story... The Awesome Young Tippers

One evening last year, I had a big group of attractive, well-dressed young people sit in my section. I took a deep breath, checked everybody's ID, and then took their drink orders.

As I was dropping off drinks and collecting money, every single person gave me an extremely generous tip. They were my favorite group to serve that week as they were polite, more than generous with the tips, low-maintenance, and quiet.

When it was time for them to leave, I thanked them for coming in and one of the girls had praised me for the great service.

I told her that I appreciated the nice compliment, and she explained that they all work in a popular bar downtown.

Romana's Story... "Want to Go Out On Date?"

About five years ago around the Christmas season, one of my young customers, whom I ask for ID on a regular basis, said to me, "I was wondering if I could take you out to dinner sometime?"

I was surprised because I didn't see this coming, and responded with, "Honey, I'm very flattered but I'm married."

"You are?" he said, looking embarrassed.

I said, "I also have a twelve-year-old daughter."

He sure is a cutie and he now comes in with a very pretty girl his own age.

The Bad Boys

Who are the Bad Boys?

The bad boys are the guys that come into the bar with loads of cash in their pocket. I'm not talking about the guy that deposits his pay cheques or flashes his money around. Don't ask the bad boys questions on what they do for a living as it's none of your business because you don't want to know anything anyways. It's safer this way.

They're usually the ones that make your night by over-tipping. They don't want any change back and these are the guys you'll bend over backwards for, so keep right on top of the service! If they're having a drinking marathon, be there every spare moment you can. When one drink is half full, don't ask the one guy if he wants another drink, ask if they want another round. Nine times out of ten they'll say yes. This is the group that will make your sales high and you'll make some great tips ... best of both worlds!

Do yourself a favor and, like I've said before, don't get involved. If you're asked by a customer where he can find blow or weed, just say you don't know. People push it a little further and say, "Oh, come on. You know! You're a waitress and all waitresses know the right people. There's some money in it for you!"

I respond with, "Sorry. I can't help you. I don't get involved with that sort of thing." Lie if you do know as the person could be an undercover cop. Just do your job and serve drinks.

You'll find that you'll never have any trouble with the bad boys because they like to lay low and most don't like to bring any attention on themselves. If you do start to have any type of trouble, talk to your manager and ask what the next plan of action is. Sometimes the last resort is to call the police and get them removed out of the building. Don't get all heated and hissy with some of these types of people as you don't want to end up getting physically hurt, because it's not worth it.

I heard a story on the radio last summer about a server in a nice restaurant having trouble with a group of guys. She got all heated with them and was yelling at them to get out of the restaurant. One guy broke a beer bottle and smashed it into her face. You never want to feel like you have that amount of power over a group of people. Don't forget that people are drinking and some are doing drugs, some are "nuts" in the first place, and some just don't accept a woman yelling at them and telling them what to do, especially in front of their boys. With all the problems associated with gangs and fighting, be more conscious of your safety. If you must, call the police.

Romana's Story... The Bad Boys

I have thought long and hard through all my stories about my Bad Boys, as I have many! How could I not? Some of these people still pop in now and then, some have moved, a few have passed away, and a couple have vanished.

I have decided that I would rather not write about any of them. They are low-key people who lead fast-paced lives. They treat me like gold, tip me more than generously and I respect their privacy. So, I move onto the next chapter ...

The Rude Customer

Of all the customers that I have to deal with on a daily basis, the rude customer is the personality that sucks the life and energy out of me. I can handle bitchy women, the drunks, crazy party animals, and the guys that constantly hit on me, but it's the dark entities that steal my positive energy and tire me out. They cause me to become snippy towards other customers, which end up affecting my tips.

These people seem unhappy with their lives and themselves, and have a bitter attitude towards others. They're disconnected from the regular folks and when you come face to face with them, you can feel the negative energy seep out of them almost immediately. They don't smile, their appearance is stiff, and they stare straight ahead with piercing eyes. When they talk, it's almost with attitude as if you're annoying them with unnecessary questions, like asking what drink they'd like to order.

Same Scenario; Two Different Types of People

Scenario #1

Me- "Hi! How are you tonight?"
Him- "I'll get a Budweiser."
Me- "I didn't ask what you wanted. I asked how you're doing tonight!" I'm smiling and saying this in a joking and light-hearted way.
Him- "Oh, I'm sorry! I'm doing great. How are you? I'll get a Budweiser please." He smiles and looks embarrassed.

186

This person isn't rude; he must've been on auto pilot and the only thing that seems to be on his mind at the moment is beer.

Scenario #2

Me- "Hi! How are you tonight?"
Him- "I'll get a Budweiser."
Me- "I didn't ask what you wanted. I asked how you're doing tonight!" I'm smiling and saying this in a joking and light-hearted way.
Him- He'll glare at me and repeat, "I'll get a Budweiser."

I'm sure he's thinking that I'm a smart ass, but that's okay because I'll walk away and get his beer. I'll also make a point of neglecting him for the rest of the night because I don't need people to treat me like dirt. If he tries flagging me down for a second beer, I'll look right through him as if I don't see him and this ensures he has to get up out of his comfy chair and go stand in line for beer for the rest of the night. If he doesn't have common courtesy and good manners to not snap at someone who is there to serve him, he deserves to get it himself. I don't need his tip that bad.

The Demanding Customer

The other type of rude customer you may encounter is the guy who is rather demanding.

Me- "Hi, How are you tonight?"
Him- "Ya, I'll get a pint" he commands as he raises his eyebrows and many times I've even had him snap his fingers at me.
Me- "Sure. And the magic word is?" I'll mirror him by raising my own eyebrows and snapping my fingers, then I stop and smile sweetly.

As a result, I've evened the score so he knows I'm not someone to intimidate. If he leaves me a tip, I'll dismiss it and keep the drinks coming, but I won't spend much time doing small talk with him or joke around. At this point, it's all business.

The Guy With No Manners

If it's one thing that makes a server cringe, it's the guy that yells "Hey!" to get your attention.

Depending on how busy I am, I ignore him and keep walking or I respond with, "Hay is for horses and kinky women! I don't respond to hey!" Usually the person apologizes and I'll respond with, "That's ok, I'll forgive you!"

I couldn't believe my ears one night when a young punk said, "Well, what am I suppose to call you?"

I retorted with, "Well, *excuse me* works. Or even *waitress*. Or how about my name, it's Romana!" He was lucky that I even responded to his rudeness, because when I'm busy I won't even stop and waste my time explaining to people how disrespecting that sounds.

The Jerk

From time to time I have creeps say to me, "Shit, you got nice tits!"

When the other servers and I talk about why a guy would make this comment, we all wonder what's going through his head. Does he wonder that we think, "Oh good! I'm glad he told me because I wasn't too sure if they were nice or not."

There are a couple of different ways I've handled these guys. If the guy says it basically with his tongue drooling and acting like a pig, I like to respond with, "You know what? I'm someone's wife and mother! I don't think my husband would appreciate you talking to me like that." I'll usually get an apology and the guy always looks around as if to find a huge bodybuilder standing behind him while ready to grab him by the neck. I get a kick out of it as I watch him squirm in his chair.

If the guy says it matter of fact, I say "My husband thinks so too!" and I walk away before he has a chance to respond or even order a drink.

I know of girls that have asked the guy, "Do you have a wife or girlfriend?"

If the guy responds with "yes"

The server says, "I wonder why!"

If he responds with "no"

She says, "I'm not surprised!"

188

You have to have a sense of humor in this industry. If you know this would grate on your nerves and you couldn't handle it, maybe this isn't the type of place for you to work. It took me a few years to grow a thick skin and stop coming home at the end of my shift in tears because I've learned to just deal with it and take things as they come. When I leave work after a shift, I leave it all behind and don't dwell on it. I like to entertain Rod with stories about the crazy people I dealt with that day and leave it at that.

A regular asked me once how much I make in tips on a regular basis. I responded with, "Well Bob. If I give you a small number, you're going to think that I'm an idiot for putting up with all this. If I tell you a big number, you're going to stop tipping me!" He loved my response!

Many times customers ask me if I make good money. I tell them that it's the only reason why I work where I do.

They say, "Good. You deserve it, because to deal with some of these people on a daily basis, I don't know how a woman handles it." I'm glad that someone notices!

The High Maintenance Customer

You'll encounter the guy that thinks everyone is against him or he's not getting his money's worth. These are the people that don't stop and think before they yell at the server as they imagine that everything is our fault.

"Hey! When the hell is there another stripper on? I've been sitting here paying close to six bucks for a beer and I've only seen one peeler! What the hell is going on around here?"

To this person I respond with, "Excuse me, but I do not respond to *hey*. And just so that you know, the dancer called in saying she'll be late so it throws off our entire schedule. We're doing our best in getting another girl to take her show."

"Hey, why is it so cold in this room? Don't you guys have the heat on?"

"Why are you guys showing motorcycle stunts on the big screen? Why don't you change the channel to the golf championships?"

"Why do the fries have salt on them?"

This customer will always seem to find something to whine about. Do your best to try and win over the situation because you do want to make him happy and, in the end, you still want to make a tip. For example, if the room is cold, tell him you'll turn the heat up. If he doesn't like the motorcycle stunting show, tell him you'll get the DJ to turn the channel to the golf championships on the TV set close to him. If the fries are too salty, tell him you'll ask the cook to make him a new batch with no salt on them. Sometimes you have to grit your teeth and make the customer happy, no matter how annoying and demanding they may seem.

In this business, the customer is not always right as you've been taught to believe. People don't have the right to come into your place of work and treat you like their slave. You don't deserve to be yelled at, have them demand things from you, or disrespect you. Of course you don't want to be unprofessional and scream back at them, but you want to be firm, keep the upper hand, and stay in control. If I can't seem to smooth over a situation and end up with more problems with the complainer, I'll ignore them for the rest of the night. If they're so rude to the point of upsetting me and getting me close to tears, I'll end up getting the doorman or DJ to ask him to leave.

Romana's Story... "From Now on, Get Your own Beer!"

Years ago, I was starting my nightshift and did my first loop around the room, which resulted in a big order. As I was waiting for the bartender to get my drinks, the dayshift server, that was just getting off, asked me to drop off a Kokanee to the older gentleman at the stage in the red coat. I rang the drink in and proceeded to wait for the rest of my order. I heaved my heavy tray of drinks onto my arm and decided to drop the Kokanee off to the old guy in the red coat first.

I put his drink down and he snapped at me, "It's about time. You took long enough!"

As I took his money and handed him back his change I said, "I just started my shift and I got your order from the other server. With this big drink order, I thought I'd drop off your beer first. I don't appreciate being yelled at when I'm doing you a favor and delivering you a beer, so I suggest that from this day on, you get all your drinks at the bar!"

That was almost five years ago and yes, I see him a couple times a week.

190

The Drunk

Signs of an Intoxicated Person

It's illegal and looks bad for the bar when customers see someone stumbling around and they're still being served alcohol. While you're worried about their safety, there could also be a chance that a liquor inspector might show up unexpectedly. The more a customer drinks (especially at a fast pace), he becomes intoxicated and, as a result, must be cut off.

There are many reasons why a person can get intoxicated much more quickly than the average drinker. Some explanations are:

- he drinks while on an empty stomach
- the person is mixing alcohol and illegal or legal drugs
- the customer is drinking doubles in short glasses or consuming martinis, which automatically contain two ounces of alcohol, at a fast pace
- he's drinking large amounts of shooters while drinking a beer or cocktail

Keep in mind that a drunken person walking will be easier to recognize than the drunken person sitting at a table. Indications that point at the customer who's in a drunken state are slurred, mumbled, or loud speech, or even opposite: fast talking. Coordination isn't present, such as trouble picking up change off the table. Eyes may be half closed, glassy, bloodshot, blank stare that is staring at nothing in particular, nodding off as if falling asleep, and may jerk his head back up. The complexion may be beet red in color and as he sits in his chair, he may sway side to side and not sit still. Throwing up at the table is a big sign as he is usually too drunk to make it to the restroom. As he walks, he may weave, stumble, or shuffle, and even walk into a table or another person. As he walks with a drink in his hand, it may spill all over his hand because he can't seem to keep his hand steady.

Ethically, it's really bad judgment for staff to continue serving a person in an intoxicated state because of the fact he keeps over-tipping. I've seen it on more than one occasion.

Some servers are worried that they'll make the wrong decision by thinking the customer isn't that drunk yet. If you even have a small suspicion, cut him off sooner rather than later. Later could end up being too late. Besides, even if you're wrong in your decision, all staff members must honor that and stand behind you.

Once in a while, a customer that enters your bar is possibly mentally handicapped or has some other disability that makes him seem slower. Sometimes these people will usually visit the bar with a friend or family member who will let you know of their state should you have any concerns.

Be especially aware in summer weather. I find a lot of people spend the day in the sun and love to finish off their partying in the bar. They're out drinking and sitting in the sun all day which can be very dehydrating to their system.

Stand Behind Your Coworkers

Years ago, we used to have a bartender that would still serve customers when I told him that they were cut off. It makes me look like I don't know what I'm doing when staff goes against my decision. In the end, the person ends up becoming more of a problem while they get more intoxicated and I'm always the one to have those famous last words with that bartender, "I told you so!!"

I'll let the drunk know that he is cut off, as well as all staff from the bartender, DJ, doorman, and all servers, to the shooter girl. If the person is drinking solo, it's up to the server serving him to make sure he has a safe ride home. Offer to call the person a cab or ask them if they need a phone to call someone for a ride. We have a company that can be called and they arrive to pick up the intoxicated patron and their vehicle and can deliver them both home safely.

Watch out for large groups such as stag parties. I find that these people want their friend to get so inebriated that they can't stand. So, to cut off that person without cutting off the group will be trouble. I have found in the past that if the whole group is not cut off unless the drunk is taken home, they'll continue sneaking alcohol to him. Pretty soon, they need to carry him out or he ends up puking all over the place and it's not a pretty scene.

My regulars have a lot of respect for me, so if someone is to be cut off, I let the friends of the drunk know. They honor that and the only person that would have a problem with being cut-off is the person himself. So, I have found a way to make everyone happy. Read to find out how.

The Strategy of Serving the Drunk "Pretend" Drinks

If a customer ends up being "cut off" and you give him non-alcoholic drinks for the rest of his visit by pretending that they contain alcohol, there are some good reasons for this.

1. It keeps the drunk from getting drunker.
2. It keeps the peace with the drunk because he won't be arguing with you as to why he is being cut off. He's quiet and kept happy and he thinks that he's still drinking with the group.
3. You want this party to stay if the rest of the group is not a problem and they're tipping well. Your sales will increase and so will your tips.
4. By letting the group stay and continue having fun, you have happy customers that will return. If you kick out the drunken patron, most of the time the rest of the group will leave too.
5. If you cut off the drunk and refuse to serve him and the rest of his friends, the whole group will get mad and leave. You'll look like the bad guy.

Do not charge the intoxicated person for the drink if it's a virgin drink because it's only some juice and ice. If he tries paying for it, tell him it's been looked after by someone already. You're making money off his friends, so giving some virgin drinks away isn't a big deal. Usually a friend in the group will pay for the non-alcoholic beer, if a "beer" was ordered by the drunk.

If the drunk complains that the O'Doul's/mocktail tastes funny (of course it does as it contains no alcohol!) and they want something else, take the drink back to the bar and top it up with more juice or pour the beer into a fresh frosty pint and return it to the customer. Generally, about 99 percent of the time, he won't complain anyways because he's too drunk to even notice or care. When giving the virgin drinks to a person who is cut off, let other servers and even the manager know, so in case the liquor inspector or police show up, everyone knows what is going on.

When You Should Ask a Customer to Leave

I cut off a whole group of heavy drinkers when I have a feeling that trouble is starting to brew. If they're all getting out of hand, they're being loud or rude, or other customers are starting to complain in the room, then I want them all to leave. This is the time when I let them know that everyone in their party is done. It's better to get rid of a group like this as soon as you can because they can start to unnerve your other customers and cause others to leave. You don't want the trouble makers to stay because this is when a fight can break out.

If a customer throws up, is way too drunk, is falling asleep in their chair, or is ready to fight, it's time for them to go.

Romana's Story... "Clean the Blood off Yourself!"

I want to add this story even though the person wasn't drunk and this tale doesn't really belong in this section. I don't have a chapter called "Wierdo," so I'll add it to this particular segment.

A few weeks ago while I was working the Friday dayshift, a scruffy looking older man came into the bar carrying a big duffel bag. I told him that he had to check his bag in at the bar while I asked him for his drink order.

When I came up to the bar, my bartender said that he asked the guy what he had in the duffel and the guy replied by saying he didn't know. We thought that was an odd thing for him to say but my bartender said it didn't feel too heavy, so he checked it in and put it in the back. About half an hour later, the guy came up to the bar and asked for his bag because he wanted to grab his cigarettes and go outside for a smoke. After he was gone, my bartender said to me, "Did you see the blood dripping down that guy's hand?! I'm sure it was on his bag that I was touching too!" I pulled out my hand sanitizer and passed it over. When the guy returned from his smoke break, he was waiting to hand his bag back over the bar to the bartender.

I looked at the customer and said, "Buddy, do you have blood dripping down your hand?"

He showed me the back of his hand and I noticed a bandage with blood dripping out from under it.

"You can't come in here like that. You're going to have to clean yourself up before we let you back in."

He asked where the washroom was and when he returned, he showed me his hand as if to ask for permission to be let back in. I nodded and he went back to his beer.

Romana's Story... The Stag Party That Wanted to Stay

Not too long ago, I had a small stag at the stage and the guy getting married was starting to act like an idiot. One of his friends came up to the bar and asked me to bring the groom another pint of beer. I told him that he shouldn't have more to drink and the friend agreed and asked if there was anything to give him that was alcohol-free. I suggested that we take an O'Doul's (a non-alcoholic beer) and pour the contents of the bottle into a frosty mug and tell the groom that it was another draft we had on tap. The groom never caught on. I had a talk with him and told him he had to stop acting like a jackass and if he didn't, he'd have to leave. He didn't get any drunker, because he was now drinking non-alcoholic beer, so he settled down. The group stayed for another two hours without any problems. The other guys in the group knew that the groom was drinking non-alcoholic beer and they were fine with that as long as they were allowed to stay.

Check out Story #46 under **"100 of Romana's Unforgetable Customers"** on a similar story like the one above involving a woman celebrating her birthday.

196

"Jim, there was a price increase.
Your double rum is now $9.85"
**"Oh well. Guess it comes out of
your tip!"**

Chapter 7 – EQUIPMENT, SUPPLIES, THIS AND THAT

Holding and Arranging Your Tray

If you've never held a tray and tried balancing it on your arm, it may take you a bit of practice. Before you know it, you'll be handling it like an old pro and whizzing around the room.

Holding and Balancing Your Tray

These are the instructions for a right-handed person. If you're left-handed, reverse them.

Place all your paper money into your left hand. You'll find instructions and photos on how to do this correctly by referring to **Chapter #7, Subchapter #3 under "Holding and Inspecting Money."**

When you're ready to take your tray, start to slide it off the counter with both hands. When half of it is off, steady it while you slip your left hand underneath and then with your right hand, continue to slide the rest of the tray off onto your left hand and forearm smoothly as not to spill or tip any drinks; fingers are spread apart to take as much surface of the tray in your hand. Take the weight of it and lay it onto your forearm, moving your hand a little to the left or the right to balance it. Keep your right hand on the edge of the tray until you have it steady and the tray is balanced securely on your left arm.

As your tray sits on your forearm, you'll want your coin holder (cash caddy or ashtray) positioned on your tray where it's located closest to your body, which should be your left boob (I heard a few giggles). This is for the safety of your money and the convenience of reaching for change. You don't want your coin on the other end of the tray where you have to reach for it around tippy Corona bottles and risk dropping change into customer's drinks.

You'll know when you're holding all the weight of your tray on your wrist if it's cocked at an upward angle and singing with pain after a couple of hours. You want to feel the weight pull down on your shoulder and be supported on your forearm. The first few years of serving, I started sporting a wrist brace after the suggestion from one of my coworkers. She wore one because her wrist ached with pain and discomfort while working. I was embarrassed wearing it because it looked ugly and eventually started to look dirty and discolored but I had no choice as I was in too much pain.

I guess I started holding the load of my tray on my forearm and let my shoulder take the weight to compensate for the pain that I was having in my wrist. Before I knew it, the discomfort disappeared and I rationalized about how I started carrying the weight differently. I came upon it on my own, by accident. As you start to work with your tray in this manner, you'll find that after a couple of hours, muscles in your shoulder, arm, and back you never knew you had will start to throb or tighten with pain. It'll take you a while to build up strength in those muscles, but before you know it, you'll have people commenting on your *pipes* (biceps).

Don't be surprised when random guys will challenge you to an arm wrestle! My response is always, "No, I better not. I don't want to embarrass you in front of your friends!"

You may remember seeing cocktail waitresses in nightclubs or in the movies holding their tray high above their head. I can understand why girls will heave that tray high up in the air and meander through the room to deliver drinks safely to their customers, but I wouldn't recommend it or do it myself. I'll give you some reasons why:

- I make it a point to stop often and quickly while grabbing an empty or leaning in to hear a soft-spoken person give me their drink order. I wouldn't want to keep heaving that tray up and down so I could rearrange and place empties on it.
- Someone may bump into me, throw my tray off balance, and knock it to the ground, where I would end up paying for the drinks lost.

200

- I may get knocked into by someone and spill my tray onto a customer; they could get very hurt, not to mention it would soak and ruin their clothing. Accidents like this may result in a bar fight among guys.
- A drunk who's trying to be funny may reach over and tickle your armpit.
- You could eventually wear out your shoulder from the weight and rotating of balancing heavy loads while you maneuver your tray up and down constantly.
- In a very busy bar, you don't have your eyes on your tray as it is high up in the air. Tall guys could reach up and try to steal a drink, and this would upset your tray balance, knocking it out of your hand.

As you move around the room, be conscious of your surroundings and hold your right arm out like a blocker if the bar is very busy. If someone were to stand up or step back towards me, I have my arm out to protect my tray so they don't knock into it.

Use your voice as often as you can because it's a very powerful tool! While walking through a crowd of people, talk in a firm, loud voice so customers know you're right beside or behind them, "Excuse me! Excuse me please! Excuse me guys!" If you speak low, customers won't hear you. Always remember that you're always competing for them to hear you above the loud music, friends conversing, and everything else. If your right hand is free, touch them firmly on the back or arm as you pass by.

Watch the speed of your walk while matching it to the activity and energy level in the room. If the energy is low and the room is not busy while you're working the dayshift, slow down. I'm not saying to dawdle, but do walk with a purpose. If you're delivering to two guys at opposite sides of the room, walk straight over to them and never mind keeping to the map of your room. Deliver those drinks first, and then walk around the rest of the room, keeping care to not neglect any customers.

If you've got a lot of orders to take out because the room is full of patrons and buzzing with energy, pick up your speed, and walk briskly while making sharper and quicker motions. You'll need to start multi-tasking by reaching for empty bottles two at a time and asking customers to please hand you any empties you can't reach. You'll have your neck craned while listening to customers giving you their drink orders while at the same time you're rearranging empties and drinks on your tray, collecting money from another customer, or collecting empties from the next table. This is when you'll want to stay on the map of your room because it ensures that you get to everyone and nobody is neglected.

Be Aware of the *Helpful Customer*

It's very sweet when a customer wants to help you by putting empties on your tray, grabbing your rag off your ashtray to mop up a spill, or removing drinks. I have had all these happen to me and the guy has almost had the tray spill in his lap. Grab his hand quickly before he's had a chance to unbalance it and stop him in his tracks. You have to be fast and firm and then say, "Thanks for trying to help, but when you grab that beer/rag/whatever off my tray, you unbalance it and it'll tip off my arm and land in your lap!" People don't think and when you explain this to them, it computes in their head as not to touch your tray.

These people also reach over and drop coin onto your tray or into your coin holder. Coin has been dropped into a full beer or can bounce into a drink if they drop it on your tray, or it could land on the floor. If you hear them say, "Hold on!" and they're rooting around for a tip for you, hold out your hand before they have a chance to dump it on your tray.

Unloading Your Tray

You end up at the bar with a full tray of empties. Full in, full out, right?

Put the edge of your tray onto the counter smoothly and slide it so the whole thing sits on the surface. Don't leave half your tray sitting off the edge because as you unload it, it could tip off the counter, spilling all your change and anything that's left on your tray to the floor. Yes, this has happened to me twice and it sucks crawling around on the floor while you hunt for loonies and quarters that lay in stale beer spilled on the dirty floor. You wonder if you lost any money as coins could roll under the counter or fall into the trash can.

Drop any visa slips into your waitress box after you have advised them. I like to advise everything as soon as possible because I don't want to stand at the visa machine at the end of the night advising a stack of pre-authorization slips. This is the time I drop any fifty and hundred dollar bills after I do a second inspection of them and make sure they're real. All money type stuff is dealt with first!

Do you ring in your order before you forget any of your drinks, or unload your tray of empties first? Our waitress area is very small, so if I'm working a nightshift with other servers whom I have to share the space and till with, I'll unload my tray first as to be out of the way of the next girl who comes up with a full tray of empties. Then I start punching in my drinks into the till after I move my tray out of the way towards the bartender. If I leave my full tray in the way while I start punching in an order, the next girl who comes up with a full tray of empties will have nowhere to put it.

Working by myself on the dayshift, I ring in all my drinks first so nothing is forgotten. This way, the bartender can get busy and start getting everything I need onto the counter. Then any food orders are written up and run into the kitchen. I take a quick look around the room as I return to my till to make sure I haven't forgotten anyone and to check if any regulars just happened to come in and sit at a table while I was placing a food order. This is when I may end up punching in the remainder of any other drinks.

Unload your tray and place all empty bottles in their proper case. If you fill a case, dispose of it immediately so you don't leave it for another server. Empty ice and straws from dirty glasses are dumped into the sink and then the glass is placed upside down on the glass washer. Turn on the glass washer if it's near full. Any garbage collected at tables is thrown into the trash can and not into the sink. If you have a spare moment, run hot water into the sink to melt any ice and make more room. Dirty straws left in the sink after the ice has melted are thrown into the garbage. Give your tray a quick wipe if it has any spills on it before reloading with the next load of drinks.

Take a peek at your change inventory. Do you have only two quarters left and need to buy another roll from the bartender? I always like to have plenty of fives, tens, and twenties on hand for change. People will pay you in fifties and hundreds, while others will ask to buy a bunch of five dollar bills so that they can tip the dancers on stage.

I hate when I need to run back to the bar to buy change as it's such a big time and energy waster. If you need to run back to the bar in a hurry, *take your tray with you*!! Don't set it down and leave it behind at a table with customers. I hear horror stories of people getting drugged by having someone slip something in their drink. Keep an eye on your tray at all times. If I was a customer and I saw my drink on a server's tray and watched her leave it at a table full of random people as she ran to the bar for a forgotten drink or to buy change, I would be slightly unnerved by taking that drink afterward. Customers aren't stupid; many eyes are on you, so think before you make a move like that.

Ok, your tray is empty and your bartender is starting on your order.

Arranging Your Tray

When I started at the bar fifteen years ago, there were two round plastic trays lined with cork that kept drinks from slipping on the surface. I trained with these trays and since I've used them all these years and they're the only trays that I've ever worked with, they're like a second skin. Unfortunately, the trays are only fourteen inches across. They're extremely lightweight and the outer lip stands straight up, being a bit taller than the lip on the standard sixteen-inch, heavier tray. I'll use the sixteen-inch tray when I'm slammed and when I can't seem to carry everything out on the fourteen-inch tray.

My fourteen-inch tray holds my ashtray full of coin and, if packed tightly, holds sixteen bottles of beer.

Ok, so let's say you're not overly busy and your order calls for two Kokanees, four Canadians, two Coronas, rye coke, rye diet, Bombay tonic, and one jug of beer. I have a system to arrange my drinks on my tray to get full use of the space, while keeping space empty to load any empty bottles I collect. Bottles are the tallest and skinniest, so I like to arrange them all on the left side, tucked tightly together against my ashtray. To save time, arrange the bottles so that you can read their labels at a glace and you can retrieve the ones wanted without hunting and turning them around to find the right brand.

I remember the first time a drink order contained ALL bottles. I stacked them tightly against one another and had to take off the ashtray and put it aside as I had no room for it. I dumped some coin around the bottom of the tray for change to hand back to customers. I made it to the first table while my arm shook the whole time from the weight and as I looked at my tray, all I saw were brown bottles! I had to hunt through all the bottles picking them up and turning them around looking for the right brand the customer ordered. (Don't forget that I don't put my tray down on a table. It stays glued to my arm until I get back to the bar with a tray full of empties.) I learned pretty quickly to arrange them on my tray with the labels facing me!

So, the bottles are arranged on the left with labels facing you. When you remove a full bottle and replace the spot with an empty, turn the empty around so that can't see the label. This will signify an empty bottle. I love this time saver, as I don't have to pick up any empties on my tray and think that they're a full beer!

I place any Corona bottles more towards the middle and let other bottles hug them. Corona bottles are easy to tip over as they are tall and skinny and as you walk with a bit of a bounce in your step, they are that much easier to upset, especially with a big hunk of lime set in the mouth of it.

I'll put two straws into my rye with the diet coke, one straw into the rye coke. A lime twist goes into the Bombay tonic and I make sure to put frosty mugs on the tray for the jug drinkers. I'll carry the jug in my right hand if I don't have room on my tray and I arrange my cocktails around the outside of the tray as most are in short glasses. This way it's easier to grab hold of a drink without knocking over taller drinks like bottles or Caesars.

My favorite orders are when I have customers drinking lots of bottles in the room. All of the same bottles would be arranged together starting on the left side of my tray, unless I know that one of my first delivery stops will be eight Budweisers. In this case, I'll arrange everything else starting on the left side of my tray and make sure I keep those eight Budweisers more to the right, crammed against all the other bottles on the left. Any system works, as long as it's easy for you.

If the only way you can remember a mixed drink on your tray is by putting four straws in it, then do it. Just make sure you remove three of the straws from the drink when you hand the drink to the customer. I like to put a straw in a pint of beer if something unusual were in it like 7-Up (this is referred to as a Shandy).

As you gain more experience serving, you'll find different methods work best for you. Use the alphabetical-order system if you have many mixed drinks on your tray that all look the same. A few other ways to tell drinks apart from one another are by putting two straws in all the diet pop drinks and lime twists into the vodka drinks, while the rum drinks have the lime twist sitting on the edge of the glass. Be nosy and ask senior servers why they arrange their tray the way that they do and how they can tell their drinks apart from each other. You may love their system and end up adopting it. Serving is a trial and error type of a job. What may work for another server, may not work for you.

Romana's Story... Dirty Boobs

I remember when ... I first started as a server in this bar those long fifteen years ago.

Back then, the servers wore tuxedo shirts as that was the dress code at the time. We wore little black bow-ties and rolled up our sleeves so they wouldn't get wet or dirty. As we wore the bright white shirts, our left boob scrubbed along the tops of dirty ashtrays we carried back then, as well as the ashtray containing dirty coins.

All the servers cruised around with the underside of their left boob looking dirty.

Cash Caddy vs. Ashtray

Fifteen years ago, the bars were full of smokers and over the years, laws were passed and smoking rooms were built. Today in British Columbia businesses, smoking indoors is no longer legal and smokers are forced to move their smoking habit outdoors.

During the days of customers smoking indoors, servers had to carry a small stack of plastic ashtrays on their tray and exchange the dirty ones for clean ones. We kept our coin in the top ashtray while the clean stack housed underneath was replaced with a dirty when needed. Now that we no longer require ashtrays for customers, we still use the ashtray as our coin holder out of sheer habit.

I ordered a cash caddy and worked with it for four months just to try something new and try as an experiment for the purpose of my book. I'd like to give you the perspectives of using both the ashtray and the cash caddy. Depending on your place of work, you might have to go straight to using a cash caddy as most bars have probably gotten rid of all ashtrays by now anyways.

Advantages of the Cash Caddy

I know servers who love their cash caddy. I love the fact that you can customize them by putting your name, stickers, sparkles, and decorations on it and girls can't mix up their trays amongst one another.

If you like keeping your coin organized, cash caddies are great tools. You can carry a lighter or a lipstick in there too. When the lid is flipped open, there's a pocket-like area on the underside of the lid to cram bills, credit card slips, and credit cards to run your tabs. Close the lid and no one can see your money. There's a little clip on the side so you can snap the case shut and, once the case is closed, there's a big handy clip on the top. A notepad or loose bills can be clipped under it, so they don't fly off your tray while you're cruising around the room. At the end of your shift, because the paper bills are neatly stacked in the cash caddy, all you need to do is pull them out and count them, which make your cash-out very quick.

Advantages of the Ashtray

This is my preference. I stack three on top of each other as this is the height I like. The ashtray doesn't take up too much space, so I can cram all my drinks up against and around it.

I don't mind messy change because when I'm busy, my emphasis is on selling. I throw it in one big mess because it'll eventually get pulled out, only to be thrown back in again. I can see into my change at all times, so I know when I'm low on loonies or quarters and when I need to buy a roll. I keep a wet rag folded neatly on top of my change to keep it covered.

My bills are folded lengthwise and carried in between my fingers. Please refer to **Chapter #7, Subchapter #3 under "Holding and Inspecting Money"** on how to fold your money properly. It feels uncomfortable in the beginning when you're not used to it, but you'll get the hang of it pretty quick. Get in the habit of not removing it from your fingers and laying it on the counter. You could forget it and walk away. I can't count the amount of times new girls have removed their bills from their fingers to do something and then walk away. DO EVERYTHING with those bills in your hand, from punching your order into the till, unloading empties and garbage from your tray, writing up bills, and even using the restroom. I take the bills out of my fingers to wash my hands only if there's no one in the restroom. If there are girls there, I do my best washing my hands with the bills intact. I'd rather have wet bills than no bills.

Disadvantages of the Cash Caddy

The cash caddy was a great little tool to have, but there were a few reasons why I preferred to go back to using the ashtray instead of continuing with the caddy.

I found that the cash caddy took up a little more room than the ashtray and I was not able to load up my tray with as many drinks as when I used the ashtray. I also now had my wet rag that wasted room by sitting beside the cash caddy on the tray.

I found it virtually impossible to write on the pad because the clip is so big and got in the way. I don't write any orders down but wanted to try for the sake of this experiment. A coworker removed the big clip and uses an elastic band to hold down her notepapers. How ingenious!

I found that because I use my favorite fourteen-inch tray, the lip is too tall and the cash caddy won't clip to the edge unless I raise it by stacking a small pile of coasters underneath.

When I opened up the lid on the cash caddy, the big clip on the lid would hit my bottles and I'd either have to rearrange or remove them when I would need to get inside it for change. If I didn't move the bottles, they would get tipped over because of the awkward clip. I learned pretty quickly to open my lid while I loaded my tray. This would make a gap where I would not place any bottles/drinks, which I found was a waste of space. It also put more emphasis on the weight being at the outer edges, and this would throw my tray balance off kilter and hurt my wrist. I didn't like the fact that customers standing around me at the bar could see inside the cash caddy when I had it open to load my tray.

I found it extremely frustrating when I needed to open the caddy to give someone change and that clip hindered me from doing so because of empties I stacked behind it. This was definitely the main thing that drove me insane, not being able to open up the caddy when my tray was full. Being slammin' busy, when I used the sixteen-inch larger tray, balancing the bottles and drinks on the outer edge was a killer on my arm. When it's loaded to the hilt with the balance being uneven, it's extremely tiring for your arm, as well as the muscles in your back and shoulder.

By having all my bills in the cash caddy, I found that I was extremely nervous about leaving my tray on the counter (even when I did clip it shut) as I ran off to put an order into the kitchen. The bartender can leave the bar to go get beer or ice and no one would notice if someone unclipped my cash caddy and ran out the door with it. Your tray is your responsibility, not your bartender's. At times when I would run off to the restroom, I unclipped the caddy and took it with me, which was unnerving for me while I didn't want it to fall into the toilet if I set it on the back. If I set it on the floor by my feet, I was scared that someone would reach underneath the door, grab it, and run out the door while I was in mid-pee.

At times when I was at the bar getting drinks, I didn't notice the change in my cash caddy being low unless I opened it to load my tray of drinks if there were many. Therefore, unnecessary trips were made by running back to the bar to buy a roll of coin.

If your shift is long or very busy, you'll still need the use of a waitress box or even an apron, as the cash caddy is not big enough to hold large amounts of money, visa slips, and interac slips.

Disadvantages of the Ashtray

The biggest disadvantage I've found was if servers are using the same style of tray and also have messy coin, you or another girl can accidentally grab the wrong tray. This has happened to me a few times. As I look into the ashtray and I notice there are only three loonies, panic rises as I realize that three minutes earlier I had bought a roll. I look across the room and realize the other server is delivering drinks with my tray and digging into my ashtray for change to hand to her customers.

Romana's Story... "You Took My Tray!"

Years ago, I was working with another server and I loaded my tray with drinks. I went to drop off my first order and as I removed the rag off the top of my change that was housed on the ashtray, I noticed that something wasn't right. My coin was too empty and the quarters were arranged in the middle where I keep my nickels. I put the drinks on the table and ran to where the other server was in her section. I had her stop and looked at her tray. She had taken my tray by mistake. I picked up the stack of ashtrays to look underneath and as I inspected it, I saw three pennies that I had placed there earlier in the night. It really sucks when this happens because it's hard to retrace and figure out what was taken from the change.

Romana's Story... Free Desserts for the Dancers

This is another story that doesn't fit in this section, but I'm adding it for your entertainment.

We had a guy that is a chef who used to come into the bar quite frequently. One day he brought in a big tray of baked goods and told me that he brought them in for the dancers. I asked the DJ to call the dancer's change room and let some of the girls know. That was all I could basically do to help him out in locating any dancers as it was Friday afternoon and I was busy. He sat there for twenty minutes with his tray of desserts and not one dancer came to sit with him.

He said to me, "Can you go get some of the strippers and tell them I'm waiting here for them with desserts?"

I replied, "No, I can't. I can't leave the room as I'm doing my job. The DJ let the girls know and they're probably busy or getting ready for a show."

Well, he looked a little upset. I guess he was expecting all the dancers to come racing into the room to get their free desserts.

Holding and Inspecting Money

How to Correctly Hold Your Paper Money

I like to hold my paper money in my left hand, with the bills folded lengthwise all the same side folded, one on top of the other, individually. This is the same hand and forearm that will be supporting my tray. Keep the folded parts of the bills touching the inside of the skin between the fingers. If I keep the open ends of the money against my skin, it feels sharp and feels like it will cut into my hand. I am also not able to straighten out the bill easily for the customer with the other hand.

My right hand is free to do all my other waitress duties such as using the till, grabbing empties, taking and giving money, and removing drinks from my tray.

I like to slip all my five dollar bills around my middle finger. My twenties are slipped around my index (wedding ring) finger, with the tens on the outside. The "fan" of money will stand up from the back of your hand.

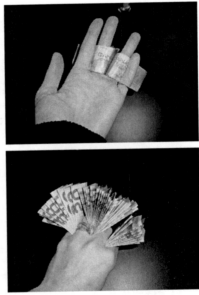

The Goal is To Retrieve and Put Back Money Without Looking

At home, grab a plate or empty tray and practice memorizing where your money is. Pretend your tray is full and, with your hand firmly planted at the bottom of your tray, you need to pull out bills from your hand without looking. Keep your tray steady and straight as you reach under with your right hand and pull out four twenties (you're giving back change for a hundred). Now you need to pull out a ten and a five. Pull your money out of your fingers slowly. If you pull too quickly, you'll remove other bills without knowing and

211

they could fall to the floor. Practice this while balancing drinks on the tray.

Hand over any bills to your customer, flattened (not folded). This way he'll be able to see the bill's denomination and there's no mistake by you giving him a bigger or smaller bill.

As you pull your first bill out from your left hand, pinch it together tightly and roll your fingers across, separating the two halves and straightening it flat. It helps if you pinch your wet rag on the tray to moisten your fingers before you attempt this. The bill will stick better to your fingers and then slide apart.

Now, as you move through the room, practice folding twenties, tens, and fives and place them back into your fingers. Practice folding, unfolding, and playing with your paper money.

Inspecting Bills for Fakes

Playing with your money has its benefits. You'll be able to feel anything unusual about it and may spot a fake bill by feel. For anything that looks or feels unusual, take it up to the bar where there's more light and inspect its color, markings, and size. If you're unsure, ask a fellow server or bartender for a second opinion.

Black light is your friend. Sure, it shows up bleach streaks on clothing and lint on black, but quick inspection of a paper bill, Canadian Citizenship card, or a driver's license under it can detect a fake. There are holograms and marks that attest to the authenticity. During down time, pull out paper money and all sorts of identification and inspect it under the black light so you get familiar with them and know what you're looking for.

I'll always do a quick once over on a big bill when the customer hands it to me. If it looks funny or unusual, I'll hand it back to him and tell him that I can't accept it. If the customer gets upset, show and tell him why you won't take it.

If you notice the color on the bill seems smudged, wet your finger on your wet rag and rub it on the bill. If the color starts to run, it's a fake and the customer is right there watching as your witness. If the bill looks okay but feels funny, I'll tell the customer that I need to inspect it some more at the bar under the lights, and if there's a problem, I'll be back for a replacement bill.

At the bar, I compare the bill to others under the light and even ask other staff members for a second opinion. Then I put part of the bill under running water. If the color doesn't run, the bill is good.

212

Because I am a Canadian girl, the information on money I give you will be about Canadian currency.

Five dollar bills are light blue in color, tens are purple, twenties are green, fifties are red, and hundreds are brown. Inspect all bills carefully and get familiar with them.

Front

The front has the face of the Queen or a Prime Minister.

The bill will have a stripe of silver that looks hologram-like on the left running vertically. The stripe has maple leaves and the amount of the bill alternating. If you hold the bill up into the light, you'll see an invisible face close to the middle of the bill. Rub your finger nail across the lapel of the Queen or Prime Minister on the bill. It will be raised and feel bumpy. On the top right-hand side you'll feel little unusual bumps, which are brail for the blind.

Take the bill in your hand. Put your pointer finger on the back side of the bill behind the lapel, clamp the edge of the front of the bill with your middle finger, and pinch your pointer finger with your thumb. Press that finger down with the bill trapped between a piece of white paper and finger, and scrub it quickly. If a line of color is left on the paper, the bill is real.

Back

Each denomination has its own scene on the back.

There will be a broken stripe running vertically on the left side of the bill in a greenish-gold type hologram. On the left and right side of the bill there is a serial number. The left side will match the right side.

Are Torn or Bills With Missing Pieces Legal?

- If a customer gives you a ripped bill in half, inspect both sides of the bill's serial number. If the numbers/letters don't match, it is considered not useable.
- If a bill has a piece missing, it's still useable as long as both serial numbers are on each side. If one letter or number is missing from a tear ripped out, it is not accepted and is unusable.

If a bill is torn in half, repair it immediately. You don't want to lose one half. I misplaced one half of a twenty dollar bill years ago, which I found hiding in between my stack of twenties in my box.

I always have scotch tape on hand for quick fix ups. If you're in a big rush or can't find tape, use the stapler and staple both halves together until you have time to tape them later.

In the office supply stores such as Staples, I have seen specialty felt markers you can buy specifically for detecting fake paper money. Our bar used to carry the markers and the problem that we encountered was that caps went missing and the pens dried out rather quickly. You can also buy money lights that, when holding a bill under them, can detect fakes. They are inexpensive and can also be found in the office supply stores.

I like to rely on myself and learn to detect the real from the fake money. It's also a handy skill to have as cash is transferred on a daily basis.

Romana's Story... "You Stole my Money!"

I remember one nightshift that I was working by myself. I got slammed and I was zooming all over the room.

The customers at one of my tables had left and because I was really busy and didn't have a chance to pick up the empties and the pile of change that was left for me, I kept a mental note to myself to do it as soon as I had a chance.

Well, imagine my surprise when I got to the table and the empties were there but my money was gone. There were two new guys sitting there. I said to the one guy, "There was a pile of change on this table. Would you know who took it?"

He looked at me and said, "Ya, my buddy here beside me took it," in a no big deal kind of way.

I said to his friend, "I had a table of customers that I had been serving and they left that money as a tip for me. You just stole from me!"

He put his hand in his pocket and dumped all the money on the table. As I scooped it up, I said "You ever pull something like that again, you won't be allowed back in here!"

Did you know that...?

The following are some random facts and fun information in relation to the bar industry.

Did you know that...

1) When you pour a diet coke, it foams up a lot more than regular coke and it takes up too much time before the bubbles settle down until you can top the glass up. When you're busy, waiting for the bubbles to settle wastes precious time that you may not have.

...grab a piece of lime twist and squeeze the juice overtop. It breaks down the bubbles very quickly and you can top up the soda and go!

2) I take extra pints on my tray to sell when I get very busy. If they don't sell, it's given to the bartender to hold for me until a customer orders a pint. The longer the draft sits behind the bar, it settles, the head disappears, and it looks flat.

...when a pint is ordered, I grab a straw and stir up the top portion of the beer to foam it up and give it some head. It looks freshly poured and the customer will never know. It's a good idea to ask your bartender to pour the pint of draft into a fresh, frosty pint glass.

3) If you can't tell the difference between a drink that has soda/7-Up and water, look closely: the pop has tiny bubbles in it, especially clinging to the straw. If your eyesight is bad, do the straw test.

4) Tonic water always glows and looks blue under the black light.

5) Diet coke looks slightly lighter than regular coke.

6) Rye looks darker than rum.

7) When you make a paralyzer (vodka, tequila, sambuca, or banana) drink, it could curdle if you don't follow these instructions:
Scoop ice into glass
Put shot of liquor in glass
Pour the coke in (about three-fourths full)

Wait until the coke settles and stops fizzing
Lightly pour the cream or milk in to fill up the rest of the glass.
If you pour the cream in before the coke or pour the cream in while the coke is still fizzling, there's a good chance the drink will start to curdle.

8) If a customer asks you for a drink in a tall glass with no ice, watch your straw as you walk with your tray. There is no ice to hold the straw in place and by the time you arrive to the table, the straw will be laying on your tray or on the floor.

9) You should keep a box of baking soda on hand to neutralize and clean any stinky trays that have a cork liner. Sprinkle a small amount on the surface and then add some hot water. Take an empty glass, flip it upside down, and rub the soda into the tray. Rinse and wipe dry. If you don't have baking soda, I find that soda water works pretty good too. Baking soda can be used on any tray to kill the stink!

10) Kitty litter is good for soaking up puke on surfaces and it also neutralizes the smell. Sprinkle it onto the area, let it soak, and vacuum it up later.

11) When soda pop is poured into a glass and it goes flat, there may be too much bleach in the dishwasher where it coats the glassware while being washed. You'll know for sure when customers start to complain about a harsh bleach smell while taking a sip out of the glass.

12) I am an avid recycler at work and home, and I would regret not making at least this comment before I get this book out into the world. I keep an empty box at work beside the empty bottle cases and everyone throws all their recycling into it (plastics, paper, pull tabs, water bottles, etc) and then I take it home every evening and add it to my recycling at home.
Every little bit helps to save our planet.

216

13) When you open a can of juice such as pineapple or tomato, immediately pour it into a plastic container. If it's left in the can, within a couple of days it will start its oxidization process and go bad, and it will also start smelling of tin.

14) If you get a couple of drinks confused, use the "straw taste test." This is when you take a straw, dip it into the drink, and cover the end with your finger. Keeping your finger over the straw, bring it to your mouth, remove your finger, and the liquid will fall out.
If you still can't figure out which drink is which, ask your bartender. This is a great way to sample new drinks that you've never tried. Try not to let customers see you do this though!

15) A friend of mine who was in the military once told me that a clean passport can be worth over $25,000.00 on the black market! Try not to take your passport to the bar in case you lose it.

16) Sometimes glassware can crack when you pour hot water or coffee into it. To keep this from happening, put a metal spoon into the glass, and then pour the hot liquid in. The spoon diffuses the heat and keeps the glass from breaking.

17) Some establishments will not allow customers to be served while wearing a wife beater. My bartender went to Australia with his wife and he said that when they went into the bars there, there were signs that read, "No Singlets Allowed." He had to ask the bartender what that meant and was informed that a singlet means a wife beater. For those of you who do not know what a wife beater or singlet are, it's a man's tight tank top style shirt, which is usually ribbed.

18) A bill with a hole ripped in the center was more than likely on a stripper's nipple. A dancer receives a bill on stage as a tip and rips a hole into it so that she can poke her nipple through it and parades around on stage with it. The guys love it and this gets the crowd throwing more money on stage for her.

19) Ice in a drink makes it harder to spill. If you're carrying a full tray of drinks and there is a martini, glass of wine, or drink with no ice, you may want to carry that drink in your free hand. You will have a better chance of it not spilling this way. If you're carrying out more than one drink with no ice, you'll have no choice but to carry it on your tray. You'll have to be steadier with the tray and walk smoothly so they don't spill.

20) Lime cutters save large amounts of time and product. It's a two-piece metal contraption that, when you place a full lime or lemon on the metal section and slam down the top part over the fruit, it sections it into eight evenly cut pieces. It's fast and keeps all pieces cut to the same size. In the past, staff would hand-cut limes and the pieces ended up either too large (to fit into a Corona bottle) or too small (consisting mostly of rind).

21) When setting down dirty jugs used for draft beer onto the glass washer, you should put the jug down with the handle facing the direction the glassware is traveling. If you set them down the opposite way, the jugs fall down on their side and then they won't get the interior washed.

22) Contrary to what you've heard, bars do not "water down" their alcohol. When a shot is poured off the gun, it is calibrated, which means that when you press the button for a liquor, it pours out exactly an ounce. Sometimes the measure is off and it pours short of a shot. Other times it goes the opposite way and over-pours.

23) My new bartender gave me a really neat idea. He said that when he worked at the nightclub, during a special celebration like a birthday party, he would take a short glass and pour some tonic water into it. Then he would light a tea-light and set it into the glass carefully until it floated. With the black lights in the bar, the tonic water glowed in the dark with the little tea-light. Setting a few of these out gives a nice little ambiance! He also mentioned that if you add a shot of cranberry juice, it gives off a reddish glowing hue and a shot of lime cordial makes the liquid glow green. Neat effect to have around the Christmas season, I'm sure!

218

24) Sometimes draft beer can foam like crazy. It may have something to do with someone recently moving the keg and stirring up the contents before it was hooked up. A short while ago, our bar was having that problem, so I decided to pick the brain of the guy who came out to try and fix the problem. He informed me that sometimes the beer is not at the right temperature. It should be less than 40 degrees Fahrenheit, and 38 degrees is perfect. The speed of the pour should be checked as well because too fast or too slow will cause it to foam.

25) Guys love to high-five each other and I have high-fived my share of people at the bar. I was recently told by a customer that the secret of never missing hands when you high-five someone is to watch the elbow of the person you're smacking hands with. He said, "Don't look at the hand, but do look at the elbow and you'll never miss. I learned this tip from a guy in a bar in Whistler." He commented to me.

I now try it all the time and I've never missed yet!

"We have a bet going...are your
boobs real?"

Chapter 8 – THE MANY FACES OF THE SERVING INDUSTRY

The Beer Barrel Girl

What Does a Beer Barrel Girl Do?

Beer barrel girls are found working in dance clubs and strip bars. I worked as a beer barrel girl at the bar that I did my first bikini contest at and I was very fortunate to learn some handy tricks from one of the best beer barrel girls around: the girl that ran the bikini contests in the area. (I remember her having the title of Miss Canada. The year, I can't remember.) Watching her work the beer barrel, I followed her lead.

If you're not sure what a beer barrel girl is, she's the girl that stands beside a beer tub and sells bottles of beer sitting in ice when you first set foot into a bar. She'll be good looking and is good for the bar because customers don't have to go stand in line or wait for a server to grab their first drink. Sometimes customers have their heart set on the special cheap drink or a cocktail, but if she's very persistent and good at her job, usually the customer can be swayed to buy what she's selling.

The advantages of being a beer barrel girl:
1.   You don't have to walk around the room to your customers. They come to you.
2.   You don't spend time wiping tables, picking up empties, and pushing in chairs.
3.   You stand there and dance between customers, and look pretty.
4.   You're offering a product NOW to your patron. They don't have to stand in a line up or wait for a server to get a drink.
5.   You get to flirt and talk to all the hot guys and you won't get in trouble for spending time talking to them if they hang around your beer barrel. You're chatting with and working the customers (this is called customer relations).

Some disadvantages of working the beer barrel:

1.   You're limited to the brands of beer in your tub. You can't offer every type your bar carries.

2.   You can't cater to every customer as you don't serve cocktails or draft beer.

3.   If you get busy and run out of beer, you may have to wait until a doorman or DJ has a spare moment to get you another case of beer. Same goes for running out of change or small bills.

4.   If you need to use the restroom, you can't run off until someone watches your beer and money.

5.   Once your customer buys a beer and leaves, he may continue ordering from the server. When people find a chair, some won't leave the comfort of it until they need to use the restroom.

6.   The beer tub is usually situated near the door and the cold will affect you during the chilly months as the door is being opened and closed constantly.

Maximizing Beer Barrel Sales and Making Big Tips

The following are some helpful pointers to remember for a beer barrel girl so she can maximize her sales and make some fantastic money.

You're one of the first girls the customers notice when they walk into the bar, so you want to be dolled up to the nines! You want full make-up and hair done, while wearing a cute little outfit. You don't want to look trashy, but you do want to look classy and hot. I've seen beer barrel girls making the mistake of wearing ripped up shorts and beat up sneakers ... ugh!

Depending on the bar, you may be required to get your own ice, or a bus boy, DJ, or doorman may get it for you. I always took initiative and got my own supplies. Other items needed for this job are a bottle opener, a few dry rags, a wet rag, and an empty beer jug or small pail for bottle caps. Don't forget your tip jar!

If you get to work early and it looks like it's starting to get busy, get started right away. If I could be making money, I'll make it if I can, so I don't stand around waiting.

Use a cash caddy or ashtray to hold your coin. All paper bills are held in my fingers for safe keeping. I don't like to leave paper money sitting in a jar or in a bill organizer. A fight could break out nearby and I would hate to see my bills fly to the floor. People are constantly mingling around and while you have your head turned, someone could end up robbing you.

Lights, Camera, Action!

Ok, so you're standing there and people are walking in through the door. They walk right by you towards the bar. Why are people not stopping to buy a beer? I'll tell you why: you didn't open your mouth to say something. Don't forget to smile! You want to look approachable and friendly.

I would call ... "Hi guys! Come on over! I've got nice cold beer on ice!"

If people keep walking, I don't stop because that's a potential sale. "Hey guys! Stop for a moment! Come over! Please come over!" Usually they walk over to me and sometimes they'll say that they want a pint of beer. This is where I chime in, "Well, my beer is ice cold, I have a nice assortment of brands and it's only $5.75!" Don't be afraid to tell them that you have a good assortment, even if you only have three types. Also, they don't need to be told that if they bought the same beer from the bartender or server, they would pay the same price.

Most of the time, they'll break down and buy their first beer from you if you're persistent enough. I find that most people don't like to mix their alcohol and once they start drinking one thing, some will stay with the same drink all night. If you persuaded them to buy a bottle of Budweiser, this is what they may end up drinking for the rest of the evening. If the customer likes you and you're friendly, he'll usually return to you when he needs another beer, even if it means getting out of his comfy chair. Your beer is cold and he will get it right away instead of standing in line at the bar or waiting for the server to run off and get it for him.

I like to make small talk. This way the customer doesn't feel like you're kicking him to the curb once you get a hold of his money. If you end up with a little line up, fire through everyone as quick as you can. You don't want people thinking that if they stand at the beer barrel or the bar, either way they're in a line up to wait for a drink.

I found that if I tell customers that if I don't meet a set quota to sell a certain number of beers that evening, then I get in trouble with my boss, a written warning, fired, whatever; I've used them all. You will usually not have any trouble selling to men, unless the guy is a crabby old man, but even then you can turn a grouchy old man's attitude around. Try something like, "So, Handsome, how are you doing tonight?" as you smile sweetly and look him in the eye. If he's close enough, touch his arm. If he's standing there with a lady friend, keep your hands to yourself. Women can get awfully territorial about their men.

Girls love compliments, especially if it comes from a nice-looking, well put-together girl. I like to admire a girl's shoes, purse, necklace, bracelet, or perfume and comment to her about it. Who cares if it's something you would never wear. Tell her how pretty it is. She will love you for it and it makes her feel good. Sometimes, you'll get a sale out of her friends or boyfriend. Who knows, she may even be another server which is a big bonus because fellow servers usually always tip well!

When you stand at the beer barrel, keep calling out to people as they walk by, walk in, or walk out. As customers are leaving, call out to them "Have a great evening you guys! Thanks for coming!"

Your boss will love this as it's very friendly. If you're happy and friendly with a good energy, people will approach you.

Be nice to your porter/helper (the person who is running off to get you more beer or relieve you so that you can run to the restroom). I like to give him a nice, sincere smile and say, "Thank you so much, Tom. I really appreciate your help!" I like to touch him on the arm as it's more personal. He'll be more inclined to come by more often and ask if you need anything. This is more powerful than just mumbling a quick, "Thanks."

In between customers, enjoy the music, smile, and dance. You want guys to check you out. This keeps them coming back to buy more beer. Keep your area clean and neat. Load any empty bottles that you have around you in your empty cases.

If you notice people blocking your beer barrel, ask them to kindly move. You want customers to see your beer barrel and what you have to offer.

226

When it's time to pack up, clean up after yourself. Take away all garbage and dirty rags. Put away all cases containing empties and dump bottle caps into the trash can. Run the beer jug or pail through the glass washer and finish up by wiping down your area. Ask someone what you should do with the ice in the tub. If it's to be dumped outside or in a sink, don't forget about it and expect someone else to get rid of it for you. Some bars will want you to leave the ice so that it melts overnight and it's removed the next day.

At the end of a shift, everyone wants to just clean up as quickly as they can, do their cash, and leave. No one likes to clean up after others, so if you leave a mess behind you, someone else ends up dealing with it. Coworkers will learn pretty quickly if you're a high-maintenance girl or if you do your job and then some. I can assure you that you won't want the reputation of being a princess because people will not enjoy working with you.

Don't forget to tip out your porter/helper. Find out what the average tip-out is and, if you can, always give more. This is a great way to win over other staff. As you tip him out, you can even make a comment like, "Thanks for all your extra help tonight! Here's an extra twenty bucks."

You know he'll be all over you the next time he's to help you. The quicker he gets you more beer when you run out, the quicker you're able to start selling more product and making more tips!

The Shooter Girl

The Shooter Girl's Job

The shooter girl (or shot girl) is the girl who wanders around the room and sells shooters. She's the eye candy and provides customer relations by schmoozing with patrons and working them to loosen their purse strings. She's the fantasy girl who keeps the guys in the room by hanging out and chatting with them. She attracts attention and is pleasant to look at when there are no dancers in the room in between shows in a strip bar. Shooter girls are found working in dance clubs and show lounges (strip bars). This was my first job in the bar industry.

When I got hired to sell shooters, it was mandatory that I wear a swim suit. Nowadays most shooter girls that you see working in a nightclub are dressed in club wear, and the ones that are making really good tips are dressed in lingerie. The more skin you show, the more money you make and that's the fact. Guys will buy shots from the shot girl if she sits down and chats with them. Most have a fantasy that there might be a chance that she will go home with them. This is a job that requires you to flirt and work the clientele if you want to sell shots and make some great tips.

It can get quite tiring and make you feel restless if nobody wants to buy shots after you've walked the room a few times. Sometimes you end up with a crowd that wants to sip on their drinks and are not in the mood to party. Many years ago when we were showing the big Mike Tyson boxing match on the big screens, I was selling shots that evening. The bar was packed full of people and not one person was interested in buying shooters. I felt antsy, nervous, and worried. The servers were running out with trays of drinks and I didn't understand why this crowd didn't want a couple shooters. It was a different kind of crowd that night that consisted of customers that just wanted a beer or cocktail and to concentrate on the fight shown on the TVs. I tried being persistent and did my best to work the room. Eventually, the fight was over, the bar had a change-over of customers, and I was back to selling shooters.

How To Be a Successful Shooter Girl

To be a shooter girl, you have to be friendly, outgoing, and energetic; you have to promote the bar, work the room, and party with the crowd. Remember that you are the fantasy girl. You want to talk, walk, and act sexy. This isn't the time to talk like a truck driver, burp, and talk about farting.

If the room is pretty mellow, this is a time to sit with a group and strike up a conversation. You have to be aggressive in selling your shooters. If customer after customer tells you that they aren't interested, you will have to be a little pushier.

Communicate with the servers and see if there are any stags, birthdays, or celebrations in the room. Usually, these people are out to party and spend large amounts of money.

If the room is hopping and you're selling a lot of shooters, take advantage of this time, stay on your feet, and go! If the guys want you to sit and chat, explain to them that you're busy right now and customers want shooters. You'll be back to hang out and chat when the crowd slows down. You don't want the servers running out with shooters that you could be making sales and tips on.

When you run low on shooters, it's time to go back to the bar and load up your tray. This can be quite a challenge as there are servers and customers at the bar waiting for drinks and it can be quite a while before your order is filled. Go to the bar to refill when most of your tray is near empty. It's a waste of time when a shooter girl makes a trip to the bar for two shooters that she doesn't have on her tray. A good shooter girl persuades customers to buy shooters she's carrying at the time. If a group that is partying and drinking lots orders a dozen jagerbombs, go get them!

My Friday dayshift bartender knows how to use his slow periods wisely. He knows what each shooter girl likes to start with on her tray and when he has some spare time, he'll fill the tray before she starts her shift. It's a great time saver because she can ring in her order as soon as she comes in, grab her tray, and go. It's wonderful for the servers because there isn't a shooter girl standing in our way while we're trying to ring in and get drinks from the bar, especially if we're busy.

In the past we've had shooter girls that would take a quick walk around the room and then hide in the corner and moan about how nobody wants to buy her shots. I can assure you that they didn't last long in the job. In this business you have to constantly work the room, not hide out and stand at the bar complaining that you're not selling shooters. The only ways to making some sales is by being personable, friendly, and being persistent while trying to sell, sell, sell. You are a salesperson and you are there to sell shooters for the bar.

You don't want to walk up to a table, just start dumping shots on the table, and say, "Ok, how many shots do you guys want?" I've heard from several customers that some shooter girls in the past had tried using this tactic and the guys got really upset with this pushy sales move.

The shooter girl has to be professional. If she drinks, she has to be careful and watch her intake. It looks bad for the bar if she stumbles around like a lush and spills her tray because she's too drunk to hold it. When the shooter girl is drunk, she's not aware of over-serving, proper identification of young customers, keeping her business mind on for strategically selling her product, properly balancing and carrying her tray without spillage, and being aware of the drunks who wanders into her. It is a job and as much fun as it is, it should be treated as such.

Some bars pay their shooter girls an hourly wage, and most pay them on a commission basis. She will buy some of her shooters at a cheaper price, and sell them at a profit. Sometimes the premium alcohol will be bought at the same price the server sells it at. In this situation, she hopes that since she isn't making a commission, she will at least receive a decent tip.

When there is a shooter girl working, and people order shots from me, I'll say to them, "I'll send over the shooter girl because she sells them at a cheaper price. And I'm sure you'd love to get served by a half naked girl anyways." I don't mind helping her this way so she can make money. I do get annoyed when people want shots and I need to run outside to the smoke pit, or into the staff room while she's texting and checking messages on her phone or eating. I'll run for her a few times, but after the third time I'm tired of trying to hunt her down and I'll just start taking the shots out myself. I don't think it's fair that in order for her to make some money, I'm running around looking for her. Remember this if you are a shooter girl so that you don't annoy your fellow servers.

If the room is busy and the shooter girl is on the other end of the room, do your customers a favor and take the shooters out yourself. I've had customers get upset and ask me to please not call the shooter girl over because it just takes too long for them to get shooters. If people want to drink and spend their money, I will help it along.

Some Shooter Selling Tactics

Here are a few things to say to try and convince customers to buy a shooter or two.
- "Hi guys! Anyone ready for a shooter?"
- "I hear that this is a stag/birthday party and you guys are out to celebrate tonight! How about starting out with some pussy licker shots?"

230

- "Who loves dirty hookers or blow jobs?"
- "Guys, can you help me out and buy some shots tonight? I'm new and want to look good to the boss" or "I have a quota I need to sell tonight or I get fired/written warning."
- "Guys, can you pleeeeease help me get rid of some of my shots?"
- "Ok, who wants what? I'm not taking a no for an answer. You guys gotta buy at least one shot from me today or I'll just keep on coming back and bugging you!" (Make sure you smile sweetly and give them a big wink.)
- "Hey guys! Did you know what day it is? It's shooter Tuesday/Saturday (whatever day it is) and that means that everyone has to buy a shooter today to celebrate!"
- "Ok ... 'cause there are ten of you, I'll give you guys a deal! If you buy nine shots, I'll give you one for free!"
- "Hey guys, if I can arrange a poster from one of the dancers for the groom, will you guys buy a round of shots from me?"
- "There are some girls on the other side of the room that think you guys are hot! You guys want to buy them some shots?"

You can actually have a lot of fun to try and figure out how to persuade people to buy shooters from you. By making it challenging and turning it into a game, before you know it, you're having a blast and making tons of money!

The Food Girl: Food Service

Although this chapter is titled for the food server, almost all of the tips can be used by the cocktail waitress who serves food alongside drinks.

A taste of how our bar runs...

During the dayshift until dinner time, the dayshift server serves drinks and food. The dayshift keeps the server hopping at times, especially on a busy Friday. At six o'clock, a food girl comes onto the floor who solely takes over all food orders for the rest of the evening. For the dayshift server, selling food is not frowned upon. This shift is pretty mellow at times, so selling and dealing with food is a good thing. It keeps me busy, the day flies by, and it is another item to sell during the shift to make some extra tips.

Greet Your Customers and Always Ask If They Want a Menu

As customers walk in and sit down. I'll greet them with "Hi guys, how's your day going?" I'll ask them what they'd like to drink, and ask them if they'd like to see a food menu. If they hum and haw, I'll usually reply with, "They make awesome food here. If you've never eaten here, you've got to try it. I'll bring you guys a couple of menus and you can have a peek inside." Most of the time, I place a food order which equals tips for me, and my food sales are higher! By asking every single person if they want a menu, you are selling food for the kitchen and there's a chance that you can make some extra money with a tip.

Scan all menus before you run them out to any customers. You don't want to hand over anything sticky, wet, and dirty or damaged. Handing customers soiled menus may turn them off of the kitchen, thinking it's dirty back there too. All menus should be wiped down with a clean cloth and warm water every few days.

Patrons occasionally ask what I would suggest they try on the menu. I usually ask them if they're extremely hungry and if they respond with a yes, I steer them away from the smaller portioned items. I'll suggest menu choices that customers rave about and that are hot sellers. If a customer orders the steak sandwich and really enjoyed it, I'll mention that it's on sale Thursdays. They may come back for lunch on a Thursday and possibly bring friends. You've just helped the business, your sales, and possible tips for you!

Some bars will want their servers to punch all food orders into a till. At our bar, we handwrite all food orders onto a guest check book. In this situation, it's important to have legible handwriting! You don't want the cook trying to decipher a food bill for three minutes and wonder if it says cheese burger or cheese bread.

Also, learning some shorthand is a time saver. When I want to write honey garlic wings, I write *HG wings*. *B/C Burger* is a bacon cheese burger. I don't write *Chs. B.* for cheeseburger anymore as the new cook made cheese bread for a customer once. I write *Chs. Burger* as there is less room for error. When I write out steak sandwich orders and someone wants sautéed mushrooms, I write *w/saut. mush.* Every individual will have their own version of shorthand, so when I figure out some new shorthand, I'll always let my cook know what it stands for. If you keep the lines of communication open, it saves time and keeps mistakes from occurring.

Think About Your Menu Items When Customers Order Food

You have to think about the menu item when customers are ordering food. If someone orders a steak, ask how they would like their steak cooked. Would they like fries, soup, or salad? With the salad, ask what type of dressing they would like. How about trying to up-sell and ask if they would like sautéed mushrooms or even sautéed onions for an extra two dollars. What about some gravy for the fries?

When a customer orders food, make sure to carry out all napkins, utensils, and salt and pepper. Taking out any ketchup bottles, wipe up any runny ketchup spilling down the side of the bottle, as well as screw the cap on straight.

Take a moment to think about the food order. It's annoying for the customer when they're sitting there with soup and a sandwich, and you've forgotten the soup spoon, or a fork for their salad. Set them up right away, so you don't forget. You don't want their food sitting in front of them while they're watching you cruise around the room with their napkins and cutlery on your tray. Taking napkins out, place them in a glass so they are kept clean and dry. Nobody wants wet napkins from beer spills on your tray!

Use common sense; if three people order three pounds of wings, don't bring them one napkin each. Bring them a small stack. Just as you wouldn't bring a stack of napkins to one person who orders a basket of french fries.

Other Little Food Service Tips

ALWAYS ask how the food is, as you pass by. Don't overdo it and ask three times. It's annoying to a customer as he's trying to eat and enjoy his meal. By asking how everything is, you may be asked for more dip, napkins, or a clean fork. Maybe there's mayonnaise on the burger when they specifically ordered it without it. Maybe the order was wrong? When a patron orders food and he is adamant about not wanting mushrooms, mayonnaise, etc., I will ALWAYS ask if they are allergic. If they are, I write it boldly on the bill, as well as verbally let the cook know. This way there are no mistakes and no calls for an ambulance!

A few weeks ago, Rod and I popped by a neighborhood pub for a bite to eat. I ordered the Greek wrap and he ordered the fajitas. While Rod is not a picky person, he informed me that the meal had no flavor to it and was not very good at all. He ate two out of the six fajitas and pushed the rest aside, commenting that he didn't enjoy it. I was expecting the waitress to ask him if there was a problem with his meal. Instead, she said "Had enough?" while she grabbed the plate and zoomed away. Clearly, the meal had barely been touched so I was amazed as to why she hadn't asked if there was anything wrong with it. This is a good way to upset a customer and lose a tip.

Never run off with a plate when the customer is not there unless it is completely empty or has dirty napkins and garbage piled on top of it. Always ask, "May I take this away for you?" Be considerate. They may still want those last two bites of their salad.

Take away dirty dishes as soon as you can because customers don't want to sit there staring at a dirty plate. If I'm busy, I'll tell them that I'll be back in a minute to take it away. I want them to know that I am aware of the dishes and they will be taken care of momentarily. If I'm extremely busy, I ask the DJ if he has a moment to grab them for me.

Dirty dishes are taken straight into the kitchen and, if I have the time, I'll scrape off the food. Then I set the plates into the dish rack and rinse them off. When the rack is full, I run it through the wash. The kitchen staff is always really appreciative of this help and it leaves them more time for prep work or other tasks. If I'm really busy, the dishes go into the bus pan.

When a food order is written on a guest cheque, I give the back copy to the kitchen so they know what the order is and where it goes (make sure you write the table number).

When I run into the kitchen with a food bill and there is nobody in sight, I yell, "Order up!" or "Hello!" This is my signal that I'm putting an order in.

234

I have a little system that I use, which works well. Any tabs running, I write the food amount on the tab and slip the kitchen bill into a glass that I keep for all paid kitchen bills. When someone pays me for their food immediately, the kitchen bill is slipped into the glass to get out of my way. Any unpaid bills are laid by my till if I'm the only one working. If I'm working with other servers, the bills are kept on my tray, slipped in between my ashtrays. Usually I don't have many unpaid bills as I get payment immediately, especially when I work the nightshift.

During busy nights when we show a UFC or a special event, the kitchen is usually quite hectic, and they will have one or even two food servers working. If I have a spare moment or two, I like to help out the food girls. If my right hand is free and I'm running by a table with dirty plates, I'll grab them and take them away. The room looks less messy (boss is happy), it gets out of the customer's way (customer is happy), and you're helping out the food girl (food girl is happy). This way, when I'm slammed, the food girl will be more inclined to help me out and grab empties or wipe a table for me when she's not busy.

When I'm asked to grab a vinegar bottle for a customer, I always hold it up to the light and do a quick inspection of the contents. I'm looking for any fruit flies that happen to get into the bottle overnight. This habit of doing a quick check before any vinegar bottle leaving the kitchen is a good habit to embrace. Even the cleanest of kitchens will unfortunately encounter these unnecessary annoyances.

When a customer leaves on his bill without paying, it's called *Dine and Dash* or *Eat and Run*. For more information on this subject, please refer to **Chapter #9, Subchapter #5 under "What to do When a Dine and Dash Happens to You."**

If there is no kitchen girl working during a nightshift, and I'm stuck taking food orders, I always ask customers to pay me for their meal before they receive it. I collect money for the food when I bring their drink and napkins. The nightshift gets busy and people move around the room a lot. I concentrate on serving drinks and I don't want to worry about forgetting to collect money on the food. Unfortunately there are the scammers that are happy to receive a free meal and the server ends up paying for it.

The Bartender

The bartender is the boss man in the room. He's in charge of everything running smoothly if the manager is not around.

The Bartender Helps You Make Money

He's my favorite person because he is the guy who helps me make money. If it wasn't for him, I'd have to make my own drinks and run to the cooler down the hall to bring in cases of beer and other product that we run out of. He's the guy that changes the kegs when they run dry and he deals with any irate customers. He's the guy that leaps over the bar to help the doorman if there are any fights and he works with the DJ in any dancer schedule changes. He calls taxis for customers when I ask him to, and he's the one to listen to the drunken guy sitting at his bar blubbering about losing his job or about his wife being ready to leave him. The bartender doesn't have the luxury to walk away because he's stuck behind his bar. The bartender is the guy who is pressured to get drinks ready for all servers. He makes shots for the shooter girl and he's the one who feels the pressure of the line up of people staring at him to serve people faster. He must always move fast when it's busy, and to think two or three steps ahead on everything. He's always got to stay focused, be good at multi-tasking, and stay in control.

If I make exceptionally good money or find an unusually large amount of money on the floor, I will tip him out more than what I normally would have. I like to treat him well as he will be the guy to promo me a birthday shot for a customer or even promo a drink or two for my husband when he comes in. He's also the guy to give me the heads up on the crazy customers that come in and go to the bar for their first drink, and throw that ten dollar tip into his tip jar!

Remember the 80s movie *Cocktail* with Tom Cruise? In the movie they portrayed Flair Bartending.

"Flair bartending is the practice of bartenders entertaining guests, clientele, or audiences with the manipulation of bar tools (e.g., cocktail shakers) and liquor bottles in tricky, dazzling ways. Used occasionally in cocktail bars, the action requires skills commonly associated with jugglers. It has become a sought-after talent among venue owners and

236

marketers to help advertise a liquor product or the opening of a bar establishment. Competitions have been sponsored by liquor brands to attract flair bartenders, and some hospitality training companies hold courses to teach flair techniques. – Wikipedia"

Help Out the Big Man

If I have time, I like to help out my bartender. I offer to put visas or interacs through for him if he's busy. I'll push in the chairs around his bar so that the bar looks tidy and inviting. While I'm at it, I'll give the area a quick wipe. If he has a line up at his bar and he's busy, I offer to go get him ice or a case of beer needed from the cooler down the hall. When the room is busy and my section is caught up or has low energy, I'll hop behind the bar to unload the glass washer and put glasswear away for him.

The bartender is the last guy to leave for the evening as he has to restock his bar at the end of his shift or to do inventory at the end of the month.

Don't Steal Your Bartender's Customers

The one thing that irks me is when I see other servers steal my bartender's customers. He will agree with me. Let me explain...

If there are a couple of people standing at the bar and they're waiting to be served, sometimes someone will step out of line and say to the server at the till, "Can you grab me a drink while I go sit down?" Some of the servers say "Yes."

What I will do is say, "I'm sorry, but I'm not allowed to serve people at the bar. Your bartender will be with you in just a moment."

If you take that customer's order, you may have just taken a tip that the bartender could've made. You'll also upset the customers that have been standing in front of him for the past couple of minutes waiting their turn to get served.

The only way I'll take the customer's order is if he throws a fit (the bartender will usually nod at me to take the order out), if the person wants to run a tab with a server and doesn't want to keep getting up to go to the bar, if he's sending some drinks over to another table, or if the customer has a bunch of drinks he needs taken out and he can't carry them all.

One of our busiest shifts in the week is our after-work crowd on Friday afternoons. The guys run in to have those after-work, hello-weekend beers. We're busy serving food and drinks, and there is double the amount of servers as well as a shooter girl by 4:00 pm.

The shooter girl takes up much of the bartender's time as well as room at the bar, so he likes to make her tray of drinks ahead of time. When it slows down after lunch time, he makes the shots, places them on her tray, and then slips it behind the bar until she comes in to start her shift. Before she grabs her tray, she rings in the shots and off she goes. There's no holding up the bar and making the servers or customers wait for her to get her shots made.

A Bartender's Story.... "Here's Lime in Your Eye!"

I'm giggling as I'm writing this! My dayshift bartender told me about the crazy guy that came into the bar on his nightshift last week.

A customer entered the bar and walked straight to the bar and said, "I want some alcohol but I have no money."

"Sorry buddy. You gotta go," he's told.

"I'll tell you what. If you buy me a shot of tequila, I'll let you squirt a lime in my eye," he says.

"You got yourself a deal!" my bartender said as he grabbed the tequila bottle and slams down a shot glass.

The guy downs the shot and then leans back over the bar. He opens up his eye using the fingers of both hands to expose his eyeball. The bartender takes a piece of lime and squeezes the juice into the guy's eye. The crazy guy lets out a long scream and then stumbles out of the bar.

My bartender said, "I would buy that guy a shot every day if he'd let me squeeze a lime in his eye!"

I laughed for twenty minutes after hearing this story!

The DJ

The DJ is "The Man!"

The DJ is the man that is probably looked at with much envy by most patrons. I have heard many comments from the younger generation such as, "Oh my God, I would kill to work as a DJ in a strip bar!" "Man, a strip bar DJ has got to be the best job on the face of this planet!" "I bet the DJ gets to screw any stripper he wants."

238

The older generation seems to have a little more respect for the DJ. These are the guys that buy him a drink or walk over to tell him he's doing a great job in picking music to fill the air between girls.

To be a good DJ, you need to be outgoing and not be afraid to talk on the microphone. You need to have a clear, precise voice while not using the phrase "Ummmmmm" and not talk like you have a mouth full of marbles.

The DJ is "the man." He's the guy that gets to talk to and hang out with the dancers. He's the one that runs to their room to check on them if they're running late. He's the lucky guy who helps them untangle a necklace or snip a loose thread from a costume and he's the one who's returning a piece of clothing from a costume that gets left behind on stage or dropped on the floor. He cues their music and sets their lighting. He's the guy to hear all their stories about their weekend as well as the girlfriend she's fighting with at the moment. He's also the first guy to hear that she's having her period, so she's a little bloated and needs the lighting reset and brought down.

He's also the big brother. He keeps all the guys in check and makes sure no hands are placed on them. He's the one to ask the perverts to leave the building if they're snapping pictures of the girls with their camera phones or disrespecting them with rude comments.

The DJ is Also the Bad Guy

He's also the one that has to "fine" the dancers if they show up for their shows drunk, high, disheveled (looking like she just crawled out of bed and combed her hair with a pillow), or late, or if she didn't read the schedule properly and pulls a no-show. So, the DJ is also the bad guy. He's the man to make the decision for a girl to go on stage for a full show or a half show if the afternoon is slow and there are two customers sitting in the room. He's the man that gets frowned upon by the girls if a show is cut, as well as the few customers that are waiting for a show to go on. He's got to modify the schedule if a girl calls in sick or pulls a no-show and he calls the agency for a replacement.

He's also the man with power because he has a microphone in his hand. Don't screw with him as this is a man who talks into the microphone for a living and usually has a quick tongue for anyone who likes to yell comments about how his music sucks. If you don't like the music that the dancer is dancing to, don't be quick to yell at the DJ about this as it's the girl who picks it as well as owns that skipping disc!

The DJ is also in the same boat as the bartender, such as not being able to leave his booth. Sometimes a customer shows up and leans against the DJ booth and bothers him with small talk.

Depending on the bar, he may be in charge of doing the liquor-pull (bringing cases and kegs to the main beer cooler). He needs to keep an eye on the television screens and make sure that there is always something interesting for the customers to watch to keep them from getting bored and leaving. Action shows like monster trucks, car racing, or motorcycle stunts are great to have on. Guys will never protest to shows like the Hooters Bikini Contest or Miss Fitness Competitions either.

Likes and Dislikes of the DJ Job

I asked a few of our fantastic DJs what are some of the things that they love about their job. Most love the hours; we're thankful that the bar doesn't open until the early afternoon. We're lucky that we don't start work at 8:00 am like the average person. They love that it's quite casual and since a few of them are musicians or band members, they love to listen to and pick out music. They love the fact that they get paid to help people have a good time.

There are some dislikes to the job as well. They don't like to baby-sit some of the high-maintenance, flaky dancers and dealing with the rude drunks. The same DJ that had made the comment about loving to get paid to give people a good time also hates to get paid to give people a good time. I asked him to elaborate on that and he explained that if you don't watch yourself, you get roped into partying and having a good time yourself; you start the drinking, drugs, and partying until the wee hours of the morning.

The Doorman or Bouncer

The Man With a Lot of Responsibilities

I'm thankful for the doorman as he's like the big brother of the room.

He's responsible for checking customers' identification at the door before they enter the room, which is a big time saver for the servers. If a server has any doubts, we will usually recheck it.

He's the guy that tends the door and makes sure that customers don't leave the establishment with any liquor or beer bottles. He breaks up any fights (if any are started) and removes any customers that turn into troublemakers in the bar. He's good to have at the door because it usually deters fights from starting in the first place. I've seen the drunken rowdies swing at the doorman and in return the doorman gets his arm around their neck and the troublemaker is dragged outside and thrown onto the sidewalk. He escorts the dancers and any female staff to their vehicles at night if he's asked. At the end of the evening, he'll help turn on lights and ask customers to finish their drinks and escort them to the door.

The Doorman in the Strip Bar

It's rare that fights start in a strip bar. They still do happen, but not as often as a nightclub. I have my theory as to why fights happen more regularly at a nightclub than a strip bar.

Strip bars have a mix of customers of all ages which are mostly men. People sit and don't mingle around much. Most of them are concentrating on the entertainment on stage and everyone feels like they are all part of one big club or sorority. A stag group celebrating soon has the group next to them sending their groom a shot. Before you know it, they're all partying together.

Most of the women that come into the bar are either lesbians, girlfriends, or wives of a customer, swingers that come there to start their date, female regulars that party with their guy friends, stagette parties, girlfriends that are curious about this industry, and even wanna-be strippers. Most women keep to themselves and their girl group. They don't roam around the room talking to random guys unless they know them. At times, men send over drinks to pretty girls across the room, but it's rare if they mosey over to talk to them or hit on them. In some cases where guys try and join a girls' group, the annoyed women down their drinks and leave.

So, in the strip bar, fights don't happen much. It's usually when a troublemaker thinks some guy is staring at him or a few choice words are exchanged between them. This is the kind of guy who is looking for any kind of excuse to fight someone that night. Just add alcohol and you've got an instant asshole.

The Doorman in the Nightclub

Well, we have a nightclub next door to our strip bar and I hear about the fights that happen quite often.

The clubs offer cheap drinks to gain patronage. Cheap drinks mean that customers can drink more at a faster pace and, when they're drunk, it's easier to have the confidence to approach girls. Most clientele are younger in age and the only reason those guys are at the bar in the first place is because of girls. Why do you think clubs offer no cover to all females before a certain time of the night? It's to get the girls in there and that brings the boys in.

There is sexual tension in the bar with so many people meandering around, drinking, and dancing. Conflicts happen and fights break out. Some guys turn into instant assholes when they drink and get drunk. Someone accidentally bumps into him or thinks some guy is staring at his girlfriend and he is the nut who starts throwing punches. In the club, most people roam around and it gets busy and packed with not much room to move around anyways.

With the large volume of people, there must always be doormen at the entrance at all times. It's easier for underage kids to sneak inside and hide in the mess of people. Some bars have the doormen check customers for weapons. With the problems nowadays with gangs and shootings, this is a superb idea.

The Dancers

Other terms used for these women are *strippers, exotic entertainers, exotic dancers, peelers,* and *pole dancers.*

Well my dear friends, if it wasn't for these sisters of mine, I wouldn't have a job. Over the years, many have asked me the same question ... "Ro, I have to deal with customers during the length of my show who already drive me a little crazy and then I can run off and hide until I'm on again. You have to deal with them for hours and you can't even hide from them. How the hell do you deal with it?"

I've known many of these girls for years and asked a lot of them as to how they got into the industry in the first place, so I've also done my fair share of research by talking to many of them.

When I listen to people, I hear how most people think that strippers have "daddy issues." They've been either sexually abused by an uncle, neglected, or abandoned by their father. I've heard this theory for years, and I'm embarrassed to say that I didn't give it much thought and deep down I thought the same thing.

I've asked many girls why they chose to strip for a living. I've heard many different reasons and I think that this chapter is important to write because most people look at these women as poor girls that had nowhere else to turn who ended up in a seedy and bad industry.

Why Do Girls Dance?

Girls dance because they **like the money**. As far as I'm concerned, they deserve to be well paid! I don't want to do it as I have a hard enough time getting naked for my husband or my doctor at times.

Some girls dance because they **like the attention**. Is there anything wrong with this? I can admit that I like the attention when I'm told by strangers that I'm beautiful or that I have the hottest legs they've seen in a long time. It makes me feel attractive and good. Same goes for a dancer when customers show their appreciation with applause and tips put on stage. Dancers have different stalkers follow them around from bar to bar. This is one type of attention they are not thrilled with I can assure you.

Girls dance because **they love it**! They enjoy entertaining people. Why do ballet dancers dance ballet or actors work in the movies? Hello ... they love it and they make good money doing it!

Girls dance because **they don't have other job skills**. If the bills need to be paid, they're of age and attractive, and they don't mind dancing naked in front of strange people, why not dance? They don't need to go to school for years and get training or a degree.

Girls dance because they need to **increase their household income**. Some go to school or have a part time day job. What's wrong with making some extra money on the side, especially in the evening when the kids are sleeping or even during the day while the kids are at school?

Girls dance because **they're attractive and like dressing up** in fantasy costumes. What's wrong with that? I admire many a costume or hot shoes on the stage. Why do we like to dress up during Halloween or in the bedroom and role play?

Girls dance because they're **desperate to make some good money quick**. They start work at the beginning of the week and by the end of the week they're paid. They don't have to wait for two weeks to get a pay cheque; nice little bonus when you have a purse full of tips every day.

Some girls **don't want to work physically hard or maybe they can't**. They don't want to waitress and deal closely with the public or sling a big tray of beer or work outdoors in the cold.

Some of the personal stories I was told of why some of the girls got into this industry are as follows:
- One girl said that her boyfriend entered her into an amateur contest. She won and said it was an easy way to make a hundred dollars. She started entering all the amateur contests and realized that it was an easier way to make money than kill herself at an hourly job.
- One girl said that she worked a construction job and took pole dancing lessons in the evenings for exercise. She got laid off from her construction job and couldn't collect UI because she was self employed. She saw an ad in the paper about amateur pole dancing contests and thought, "Hey, I can do that." She eventually quit her day job when she realized that she made three times more money dancing than working construction.
- One girl said she remembers being a little girl and always said that she wanted to be a stripper. She didn't know what that meant, but she wanted to dance in front of people.

The dancers are caring and generous people. Over the years, I've had expensive perfume, drinks, and flowers bought for my birthday, and flowers for me when my cat died. I always seem to be raising

244

money for a cause such as helping abused or neglected animals and I can always rely on many of the girls to help me out and contribute to my cause. They are the first people to buy a baby gift for a bartender when his baby is born and to surprise staff with a slurpee or ice cream bar on a hot summer dayshift.

The Negatives to Dancing

Dancers deal with occasional verbal abuse from some patrons. It requires a girl to cover herself in a "thick skin" as soon as possible.

Usually a typical schedule for a girl starts on a Monday and ends on a Saturday night. They work for six days straight and their Sunday is usually spent on catching up on their laundry, household chores, or traveling to the next club.

Money must always be spent on hair color and cuts, tanning, hair removal, shoes and boots (heels break and need mending), costumes (almost all are custom made), traveling (gas, car, hotel), and eating out (most girls are on the road; therefore, they don't eat a bag lunch).

Imagine traveling and living out of a suitcase. I can tell you right now that this wouldn't be the kind of life for me. I like to sleep in my own bed, kiss my husband every day, hug my daughter daily, ride my horse, and cuddle my cats and dogs. I enjoy structure and routine and like to know where I will be every day and with whom.

During the summer months, the girls sweat like crazy from the warm weather and they freeze in the winter. I'm always thankful for a nice warm sweater in winter and pity the dancers when they need to get naked.

The popular girls get recognized all over the place. One of the girls had told me that she was standing in line for a beer at a hockey game with friends and a group of guys started yelling her stage name and that he had her poster on his wall. This could be a bit of a problem if a girl is out with her parents and keeps this job a secret from them.

Private Dances

A private dance is a show that a dancer will do for a customer in a small private room where there is no physical contact. A lap dance may encounter physical contact by the dancer grinding herself on the customer.

Many times guys ask me how much the girls charge for a private dance. Every girl and every bar is different. Some bars may set a standard fee.

Some girls refuse to do them in the first place and I'm asked why. I'll tell you why ... some girls are married, some are engaged, some have children, some feel that getting on stage is enough, and some girls have told me that they feel dirty. Whatever the reason, they just aren't comfortable with it and refuse to do it.

Is The Story Real or a Myth?

There's been a story I've heard for many years. I am told by some dancers that the story is untrue. The story goes as follows...

Many years ago, a dancer was working at a strip bar for the week. She had the flu and wasn't feeling well. She went on stage to do her show and while she was spinning around the pole, she ended up spraying diarrhea all over the guys sitting at gyno row.

Real or fake?

**"Sorry, I can't afford to tip you
tonight"**
…Then why the hell has he been buying
drinks for his friends all night?!

Chapter 9 – THE DOWNSIDE OF SERVING

The Bar Rules

Yuck, the dreaded bar rules. They're there for a few reasons which are to keep everyone on the same page and everything in check.

Why are Bar Rules Important?

Rules exist for safety and privacy. Customers not touching the girls or using their cell phones at gyno are usually enforced. Most cell phones have a built in camera and video recorder and this makes it too easy for someone to post a picture of a dancer during her show onto the internet without her knowing. This rule is followed to respect her privacy as some dancers have children and sometimes their family members don't know what they do for a living. On the other hand, she's there doing a show so if you're sitting at gyno you should be paying attention to her and not texting away to a buddy.

Our establishment doesn't mind photos taken in the bar unless there's a dancer on stage at the same time. Female customers seem to be the only ones running around with cameras anyways and they can get quite defensive when asked to put their camera away. I like to explain to them that they're in a strip bar and there are many customers who want to be kept anonymous. They have wives and girlfriends who don't know that they sneak in here from time to time and we want to respect their secrecy. Most people are pretty understanding when you explain this to them. If they don't put the camera away, they're usually given a warning of being told to leave if it happens again.

Some bars don't allow bikers to bring their helmets into the bar because they can be used as a weapon in a fight (so I'm told). Helmets can usually be checked in with the bartender or left outside on the owner's bike depending on the bar. A bar that doesn't check in and allow helmets into its establishment at all uses this as an excuse to deter the hardcore bikers from coming into the bar in the first place. Since these guys don't want to leave their helmets outside on their bikes to get stolen, they'll leave and find another bar to drink in. As bikers check in their helmets and jackets, they blend in better with the regular clientele and don't stand out as much, which may intimidate many women and some patrons. Some bikers may wear their club's patch on their jacket or vest which could start trouble with other members, so no "colors" is another rule that many pubs and clubs keep. I know many of the local bikers and they know about and abide by our club's rules. They respect it and still visit, but without the label.

Every bar will have its own set of rules. Enforce them when you need to because if you let people get away with it one time, they will try to get away with it the next. It also upsets me when a customer says to me, "What's the big deal? The other waitress on nightshift lets me do it all the time!"

Don't be afraid of approaching customers about your bar rules. If you find someone with their feet on a table or chair, tell them to remove them immediately. This is your place of work, so be proud of it and respect it. If someone brings in their helmet and sets it down on an empty chair, ask him to please check it in with the bartender or remove it from the building. If wife beaters (a white undershirt in tank top style) are not allowed, ask the customer to kindly put on another shirt, put on a jacket, or give him an extra beer shirt you have as promo.

Another standard rule is that every single customer that enters the bar must buy a drink. This doesn't mean that it has to be alcoholic. It could be a bottle of water, a coffee, a soda, or juice. Some people get upset with me when I tell them this. I explain that since we don't charge an entrance fee (cover charge), this is a rule enforced by management and is the way we pay the dancers.

The Carelessness of Drinking on Shift

Drinking on shift is illegal and can get you fired. A liquor inspector can come in at any time and do a walk through.

Alcohol relaxes a person and causes motor skills and mental alertness to decrease. You'll have a hard time memorizing, it will make you feel tired, and your ability to make proper work decisions such as monitoring your customer's level of drunkenness will diminish. So, if a customer is kind enough to buy you a cocktail or a beer, drink it after your shift.

The Stupidity of Stealing

I hate to write about this section as everyone already knows that stealing is bad. I feel that this is an important subject to touch upon as there are many different ways of stealing.

If staff steals from customers, these customers will eventually stop coming into the bar and the bar ends up shutting down because it goes broke.

If staff steals from the bar, the bar eventually goes broke and shuts down.

If staff steals from other staff, good servers will eventually leave and go find work in another establishment. Remember to treat this as your business too!

Padding a tab is when a server charges a customer for drinks that he didn't order or consume. People are not stupid and they know when they are being scammed. If you're in the habit of padding tabs, customers will complain to management and you will be watched, eventually caught, and then fired. Karma has a way of catching up with you.

Calling out an order and not ringing in those drinks. The server pockets that money from the customer. This results in inventory being out and all staff being monitored and watched.

Stealing customers' or coworkers' personal belonging such as wallets, cell phones, jackets, etc. I know how thankful customers are when I pick up a cell phone left behind or a dropped wallet on the floor. The person gushes with the gratitude.

One of my regulars brought his brother, who was from out of town, into the bar for a Friday afternoon. My regular said, "This is my favorite waitress of all time! She's the one that found my wallet on the floor and gave it to me!" To this day, he leaves me very generous tips.

Picking a tip up off a table that you didn't serve and keeping it for yourself. If you start a shift after a server leaves, or you take over another server's section and a tip is left on the table that you didn't serve, be honest and give it to her or leave it in her box. She obviously worked hard for it and someone appreciated her service.

251

Romana's Story... "Help Me Someone. They Won't Leave!"

Many years ago while I was working a Wednesday nightshift, I noticed a group of four bikers walk in. As I was passing by them near the front doors, I noticed that they were all wearing their colors (emblems). I said, "I'm so sorry guys, but you can't wear your colors in here." I like to let guys know this rule right away so that they don't sit down at a table and make themselves comfortable. If they're standing and then leave the room, it looks like it was their decision to leave in the first place. I find that once they sit down, I have a hard time getting them to go. They must have been from out of town and not from around our area as I didn't recognize them and all the local bad boys know of our rule.

The guys continued into the bar and sat down at a table. My stomach was turning into a big knot as I walked over and repeated myself and added that I'm not allowed to serve them with their jackets and vests in the building. I tried to be very sweet and use my soft charm, but they continued to order drinks as if they didn't hear what I said. I turned and walked back to the bar.

The bartender and DJ didn't want to deal with them and I didn't want them to either, so I knew I had to deal with this myself. We all agree that it is much easier for a woman to deal with these men than a male staff member. We called our manager at the time and then I went to hide in the kitchen. As I stood in the kitchen, I thought back to the many bikers I've had to deal with. Most were pretty good and left without causing too much of a stink.

My manager was at home for dinner and only a few blocks away but he was down in about three minutes and went over to the table where the four were sitting. He sat down with them and chatted for almost ten minutes. I continued serving the rest of my customers. Ten minutes later he was shaking their hands, and then they all got up and left. I couldn't believe it.

"Oh my God, what did you say to get them to leave?" I asked him finally feeling relieved.

"I explained that I had a business to run just like they did and I respect that. I also told them that society, not us, sees you guys as criminals and this makes it very difficult for us when the cops come in and see you guys drinking in here. It puts us under a microscope.

252

Also, when some customers see you guys in here, they immediately down their drinks and leave, which is bad for our business as you guys are intimidating to these people. That's basically it. See you in half an hour." Then he left and went home to finish his dinner.

The Legalities

Serving It Right

Before you're allowed to work as a server in British Columbia, you're required by law to take *Serving It Right.* (servingitright.com)

It's a wonderful self-study package that informs a person of British Columbia's responsible serving program. Once you've read the materials and do the exam online, by mail, fax, or in person, you must pass to receive a plastic certification card. A person holding this card is legally allowed to work in an establishment that serves liquor. The course is extremely helpful and will shed some insight on the importance of being responsible in serving alcoholic beverages to the public, the consumption of alcohol, and some of the legalities involved.

It's a good idea to get your certificate if it's needed before you apply for a job. This way, you could be hired instead of someone else who might have been chosen (who doesn't hold the certificate yet) but they chose you because you could start immediately. If you're outside the province of British Columbia, you'll want to find out about your provincial serving laws or the laws in your state or country.

The following is some helpful information regarding decisions a server must make in relation to the identification process and safety of her patron. This is from a British Columbia standpoint. You'll want to check with your manager or head waitress to find out about any identification that is acceptable or unacceptable at your bar.

Asking Customers for Identification

To aid you in checking identification that you have not seen before (out of province) and you're not sure if it's valid or not, your bar can get hold of a manual that shows examples and explains in detail

253

what other province's driver's licenses look like in Canada. We also have a second manual that shows driver's licenses from the United States. Keeping the manual handy, you're able to compare out-of-province driver's licenses to see if they're fake or real.

Our bar wants us to check identification on anyone that looks thirty years old and younger. I have asked people for their identification only to find out that they're older than I! Other times I'm looking at someone thinking, "They've got to be way over the legal age," only to second-guess myself and decide to check anyways. Many times I'm amazed to find out that they had just turned nineteen and already look like they're much older than I originally thought. Never be ashamed or embarrassed to ask someone for their identification. Your job is on the line.

Before the start of a shift, know the exact date. Once in a while I have this feeling that something looks "off" about an ID while I'm inspecting it. As I let it sink into my brain, I realize the person is underage and they're hoping that you don't know how to count. When I call them on it, some say, "Oh, I thought the legal age is 18. I'm from Alberta."

My reply is, "Then why are you carrying a B.C. driver's license?"

In a group of young people, if one or more of them look underage, don't single that one person or people out. I ask every single person in the group to pull out two pieces of ID. The reason for this is that the younger-looking patrons in the group could "borrow" that older buddy's identification if they forgot theirs or they really are underage.

When I start to inspect everyone's ID (I'll explain in detail how to check IDs later on in this chapter), I'm actually reading the first and last name to myself as I'm reading the rest of the ID. This way, if John Doe gave me a driver's license and a care card and then the fifth guy in the group also named John Doe gave me a passport and a credit card, I will have made the connection. I know that one guy in the group gave his buddy some of his other pieces of ID. This way I ask everyone to kindly pull out their identification for me a second time. Don't be embarrassed to make them all go through this process again. If you hear groaning and protesting, they know they've got a smart server they can't fool! It's a good feeling and it's impressive, even to the youngsters. When young people can constantly fool a bar, the word will spread to their friends and more of them will attempt it as a result.

Acceptable Forms of Identification
There are many forms of identification out there and you want to be able to distinguish the fakes from the real thing.

Looking for the Fakes
Looking at a driver's license, you want to keep an eye out on anything that looks peculiar. Years ago, kids had been altering their driver's licenses and their B.C identification cards' last digit by scraping it from the number eight to a six. If you take the license and check it from all angles by letting light shine onto it, you'll be able to see scratch marks. I've asked kids how they would explain this to a cop if he were to notice this. Nobody had an answer for me, just a shrug of the shoulders.

Take a second look at anything you don't recognize. I have seen ID that was signed with BLUE pen! I look at them and say, "Honey, I'm sorry. You really got ripped off on this ID. Where did you get it?"

He knows he's been busted. "Downtown" he says as he looks at me sheepishly.

"How much did you pay for it?"

"$50.00"

"Come back when you're 19." You really do have to laugh and can't blame them for trying!

If you really are unsure about a piece of ID, take it to the bar and ask the bartender or another server to have a peek at it and give you a second opinion.

A Canadian Citizenship card needs to be taken under the black light where you will notice a glowing hologram of the maple leaf.

Years ago, three young guys from Guatemala came into the bar and they handed me Guatemalan ID. One of our doormen was originally from Guatemala and while he was having lunch in the bar that day on his day off, I was able to ask him to have a look at the ID. What they had given me wasn't considered a piece of government ID. My doorman was able to communicate to them that they were not allowed to stay with that form of ID unless they showed us a passport. They left.

255

Always get a second or third opinion. If you're unsure, it's better to tell the person to leave than serve him and the liquor inspector or cops end up coming in.

During slow times, pull out any identification you have in your wallet and take it into the dark of the bar and then into the black light. Play around with it and inspect it further under different lighting so that you have an inkling of what a real ID looks like. Some bars keep an altered ID in a box or drawer somewhere and you can take this out and inspect it as well, to get a better understanding of what the fakes look like. If you don't have a Canadian citizenship card, ask regulars in the bar if you can take a peek at theirs and tell them what you're doing. You just want to get familiar with all sorts of ID.

When asking someone for identification, their main piece should be Government issued with their picture and signature on it. It should not be expired. A passport is fine and dandy, but if the person looks like they're five years old in the photo, it's not acceptable as it's expired. Same goes for a Canadian Citizenship card, which I myself have and I'm eight years old with braids in the photo! I've obviously never had it updated and it still has my maiden name on it.

A primary piece of identification must contain the customer's name, signature, and a picture.

Acceptable- Driver's license, passport, B.C. identification, Firearms Weapons card, Indian Status card, Military identification, Canadian Citizenship card.

I will accept a school ID if he has no other picture ID, but it must be backed up with at least two or three other pieces.

I will accept a credit card with a photo on it, but it must be backed up with at least two other pieces of identification.

Not Acceptable- Gym membership identification, Costco card, etc.

A second piece of ID must include the customer's name and a signature on the back.

Acceptable- A bank card, credit card, Care card, S.I.N. card.

Not Acceptable- A blank bank card with no name imprinted on the front, Library card, Air Miles card, Gas points card, Blockbuster card, etc.

If you're unsure, ask another staff member. It's better to be safe than sorry. I will not accept any photocopied identification as it could have been altered in some way, then photocopied, and you wouldn't be able to tell. If you're young and expecting to be asked for ID, you should have it on you at all times anyways and definitely not have anything photocopied.

Every single person needs to carry some forms of ID on them. If that person got in trouble or an accident, the cops may need to get a hold of a wife or parent. Even if you look like you're eighty years old and you don't have one piece of ID on yourself, don't be surprised if you won't be allowed into a pub or bar.

What to look for:

Photo:
When someone hands you their primary piece of ID, you want to make sure you take a good look at the person and then at the picture. Don't worry about hair color as people color their hair and change their style all the time. Look at the overall face shape and compare the nose. If you have any doubts, ask for a few more pieces of ID or ask a coworker for a second opinion. If I have any doubts that the ID belongs to them, they are told to leave.

Birth date:
Make sure that you know today's date. Anyone who turns legal age tomorrow is still underage as of today. Don't give the poor guy a hard time as he's probably trying to get in on a Saturday night and hang out with his buddies and his birthday is the next day on Sunday.

Expiry Date:
Any ID that has an expiration date should be honored. If it is expired, it is considered not valid.

Secondary piece of ID:
The piece should have the customer's name and a signature that you can compare to the photo ID. A care card is a great second piece of identification as it contains the person's name and birth date, as well as their signature.

***ALWAYS remember...** if you have any doubts about a person's identification, you have the right to refuse entry.

Dealing With Problem People

The problem customer is the person that must leave the premises before they're given a drink. Not only are these people a pain in the neck to deal with, they could also be a liability to the business. Problem people include:

Barred Patron
This is the person that has caused problems in the past such as fighting, vandalism (vandalizing vehicles or the restrooms, for example), harassing, or threatening staff and other customers. When a person is barred, it means they're not allowed back into the bar, sometimes on a probationary period, other times forever.

Intoxicated Patron
Sometimes a drunk that has been drinking in another establishment, and has been cut off, may come straight to your bar if he wants to continue his drinking binge instead of going home. That person needs to leave your premises immediately or you're responsible for them once they're served a drink. Call a cab for this person and get him home.

Customers Ordering Many Drinks in One Sitting
When a customer sits down and orders a jug of beer, I need to ask him how many glasses are needed. Sometimes friends are joining him so he may respond with two or more. Then there are times where he will say, "Just one for me."

I was told years ago by a couple of senior servers that it's illegal to serve a jug to one person at one time. This makes sense as it is a large amount of alcohol for one person at one time and some people have a hard time monitoring their drinking at a moderate pace. I'll let the customer know about the rule and I'll bring two empty glasses so he can keep the extra glass beside him so it looks like someone is joining him. Before I bring the jug, I try to persuade him to buy a pint instead, by saying "It's nice and cold because it comes in a frosty pint glass!"

258

Being vocal by letting other servers and bartenders know that the patron is drinking a full jug to himself will keep everyone aware and it ensures that others will keep an eye on him as well. Shooter girls should be especially watchful over any large amount of shooter consumption this lonesome drinker may consume on top of the jug.

Ask your manager or senior server about serving triples in your bar. I tell customers that we don't allow it. There really is no reason why a person needs to drink triples other than to get completely loaded. You don't need the loaded customer sitting in your bar, puking on the stage, and passing out. I'm aware and get antsy when a person orders double cocktails in short glasses with lots of ice while drinking three or more in the matter of less than an hour. Keep conversing with your bartender, shooter girl, and any other servers to monitor any customer's vast amounts of alcohol intake.

Overservice: Cutting Patrons Off

One of the reasons that people go to the bar is to celebrate by drinking. Some people can't seem to hold their alcohol and they drink too quickly in a short amount of time. A celebration like a birthday or stag party has one person as the center of attention and things can get out of hand rather quickly if you're not keeping a close eye on the group. Most stag parties are great to serve but sometimes there's the party that simply starts to get out of hand, where guys are buying rounds of shots and drinks for the whole group and it's almost like a game of everyone wanting their turn to buy a round for everyone else. Before you know it, there are empty shooter glasses scattered all over the place and everyone has four full drinks in front of them. The cheap guys usually send drinks only to the groom or birthday boy and it is this person who ends up looking at a handful of full beers and shooters staring at him.

You as a server need to be fully aware of all your customers. A person that needs to be cut off (stop serving him immediately) has many noticeable signs. The indications that point at the customer who's in a drunken state are slurred, mumbled, or loud speech, or even opposite: fast talking. Coordination isn't present, such as trouble picking up change off the table. Eyes may be half closed, glassy, bloodshot, blank stare that is staring at nothing in particular,

259

nodding off as if falling asleep, and may jerk their head back up. Their complexion may be beet red in color and as they sit in their chair, they may sway side to side and not sit still. Throwing up at the table is a big sign as they are usually too drunk to make it to the restroom.

As they walk, they may weave, stumble or shuffle, and even walk into a table or another person. As they walk with a drink in their hand, sometimes it seems to spill all over their hand because they can't seem to keep their hand steady.

Some important information about cutting someone off:

• In a group where one person seems to be very intoxicated, I let the group know that they won't be served anymore until the intoxicated person leaves the building. The reason for this is because guys in the group will continue sneaking the drunk more alcohol even when you tell them that their friend is cut off. A few times I've let people continue to buy drinks for themselves, at the same time I threaten to kick them all out if I find out anyone is sneaking beers to the drunk. Most of them try to be sneaky and continue buying drinks for the drunk anyways. They think it's funny or they can't seem to reason with their drunken friend who is demanding more alcohol. Some guys want to get their friend so inebriated so he can't stand anymore, so my trying to be the nice guy ends up biting me in the ass. It's just easier to cut the whole group off in the first place until the drunk is taken home.

• Years ago, I had a bartender that would continue serving the guys that I cut off if they went to his bar. His reasoning was that the guy didn't seem that drunk to him. I was always the one that said, "I told you so!!" when we end up kicking him out. When another staff member serves a patron that has been cut off, it makes the staff member who cut him off in the first place look like they don't know how to do their job. Even if that server ends up being wrong in their decision, you honor that and stand behind them.

• When you cut someone off, you must let all other staff know immediately. You want to tell all fellow servers (in case this person moves to their side of the room), the shooter girl, bartenders, the DJ, and even doormen. This way, everyone is aware of this person, should he happen to leave the premises and drive away in their own vehicle, fight, fall asleep, etc.

- Always offer this person a free coffee, water, or pop. I like to engage in conversation by asking what their mode of transportation is to get home. Sometimes there's a friend in the room who is looking after them, but there are times when the person is drinking solo. Offer to call a taxi or ask if they need to use the phone to call someone to pick them up. We have a program where someone comes to pick up the customer and his car and get their car home for them safely. It's your legal responsibility as server to make sure this person has a safe way home.

- If I notice an intoxicated person walk into the bar and sit down, I greet him and if I even have an inkling of him being intoxicated, I'll ask if they have been drinking. Usually they will say that they've had a couple. At that point I respond with, "I'm sorry; you've had too much to drink today. I can't serve you. Sorry but you'll have to leave," and walk away. Don't stand there as they'll start to argue with you. Walk over to the bartender immediately and tell him what happened. He will honor your decision if the customer ends up going to the bar and tries ordering a drink from him. The bartender will be ready to tell the person to go.

- Never take a bribe for allowing someone or his friend to stay and drink if the patron is underage or has no ID. I've been offered as much as $300.00 to let a group's buddy stay while the friend has no ID to prove that he is of age.

- Never allow someone to intimidate you into letting them stay.
Example: "Do you have any idea who I am/know?!"
            "Where's Cindy? I know her. She always lets me stay!"

- Be polite when talking to someone and telling them that you suspect them of having too much to drink that day. I've had a friend of the person pull me aside and tell me that the person who he's with is mentally handicapped.

Romana's Story... "I'm Calling the Cops if you Drive!"

On quite a few occasions, I've had patrons drink a little more than they should and, as a result, I always ask them if they'd like me to call them a taxi. Some people inform me that they only live a few blocks away and they'll be okay to drive. I tell them that if they get behind the wheel of their car, I will be calling the cops.

I've literally walked out into the parking lot with my bartender and we've written the license plate (I write it on the back of my hand), the description of the car, and the direction that it's traveling and called the police.

I don't feel bad, even if this person was a generous tipper or he's the nicest guy in the world. My daughter and husband could be out driving around and if this idiot plows into them and ends up killing them, he's destroyed our lives. I've warned him that we would call the cops and we do!

Romana's Story... The Terrible Waitress

Many, many years ago we had a server that didn't look at checking ID with as much importance as she should have. She wasn't a very strong server in the first place and got confused and flustered very easily.

We were starting to notice a strong increase of underage patrons trying to attempt to get served in our bar. One night I got off work early as it was not very busy and as I was sitting at the bar, I noticed a couple of police officers walk into the bar and stand at the back of the room. When cops walk into the room, everyone seems to know. They make you a little jumpy as you're looking through your section hoping you didn't forget to ID anyone. As they stood at the back of the room, two young guys happened to enter the bar a few minutes later and sit down. I watched as the server walked over and took their order. She walked to the bar, returned with their beers, retrieved their money, and left.

As soon as she walked away, one of the police officers strolled over and I saw him exchange a few words with the two young guys. I saw

262

the kids shake their heads and shrug their shoulders and a moment later they got up and scooted out the door. The cops walked over to the bartender and told him that they will be returning to talk to the manager about the server on Monday.

Needless to say, she didn't stay with us much longer after that. But it sure did take awhile for the underage people to stop coming in as often as they did.

Other Problems with Coworkers and Customers

Problems with Coworkers

Things don't always run smoothly between staff members during a shift. When problems arise, any disputes must be ironed out and dealt with quickly so that you can both get on with your jobs. Never get into a screaming match out in the bar where customers can witness it as it looks extremely unprofessional.

Invading My Territory
During a shift, each server will be responsible for her section of the room containing tables. Look at these tables as income for that server on that particular shift. Servers are very territorial over their sections, so the sooner a new server realizes this, there will be fewer troubles.

During slow periods of a shift, if a customer were to stop me and order a drink from another server's section, I'll let that server know about the drink order so that she can take it out and receive the tip. If the room is bubbling with energy and all servers are busy, take the drinks out so the customers aren't kept waiting. Usually the other server won't mind if you tell her that she was on the other side of the room or looked like she was carrying out a full tray of drinks at the time. Don't be sneaky about it; be vocal and explain yourself.

Relieving Me from My Shift
Years ago we used to have a server who was always late starting her shift. She assumed that the time started was the time she could sit on the toilet, make a phone call, or apply her lipstick. I didn't mind in the beginning because I was making tips, but after a while I

got sick of it as she was taking advantage of me. I told her that from now on I will expect her to be on time for her shift so I can go on my break or home when I'm supposed to, not a minute later. If I kept my mouth shut, it would've gone on forever, not to mention that she was signing in to get paid her wage the time I was still working the floor. She was another girl that didn't last long with us.

Stop Holding a Grudge

Years later, an argument broke out between me and another server. She was another girl whom I remember getting mad at for showing up late for a shift too many times in a row to relieve me from my shift. One day she came in and I greeted her with a hello. She ignored me and I couldn't help myself and say, "Are you still mad at me for freaking out on you a couple of days ago?"

She looked at me and said, "Ya Romana, I am. You didn't have to yell at me."

I responded with, "Well, get used to it. You pull that again and I may be yelling at you again!" I admit that I shouldn't have lost my temper and yelled, but I didn't think that she would take it too personally.

We all have to work together and I used to joke to the regulars and staff that I see more of them than I do of my own husband. All I can say is "Get over it!" It makes working with the person you got into a fight with very uncomfortable, so stop the unnecessary drama of holding a grudge. Get on with life and get back to work.

Give Me My Money!

Customers who run tabs may have a few different servers add drinks to their tab in the course of a visit. A server may end up going off shift or on a break, there may be a shooter girl adding shots, or perhaps the kitchen girl is adding food to the bill.

If the customer ends up leaving a tip, it should be split up accordingly to the drinks that each server has on the tab.

One of my pet peeves is when I sell a tab to another server and coming into work the next day, I don't find money in my box. I hate asking that server, "Remember the tab that had the guys drinking double Grey Goose sodas at gyno? Did they leave a tip?" It's even more annoying when the response is, "Ya, I owe you a fifteen dollar tip."

Don't ever make a server ask you for her money!! It is rude, embarrassing and annoying. Even if the tip is a quarter, drop it into her box with a note saying that the quarter is from table #29 or whomever. I like to staple any paper money to the bill or scrap paper that I put her name on (this shows her who left her a tip and how much). Don't ever leave loose bills in a server's box because sometimes other servers may end up using that box if she's not working and any loose money will be collected by the wrong server. This way, if there is a paper or bill stapled to cash, the new server borrowing the box knows that it doesn't belong to her and she'll return it.

I know my regulars and it makes me a little suspicious when girls say that certain regulars didn't leave a tip that night, when for the last eight years I've known them, they've always been more than generous. Don't insult another waitress like this by lying and ripping her off. She'll eventually find out the truth. Liars and cheaters don't last long in this business.

Problems with Customers

The interesting part of this job is dealing with many different personalities while extraordinary things happen in the course of a shift.

Getting Hit On
You work in a bar; people hit on you. Get used to it! Instead of being mad about it, be flattered that people find you attractive. Yes, I said people.

I've been hit on by not only men, but women as well. I've been told on a couple of occasions that they find my raspy voice very sexy (that's what happens when you work in the bar industry for as long as I have; your voice becomes deeper and more raspy). It does get a little weird when a woman rubs your arm and tells you how soft your skin is while she leans into you or even grabs your bum! Yup, that's happened to me as well.

Working as a server in a strip bar, you will always get asked by guys "When are you up?" On occasion, coworkers still ask me, "Ro, do you still get asked when you're getting up on stage?"

"Of course I still do."

"Doesn't it make you mad?"

"No. I've been asked that question a trillion times. I guess I'm just used to it by now. I actually find it flattering."

Dealing with Customers who ask for Drugs

At times you'll be asked by customers where they can buy weed or coke. Everyone assumes that since you work in this wild and crazy industry, you have all the connections and you're involved in this stuff yourself.

I know stuff and I don't know stuff. I don't get involved and I don't care what people are up to as it's none of my business. I don't know if the person asking me is an undercover cop or a guy passing through town. I just tell people, "I'm sorry, I can't help you." The persistent person pushes with, "Oh come on, you know. Just tell me! There's a big tip in it for you!"

Like I said before, "I don't get involved, so I don't know." I can only advise you to follow the same rule. If your manager or the owner were to find out that you're getting involved in this kind of thing in their business, you'll end up being fired.

Handling a Customer with Bad Body Odor

This is a real tricky topic to have to deal with. You need to do it in a professional manner and in a way where it doesn't embarrass the customer because you want them to return.

Most of these people obviously don't notice their own offensive odor or they just don't care that they offend others around them. This problem just came up at my work a few weeks ago and the best way to deal with this person is to ask your manager to go over and let that person know that a few people have complained about his foul smelling body odor. This man apologized like crazy and said he was on his way home from work when he decided to pop by our bar for a quick beer. He downed his beer and left immediately.

I got onto this subject with my husband and we agreed that this was the best way to handle the situation because if it came from a female server, he might have taken it more personally.

Customers You Can Do Without

Intoxicated Drunks

These are the people that stumble around the bar almost knocking into your tray as they meander around the room in search of a buddy or convince a waitress to serve them one last drink. Some will start to fall asleep in their chair or attempt a fight with other patrons. This is the person you will have to babysit until a taxi, ride, or friend arrives to pick him up.

The Puker

Many times you'll be dealing with a birthday party or a stag. The mission of the friends is to get the groom or birthday boy absolutely gooned so that the poor guy can't remember his own name. I do my best to remind the groom or birthday boy throughout his visit to let me know if he needs a water, coffee, or pop. Before the floodgates open I like to warn the friends, "I do not want him puking on the carpets. I'm warning you guys that I do not clean up puke. If he throws up, someone in this group WILL be cleaning up after him!" I find that I haven't had too much of a problem if I warn the group.

The Complainer

It's impossible to satisfy every single person that sets foot in your bar. I could be working a busy Saturday night and the partiers are loud and having a great time. Then two old guys will enter and complain at how loud the music is and they can't hear each other talk. People have complained that the air conditioning is too cold while others complain the room is too hot at the same time. I've had customers grumble that the beef dip wasn't very good, yet everything was polished off the plate but the plate itself.

You'll always get someone that is unhappy, enjoys complaining, or is out to try and get a free meal or drink.

The Socializer

You'll have the one lonely guy whose girlfriend just broke up with him and he just lost his job, so he's drinking his sorrows away. Then he thinks its okay to meander around the room and join people at their tables trying to make new friends. Instead of making friends, he's slurring at everyone and interrupting circles of people trying to talk and have a relaxing time.

I'll usually lean over to someone in the group and ask if he's bothering them. If I get an indication (or someone comes up to me and asks me to tell him to leave them alone), then I'll pull the socializer aside and tell him that he can't be interrupting others as I'm starting to get complaints. Sometimes he gets the hint while other times he doesn't. If he continues to disrupt others at their tables, you need to form a plan and get him out of the bar before a fight erupts. I'll usually tell the socializer that I'm going to call him a taxi and it's time for him to go home.

Romana's Story... The Body Stone

I can't believe that I'm going to write about my next story.

A few years ago while I was working my busy Friday afternoon shift, our young cook at the time was whipping up some brownie batter in the kitchen as the kitchen orders were slow. As I stood at the sink rinsing off some dirty dishes, he came up to me and handed me a wooden spoon and mixing bowl with chocolate batter in it. I took the wooden spoon and gave it three big licks.

A very short time later, I felt my body go kind of numb and I was having a hard time concentrating. As I stood there dolling out change to a customer, I was trying to think whether I collected money on some drinks I just delivered to a previous table and my mind was going blank. I knew something wasn't right and I walked back into the kitchen and asked the cook if there was something extra he put into the brownie batter.

"Ya Ro. There's some bud butter in there. I thought you knew that I was making special brownies."

"I didn't know you were going to make them at work!" I had to get through the next hour and a half until another server came onto the floor to take over half the room. I struggled through as best as I could and by the time my coworker came onto shift, I was near normal again. You know when you're really drunk and wish you could feel normal again? This is what kept going through my mind!

I now know what a body stone feels like. I can laugh about it now, but back then I sure didn't find it too funny and I'm glad my boss didn't find out!

Romana's Story... "Want To Be my Girlfriend?"

Actually this story belongs to one of my girlfriends who used to work at my bar. A lesbian started frequenting our bar and loved to

268

sit in my girlfriend's section and always ended up being her biggest tipper. One night, the lesbian asked my girlfriend if she wanted to go into the restroom with her and she would perform oral sex on her! Of course she declined, but the girl wouldn't give up and told her that she would rock her world as she is very good at that sort of thing.

Told you that we meet some very colorful people!

Dumb Things People Say (and How to Deal With It!)

Ok, the more I thought about this section, the more I thought that this particular topic needed its own chapter. You'll notice that all the cartoons in this book are at the beginning of every chapter. Some of these scenarios have happened to me on more than a dozen occasions. When I mention the cartoon scenarios to other servers, they anxiously nod their heads and laugh at me saying, "Oh my God! That has happened to me too!" That's why they have been chosen by me as some of the craziest memories and put into cartoon format for your enjoyment.

You Have the Pull and Power in the Room

Some customers are rude and don't understand that just because you serve drinks, you should be looked upon as their slave or talked down to. I've had people yell at me to "f-off" when I cut them off or demand that I get them a drink without using their manners. If a customer is demanding and rude, they're obviously forgetting that I have pull and power in the bar. Do you think I'm going to give them a coffee or a bottle of water for free when they need it? How about a pop or a free shooter for their buddy's birthday? I'm asked to convince dancers to give posters to people because it's their birthday. If you're nice to me, I'll do everything I can to help you out. If you're not, don't hold your breath. Even for lunch draws, I'll make sure that the loser doesn't end up with a winning ticket! Yes, I throw the other half into the trash.

As server, you'll have to go with the flow and try not to miss a beat. Yes, it's annoying when you walk up to a new customer and say, "Hi guys! What can I grab for you?" and they respond with "What? You're grabbing me where?" or "What? Where can I grab you?" especially when you're smoking busy and don't have time to play this game.

Unpredictable Scenarios You May Find Yourself In

I took some of the scenarios I've explained and made them into multiple choice questions where you guess the right answer. Hope you enjoy it!

"You should change your price so that I can tip you better!"
This comment can drive a server to the edge of a cliff when she hears this one! The drink is $4.95 and after the customer hands you a ten, you give him a nickel and five loonies. What do you respond with after he makes this idiotic comment?

a) "I don't make the prices, management does."

b) The only thing you can do is laugh in his face and walk away.

c) "Are you dense? Why the hell did I just break up the five dollar bill in coin, dummy?"

The right answer is a. You should still be polite and realize that he obviously didn't want to tip you anyways. There may still be a small chance that he'll tip you next time or perhaps leave some change on the table when he leaves.

"Why aren't you smiling?"
I've mentioned this one on more than one occasion throughout this book.

a) "Because I'm working and I hate it here!"

b) Smile and say, "I'm just busy concentrating."

c) "Give me something to smile about!"

The right answer is b. In the end, you're hoping for a tip so be polite. If you don't want anyone even making this comment in the first place, put a smile on.

"Can we ask you a personal question?"
I know it won't be anything like, "Have you ever been to Hawaii?" or "Do you like sushi?"

a) "No!" and storm away.

b) "Okay, let me have it!"

c) Try to keep a little humor in it and say, "If you're going to ask me if my boobs are real, they are. No, this is not my natural hair color. Yes, I'm married, and No, I will not tell you my age." Smile and walk away without waiting for a response. You'll be smiling because they'll just sit there gaping at you.

The right answer is c. In my experiences, those are the four main questions I'm always asked so that is my response. I don't say it in a mean way, just a matter of fact kind of tone. I don't want them upset with me where I screwed myself out of a tip. (You can even try b, if you're curious).

"When are you up on stage next?" or "Do you dance?"

This question doesn't bother me in the least. It's the following question that drives me nuts: "Why not?"

a) "Because who's going to serve you drinks if I'm up on stage dancing? I don't want you guys to die of thirst."

b) "Because I don't want to show strangers my hooch."

c) "Because my husband wouldn't like it very much."

If you're still working for that tip, I suggest to be nice and your answer should be a.

"Does your husband tell you you're beautiful every day?"

I love this one because I can honestly answer, "As a matter of fact, he does!" I'll go along with my little game...

a) "As a matter of fact, he does!"

b) "No. What an asshole! Maybe I should dump him!"

c) "Actually, he slaps me around every night and kicks me in the stomach."

"If you were my wife, I'd never let you work here."

a) "Well, it's a good thing that we're not married then, huh?!"

b) "Actually, my husband hates that I work here too."

c) Start to cry and walk away.

First off, I think that this is a very rude thing to say to someone. My response to this person is a. Straight and simple. My pride is worth more than his stinking tip.

"I haven't been asked for ID in years! I feel so young!"

I feel like kicking people in the shin when they say this to me because these are the people that look like they're 12 years old, and have been frequenting the bar for only a couple of years.

a) I just hold my hand out for them to pass me their ID. Keep smiling!

b) "Ok buddy … you look like you're nine years old. So, just pass over the ID!"

c) "So, who hasn't been doing their job and not asking you for your ID?"

Right answer is a. Don't be rude as you want to end up with a tip.

"Does the girl on stage have real or fake boobs?"

First of all, I'm busy serving drinks and not paying attention to the girl that's parading around on the stage.

a) "Let me feel them and I'll let you know."

b) "I'll ask the dancer and get back to you about that!"

c) "Sorry, no idea."

A tip is what you're aiming for so the right answer is c.

"Can I see your wedding ring?"

I show the guy my ring. He tries to impress me with, "I'd buy you a bigger one."

They are dumbfounded as I respond with, "I love my ring! My husband insisted I pick out what I liked. Besides, I don't like big, gaudy-looking things."

Out of all the guys that asked to see my ring, I've had ONE guy reply with "What an exquisite cut!"

"Can I take you out for dinner sometime?"

I know it takes some guys a lot of guts to ask a girl out, so I will answer him with, "Thank you. I'm really very flattered but I'm married."

I've had a few guys respond with, "Well, then how about if we go out for coffee?" This response makes me shake my head, as I now need to explain to this guy that my husband wouldn't appreciate me going out to have dinner or coffee with strange men.

I have even had the odd guy say to me, "Well, it's not like anything is going to happen." This is when I tell this person that I really don't have any time, and any time that I do have available, I'd like to spend it with friends that I don't see enough of anyways.

"Boy! You must just love getting paid to work and watch this at the same time!"

We used to have duos on stage once a week every Thursday night. This was many years ago and the duo nights have long been cancelled as the agency can't seem to find girls that want to do it anymore. Back then, most of the girls were pretty nasty and basically did a live sex show on the stage.

I've had a few guys make this stupid comment to me when I ask them at gyno whether they want another drink. Guys have said to me, "Boy! You must just love getting paid to work and get to watch this at the same time!" They're serious. I guess they thought I had a penis under my mini skirt!

"Do I get free water or pop because I'm a designated driver?"

If the guy is a limo or bus driver for a big group of people, he gets all the free pop, coffee, or water he wants. In my experience, these drivers never abuse this courtesy and usually have only one non-alcoholic drink (probably because they don't want to be worrying about running to a restroom for the rest of the evening).

Usually, the person that makes this comment came in with one other friend. I respond with a "No, sorry."

If he starts to argue with me and say that it's against the law, I shut him down and say, "Almost everyone in this bar is driving home tonight at some time. The bar's policy is that every single person must buy one drink to be in here. It's the way we pay the dancers."

If he still continues to argue, I continue with, "I don't make the rules. And since we don't charge cover, everyone must buy one drink. It can also be a coffee, pop, or a bottle of water." I've made my point.

"Fine, I'll just get a Budweiser then." This is when I feel like kicking him in the leg.

"I thought you were driving?!" I'll say before I walk away. In my experience, this is the person that won't tip as he was too cheap to purchase a drink in the first place.

What to do When a Dine and Dash Happens to You

Every waitress at one time or another will encounter a dine and dash. This is where a customer will consume something they've ordered or run a tab without you grabbing a credit card and they leave you with the bill.

The Action Steps

First off, your heart will drop or the blood will feel like it's draining from your face. Try not to panic. These are the action steps I take to see if I can save the situation and still get my money.

1.   I leave my tray at the bar and tell the bartender I may have had a dine and dash. This way he will keep an eye on any drinks and my coin on the tray. Also, if I'm working with any other servers, they will understand why my tray may be in their way.

2.   I run to the patron's table to look for signs that they may be returning. Look for a jacket, keys, or cell phone. If there are no personal belongings and the drink is empty, it's time to form a quick strategy.

3.   I stop and glance around the room for him. He may have moved to another table to sit with friends or a chair closer to the stage. If I don't see him, I run near the bar in case he went to the restroom and then returned to pay his bill. If the bartender isn't waving me over or waving money in the air, I know the customer has not gone to the bar.

4.   Next, I run straight outside to see if he is in the smoking area or getting into his vehicle. I will even walk into the parking lot to have a better look.

5.   If I'm satisfied that he's not outside, I run back inside and ask a male to go into the washroom to see if there is anyone inside and then ask the description of the person inside.

6.   If I still can't find him, I go back into the bar a second time and look at the customers in the room again. This is just in case he returned from the restroom.

7.   By this point I am sure the person has left. On the bill I write my name and the date. On the back of the bill I write a description of the customer in detail. Then I give myself a moment and visualize

274

him in case he does come back so I know who it is. I let all servers and bartender know what happened.

8.	Some people come back later or the next day and realize they left on their bill. When this happens, I take the cash the customer gives me and the bill and staple both together. Then I drop it into the server's waitress box. What a nice surprise for her when she comes in for her next shift!

To avoid the scenario above, always grab a credit card to run any tabs. At our bar, we run many tabs for regulars so at times the servers are forced to run through the scenario above.

Romana's Story... Another Dine and Dash

My mom was telling me about a dine and dash she witnessed at a popular restaurant in town while she was out having dinner with my dad one night.

She said that there were two young girls sitting at the table next to them having a big dinner. They had ordered appetizers, a main course, and milkshakes. Mom said that she made a comment to dad about how much food they ordered. Then one of the girls stopped the waitress and asked for a glass of milk and the bill. The server walked away and both girls jumped up and ran out the door.

"May I see your ID, please?"
"I forgot it"
"Don't worry Sweetie, I can vouch
for him. I'm his dad!"

Bonus Chapter – 100 OF ROMANA'S UNFORGETTABLE CUSTOMERS

100 of Romana's Unforgettable Customers

"In any moment of decision the best thing you can do is the right thing,
The next best thing is the wrong thing,
And the worst thing you can do is nothing."

- Theodore Roosevelt

Ok everyone ... here it is! I've been asked by coworkers, dancers, friends, and customers to make sure that I have a section about the customers I encounter on a daily basis. Many of you reading this will find some of the stories a little unbelievable, but I assure you that they have happened. I can never say that this job is boring or uneventful. Even though I've dealt with many strange situations, I wouldn't change it for the world. This chapter of stories is about the good, the creepy, and, of course, the crazy.

Here we go...

1) The Horker

When it was still legal to smoke indoors, like many bars we had a smoking room. Servers would enter periodically to serve drinks, clean ashtrays, pick up empties, and straighten up. One evening as I was grabbing dirty ashtrays, I noticed that someone had *horked* into one. I took it to the sink and rinsed it out while I dry-heaved the whole time cleaning it. Later when I went back to tidy up the smoke room, there it was again ... *gob* in the ashtray! I didn't want to spend my shift cleaning out someone's disgusting mess every time I had to go in there so I had to find out who was doing this.

There were two young guys sitting in the smoke room and I asked them if they had any idea who was sitting in this particular chair when he came in to smoke. They said that the only person that kept coming into the room between dancer shows was the older guy in coveralls sitting on the other end of the room.

I stormed over to him and yelled, "If I catch you horking into the ashtrays one more time, YOU will be the one cleaning it out! Got it? That's disgusting!" Then I marched away. He later came over to me and apologized and I never found a surprise like that from him again.

2) The Camera Man

As I walk through the room doing my job, the main thing that I'm paying attention to is how full a customer's drink is. If it's half full or less, I'm asking them if they want another. So, I'm not really paying any attention to faces, who is on the stage dancing, or too much else.

One evening as I was ringing up an order into the till, a regular came over to me and said, "Ro, there's a guy on the right side of the room drinking a pint of beer and he has a video camera pointed at the stage. He has his hat sitting on top of the camera so you can't notice it."

Thanking my regular, I raced over to the creep, stood in front of his camera and yelled at him, "Shut it off! Grab your camera and get the hell out of our bar!" Startled, he jumped up, grabbed the camera with one hand and his pint with the other. I yelled after him, "You can't take your beer with you! And don't come back!" He slammed the pint mug down on an empty table as he ran out the door in embarrassment.

3) The Reliever

Years ago, we had a cheap little private dance room with saloon-style doors that was situated in the corner of the room. It wasn't very private and there was a long mirror that ran along the length of the wall so people on the outside of the small room sitting at the table beside it could see inside if they craned their neck a little.

This particular shift was the first day on the job for a new DJ. That evening, a customer sitting at the table beside the private dance room walked over to the DJ booth where I was standing and informed the DJ and me that there was a guy standing in the private dance room by himself, jerking off.

I asked our DJ if he could please go in there, bust him and tell him to leave. He looked at me for a moment, hesitated, and then got up from his stool and did his duty. What a trooper!

The customer was actually extremely apologetic and embarrassed.

4) "Call Me Sir!"

As you all know from reading this book, I always use the endearing term of *Honey* when I don't know a customer's name or I need to address him. Most guys love it when I address them with this title and many times I hear, "I wish my wife/girlfriend would call me *Honey!*"

Years ago, an older gentleman in a suit came into the bar and after I called him Honey, he responded with, "If you don't mind, don't call me *Honey*. I prefer *Sir*."

When I tell some of the customers about this story, they all agree with me that the guy is a weirdo!

5) The Chair Grinder

A very small man with a bushy moustache and dirty ball cap used to come into the bar quite regularly and always ordered a pint. He would sit at gyno and pull his chair right up under the counter, so he was as close to the stage as possible. Then he would grind his crotch into the chair, moving back and forth. We called him "The chair grinder." It's very creepy as he's obviously pleasuring himself! He must have moved or something by now because I haven't seen him in years. Thank God!

6) Dine, Drink, & Dash!

Many years ago, an older guy came in while I was working the dayshift. He ordered a pint of dark beer and a steak. When he was on his second pint, he had half an inch of beer left at the bottom and then he walked into the hall to use the restroom. He hadn't paid me yet and I had some weird vibes, so I stood out in the hallway talking with a regular and making sure he didn't walk out forgetting about his bill.

As I stood in the hallway, he came out of the restroom at a full run! He ran outside as I ran after him (my regular right behind me) into the parking lot. "Hey!!" I screamed after him. He stopped dead in his tracks and froze. Then he turned to look at me as I walked towards him and yelled, "You owe me $21.75 on your bill!"

He said, "I was coming right back. I was just going out to my car to get my cigarettes."

"I want my money! Did you know that I'm stuck paying your bill if you take off on me?!" I yelled at him, my temper out of control. I was infuriated!

He handed me the money and I turned on my heel and stormed back towards the building where my regular stood waiting for me at the doors. The scammer yelled back at me, "Hey, don't you want a tip?"

I screamed back, "I don't want your f-ing tip! I just want the money owed to me!"

7) The Married Traveler

Many years ago while I was a shooter girl, I had a regular who came into the bar every Friday afternoon. Every time he came in to visit, he loved to flirt with me. I was nice and polite to him and didn't forget to remind him that I'm happily married.

One Friday afternoon he had asked me if I was interested in going on a cruise with him, all expenses paid. He said that he knew I was married and so was he, but he wanted someone to go with him. He explained that we would go as friends and hang out, maybe go as far as holding hands. He mentioned that nothing else was expected. Ya, right! Nothing's for free!

I politely declined and told him that I was NOT interested.

8) The Flasher

Years ago, we used to have a middle aged guy come into the bar and he drank apple ciders (funny how I seem to remember what people drink after all these years). One night as he sat at gyno, he pulled out his penis to show the dancer! She called over the DJ and he was kicked out. Later on, we were told that the same guy exposed himself to the girls working in the windows of the liquor store next door and they called the police. We decided we didn't need a freak like this coming into our bar anymore, so we decided to bar him for good. He was surprised when we kicked his ass out when he came in later on that week and told him to not come back.

9) The Baby

The first few years while I was still new to serving, I struggled to keep up to the room by myself during the busy times when I was the only server on shift. I was running my butt off and quite stressed out.

One night as I was passing by a table of eight guys, I noticed that seven of them were big guys and the smallest one sat in the corner. The small guy was looking down or away from me each time I ran by their table. When I ran by a half dozen times, I finally caught a glimpse of the little guy's face and realized that he was a very young kid who couldn't have been more than fifteen years old! I stopped and lost my temper, "What the hell are you guys thinking?! Get that kid out of here now!" They started looking at one another and laughing. I didn't know what they thought was funny. It was either my yelling or the situation of the youngster sitting in the strip bar.

"Now!" I yelled at the group as my arm was shaking from the weight of the drinks on my tray and my face turned beet red from the anger. They got up and sauntered out the door.

10) The Well Dressed Jerk-off

One evening I had a super friendly older gentleman come in and order a beer at the stage. He was very polite and dressed in a nice suit. I delivered the pint and went on a break.

When I returned, I was told by the other server that she caught the older guy in the suit at gyno jerking off so he got kicked out.

In all the years of working at the strip bar, I have known about two more guys who were pleasuring themselves in our bar during my shift. Obviously they were all kicked out and told not to return.

11) Hundred Bucks for a BJ

A few years ago, a previous manager walked by our private dance room (we had a proper private dance room now built, and the little room with saloon-style doors was gone at this point) and found some unwanted visitors in there. If a customer and dancer want to use the room, management would know about it because it would have to be unlocked. Well, I guess the last person who used the room forgot to lock it up because there was some activity going on in there that staff knew nothing about.

I heard talking in the hallway as I was running some dirty plates into the kitchen and customers passing by were peeking into the room. I was curious too so I joined the few spectators standing in the hallway. The lights were on, the door wide open, and we saw a heavy-set naked woman on her knees in front of a young guy who was leaning back in the chair. He was zipping up his pants and adjusting himself by the time I looked inside. Our manager told her to get her clothes on and get the hell out of here. She scrambled for her clothes and ran down the hallway.

The guy was holding out his hand and asked our manager for his hundred dollars back. Our manager said that that lady doesn't work here. The guy said that she promised him a blow job if he gave her a hundred dollars. She disappeared and he was out a hundred bucks. What did the idiot think that we did, run a brothel?!

12) "I'm Taking You for Dinner"

I have a customer who comes in once a year or so and he is the one person that seems to intimidate me. He makes me kind of nervous as he's extremely flirty, very flashy with his money, and always asks me out even though he knows I'm a happily married woman.

One visit years ago, he walked up to the stage and put a one-hundred dollar bill down for the first dancer. She was ecstatic and after her show she ran to tell the other girls about this customer who put this giant tip on the stage for her. The next girl that came down to do her show also received a brown bill. The third girl on stage was also the lucky girl of this generous bonus. All the girls that were on stage received a hundred dollar tip that day except for one. She ran up to her room and cried. I was even fortunate to receive a hundred dollar tip for serving him and his friend a few drinks. I don't know if he was only tipping the girls that he found attractive but we all thought it was mean not to include her.

He asked me out again as usual and I did my usual speech about how I was married and my husband wouldn't appreciate me going out with other men for dinner. With a straight face he said, "I'm going to be here same time next week, so you better have a pretty dress with you. I'm taking you downtown for a nice expensive dinner." I didn't say anything, and left it at that thinking that he was either bluffing or would forget anyway. True to his word, he returned like he said he would. When I finished my shift, I disappeared into the staff room to do my cash as fast as I could and snuck out of the dancers' door without saying good bye or having him see me leave.

284

He has come in a few times over the years and the dinner has not been mentioned.

13) Stupid Kids

Years ago, there was a dancer who started showing her age but I thought she still looked great. One night while she was on stage doing a show, a group of young guys were insulting her by laughing and heckling her, saying that they could see her cellulite and wrinkles. She finished her show and ended up crying as she went up to her room. I didn't know this had happened until one of the other dancers told me. Thank goodness I was told right away because I dealt with it immediately. I was furious!

I left my section of the room, ran over to the four of them who were sitting at the stage and said, "Holy shit! You guys better get out of here fast! That dancer phoned her crazy biker boyfriend and he's coming right now with some of his friends to kick your asses!" Those kids freaked out, left their drinks, and took off. Of course the story was a lie. They didn't deserve to hang out and have a good time and bother any more of our girls!

14) Mr. Moneybags

Years ago I used to have a good-looking guy come into the bar who tipped me like crazy. I was on top of the service and made sure that he never had an empty drink in front of him.

He had this very strange habit of taking twenty and fifty dollar bills, crumpling them into tiny little balls, and throwing them across the room at the dancers on the stage. Sometimes the balls would bounce off the stage onto the floor. I think that customers always thought he was just being a creep and throwing paper at the girls. A few of the dancers had figured out that the colored balls were paper bills but most didn't. During and at the end of my shift while cleaning up, I would keep my eye open for green and red crumpled papers. Yup, I would find them now and then; bonus money for me!

15) Shove THIS Up Your Ass!

I have a customer whom I see a few times a week. To this day, we don't speak to one another and I refuse to serve him. I'll tell you why. A couple years ago, when I was just starting my evening shift, he ordered a coffee from me. I brought it out, placed it on his table, and said, "$3.50 please."

"$3.50 for a coffee?!" he said, seeming upset.

"Yup, that's the price. Sorry I don't make up the prices," I replied as I took the five dollar bill, set down the change, and then moved on.

I looped around the bar and as I returned to the bar, my bartender had a puzzled look on his face and said to me, "Ro, you know that guy you just served a coffee to?"

"Ya?" I said.

"He told me to give you a message. He said to tell Ro to take her coffee and every tip I gave her in the past and shove it up her ass."

I was so mad, but I figured it out at that moment. Instead of being upset about the price, he was mad that I had charged him. If he would've just said, "Ro, I know you just started your shift, but I've been here for so many hours drinking beers. Do you have to charge me for the coffee?" Of course I wouldn't charge him. But instead he had to be rude and immature.

I told my bartender I was going to void the coffee and be ready to throw his measly coffee money back at him the next time he came in. He didn't come in for two weeks. When he finally did, I lunged at him by slamming down the coins on the table in front of him as I yelled, "I got your message from my bartender the other day. Here's your three fifty and you can shove it up your ass!" Then I ran out into the hallway and I stood there shaking for a few minutes. I haven't served him or talked to him to this day.

16) Mr. Pull Tab

Years ago I had a customer loading money into the pull tab machine. As I served him a beer, we made small talk and I asked him if he has ever won the big money. He told me that he won large amounts once in a while. I said that I've never won any big amounts, but if I would win then everyone in the bar would know about it because I would be screaming and dancing around like a maniac.

He said, "I'll tell you what. If I win the big one, I'll split it with you."

"Sure you will." I thought to myself as I just smiled at him. I went on my break and sat at the bar eating my dinner and reading a book.

I heard, "Blondie! Hey Blondie! I won $500.00!"

He split it with me and I went home with $250.00 extra that night!

17) Profitable Mistake

The room was busy one Friday night and as I stood at the bar waiting for the bartender to make my drinks, a customer pulled me over to the pull tab machine and said, "Could you please help me? I put $4.00 into the pull tab machine, and I thought it was the cigarette machine. Can I get my $4.00 out?"

I said, "No Honey, I'm sorry. You'll have to play the pull tabs."

He told me to pick a column and try my luck. As I was pushing the buttons, he said to me, "So, if you're going to win, you're going to split it with me, right?"

I replied, "No, it's your money. I hope you're going to split it with me!"

He opened the winner ... $400.00! We each got $200.00 and high-fived each other so much that our hands hurt!

18) Watch Where You Aim That Spray Bottle

Many years ago, our bar held a wet t-shirt contest for the dancers (it was more of a get naked and wet contest) every Monday night.

Before the start of the contest, the DJ handed spray bottles out to the customers, which they were allowed to use to soak the girls with water. The contest got to being so popular that guys started bringing in their own water guns and super soakers. Before the start of the contest, the DJ would announce that the customers were not allowed to spray the waitresses, but we always got nailed anyways.

One night while I was bent over a counter taking a drink order, the guy behind me had turned around from the stage and shoved his spray bottle under my skirt and pulled the trigger! I screamed and freaked out while he apologized profusely, but he wouldn't give me the spray gun even when I demanded he hand it over to me.

Before the next dancer was up, I told her what happened. While she was on stage, she seduced the guy into letting her have the water bottle. I was standing right behind him waiting patiently when she handed it to me and I nailed him in the back of the head with a shot of water as payback. For further revenge I took the bottle away from him and gave it to someone else.

Never underestimate the power we women have together!

19) I'll Clean Your Mess for $60

I was starting a nightshift after a new girl worked the dayshift and already my shift started on the negative side. She went off the floor and left me with a big mess even though the room wasn't busy. I hate starting a shift in a pissed-off mood; it affects my tips!

As I was moving through the room, I was taking a few orders and doing a massive clean up. At one of my last tables, I moved the chairs back under table and as I glanced on the floor I saw $60.00 in twenty dollar bills! If she had done her job and cleaned up, she would've been the one that was $60.00 richer.

20) Willy

Many years ago we had a regular who came in quite often. He was an energetic little man who came in a couple times a week for a coffee and something to eat. Once he had gone on a singles cruise and returned with a little souvenir for every server. We got a kick out of the keychain he brought back for my girlfriend Kim as it said Tim. Willy was a very giving person as he would make little wreaths during the Christmas season and hand them out to servers and dancers in the bar. His visits became less frequent and he always complained to us that his daughter didn't like him coming to our bar.

He stopped visiting completely for a few years until the day he showed up with a walker. We didn't think too much of it until we got a phone call from the old folks home a few blocks away, asking if Willy was in the room. We told them that he was and had been there for the past few hours. They explained that he escaped and they were sending over a taxi. The woman on the phone asked us if we could make sure that he got in it. Willy was put in the taxi as promised, but a week later he was back.

I asked him, "Willy, did you tell the people in charge that you were leaving?"

"Oh no! They wouldn't have let me come!" he said.

I tried to reason with him. "Well, you can't run away without letting someone know! Your daughter will be worried and those people are responsible for you."

We decided we couldn't make his stay comfortable, so we decided to ignore him. He sat there for fifteen minutes until we felt sorry for him and ended up giving him his coffee. The people arrived from the old folks home a short time later and they took him away. He hasn't been back since.

21) The Frenchman

Many years ago, we had this really nice guy that used to come into the bar quite often. He had a French accent, always talked about his grandchildren, and tipped quite well.

One day while he was getting a massage from the massage girl, he pulled out his penis from his shorts. The massage girl stopped the massage right then and there and he was kicked out. The manager told him to stay away for a while.

A few months later, he returned and tried talking to the manager about being let back in. We were told that it was OUR decision as female staff to decide whether we should allow him to return. Our massage girl felt too uncomfortable for him to come back in, so we all stood behind her and decided it was a no.

Decision made ... barred for life.

22) The Classy Couple!

A regular couple had come into the bar one evening and they sat at their usual spot at gyno. They ordered their drinks from me and after I dropped them off, I went to talk to the DJ for a couple minutes. As I stood there chatting and scanning the room for anyone who may need another drink, I glanced at the couple.

She was sitting at a very odd angle and his hand was moving around under her skirt. We knew what was happening and we couldn't believe it! My poor DJ waited to see if this would stop after a few minutes but it didn't, so he walked over and had a few words with them.

When he returned to the DJ booth, I asked him what he said.

He said, "I told them that I'm really embarrassed to have to come over here to tell you to stop doing what you're doing. I'm sure you know that you aren't allowed to do that in here. Ok?" I couldn't believe that they didn't leave at this point. They obviously weren't mortified as they sat there laughing and hung out until the bar closed.

Later on when our doorman was locking up the doors, he told us that he saw the guy smacking around his girlfriend in the parking lot just before they crawled into a cab. The doorman told us that the next time they show up, he was going to have a word with the guy about him hitting his girlfriend.

They showed up a few weeks later and went to sit at their favorite spot at gyno. When the same doorman came onto shift, we pointed out the couple to him. He marched down towards them, put his hand on the guy's back and asked him to please come out into the hallway for a moment.

This was what he said to the guy... "If I ever catch you laying your hand on your girlfriend, or any other girl, for that matter, I'll drag you outside and break your arms. Got it?!"

Last I saw, he now comes in with another woman.

23) The Dickhead

One Friday night I had a table of four guys sitting in my section. They were ordering beers and tipping me well on each round.

One of the guys asked me, "So, can I take you out for dinner some time?"

I responded with, "Thanks. I'm really very flattered, but I'm married."

I couldn't believe what he said to me next. I actually had to laugh out loud. He said, "Then why the hell am I wasting my time ordering drinks from you? I might as well get them from the beer barrel girl and tip her!"

What a dickhead!

24) Santa Clause!

Every year we do a big fundraiser in our bar to raise money for the local food bank. The dancers and all the staff work for free. Years ago, the servers started auctioning off their bras so that we could try raising even more money! And no, we don't pull the bras off on stage where everyone checks out "the goods." Some of the staff goes to the washroom and then hand delivers it to the customer while other girls pull the bra off from under their top.

The first year I auctioned off my bra, it went for $300 and a year later it went higher for $500. The year after, my bra sold for $1,000 and the year after I got $2,500! The other servers also have their regulars buy their bras for large amounts of money. It's a tradition for the servers to get the guys to buy their bras where he has his time in the spotlight to look like the big man and we raise large amounts of money for this great cause!

290

This past charity was the topper … as this was still around the time of the economy being a little on the scary side, although my bra had only sold for $800, a coworker's went for $5,000! It was the highest bra ever sold at our fundraiser and we were delighted with our overall total because of it!

25) The Jailbirds

There's been many times where I have gone up to a new table full of guys and ask what they would like to drink.

It throws me off a little when the response I get is, "Can you come back in a couple minutes? Our buddy is in the restroom and we're celebrating him getting out of jail after twenty years!"

It's strange because the group seems like they are out to celebrate like it's some kind of a retirement party or something!

26) Three Stooges

Our bar has a policy that you're not allowed to bring in biker jackets or helmets. One night a few years ago, a couple of older guys came into the bar and one of them was wearing this type of jacket, which I told him he had to remove from the building. He freaked out saying that they had parked their vehicle a few blocks down the road and he didn't want to run all the way back to dump his jacket into his car.

"I'm sorry, but there's nothing I can do. That's the bar's policy." I said and walked away. They left, but returned a short time later. They were still irate about the whole thing, even though I thanked them for taking the jacket out and I brought them a round of drinks on the house. They were very rude to me, so I stopped coming near them. Because I stopped serving them, they started going to the bar for drinks. A third friend joined them about an hour after they arrived.

A few hours later, it was closing time so I was doing my clean-up duties. The room emptied out rather quickly and I was the only one cleaning, while my bartender and two other off-duty doormen were sitting at the bar. I saw the three troublemakers from earlier that evening walk towards me, but I didn't get too worried as I thought that they were coming over to apologize.

One of the men said to me, "What's your f-ing problem?"

"Buddy, time to go. We're closed now." I said to him. Clearly, they had too much to drink and they were still acting rude. Then the bigger guy walked over to me, pushed me in the back, and said, "Pretty good sex change operation!" That's when I yelled for my bartender and hollered that I was being harassed.

My bartender and the off-duty doormen ran over to me and pushed the creeps out of the bar. The guys were outside for quite a while and when they finally returned, they told me their story. One of the idiots lunged at them, so he got punched in the face by one of the doormen and dropped to the ground. There was a cop that was driving by and pulled into the parking lot. He was helping my friends and ended up tasering the second guy. The third idiot ran away on foot.

A week later I got a call from an employee that worked in the building, saying that the guys are his neighbors and that they were really sorry. He said that they wanted to come in and apologize to me. I told him that I don't want them in the building and I don't care to hear an apology. A few days later, that same employee came into the bar and asked me again if the guys could come into the bar and apologize to me because they wanted permission to come in and drink. He said that he had talked to the owner of the club and it was up to me to make the decision. I told that employee that out of all the years I have worked here, I have never had anyone lay their hands on me in a way like that (if my dad or Rod had been there and seen him push me, he would've ended up in the hospital!).

My decision (and a very good decision) ... they are barred for life.

27) The Nut

Every few days, the bartenders check our messages on the answering machine. One particular week, we were advertising a duo show with two hot-looking dancers on our advertising sign on the road up front. There was a crazy woman who left three irate messages on our machine. In the first message, she was yelling about how bad we were and she wanted our manager to call her back. Then she continued yelling for the next four minutes about how messed up the girls are for getting naked for money, blah, blah, blah.

She called back a second time and for twenty minutes she continued her tirade about how sick the customers were for feeding this industry. In the third message she continued her screaming about how her two-year-old son was sodomized and somehow this was our fault.

We kept the messages for about a month and kept rewinding and listening to them over again because we couldn't believe how crazy and mad this woman was.

28) The Crazy Lady

I was driving into our parking lot before my shift one day. As I turned off the ignition, I watched a woman walk through our parking lot wearing one high heeled shoe and the other foot wearing a flip flop. It was very unusual to watch her hobbling along in her odd pair of footwear while she talked to herself. She was either really drunk, really crazy, or both.

29) Little Hands

It was a slow dayshift and a dancer had just finished her show. Just before she walked off stage, she collected the pieces of her costume and noticed that her bunny ears and thong were missing. She came to tell me and I helped her check the floor by the stage. We found nothing and the one guy that was sitting where she threw her costume during her show was now gone. He was a Friday night regular and we nicknamed him "Little Hands" because he had unusually small hands for a man.

The DJ, the dancer, and I went out into the hallway. We wandered down the hall towards the restrooms and we stood looking inside the men's restroom (the main door is kept propped open) and we noticed feet in the cubicle. As the three of us stood there contemplating what happened, two customers who entered the building stopped to talk to us in the hall. As we stood in the hall looking inside, the bunny ears fell to the floor and the perpetrator quickly scooped them up! Our DJ ran inside and started banging on the cubicle door, yelling at the guy to come out. He walked straight out into the hallway. The dancer ripped the bunny ears out of his hands, screamed some profanities at him, and then slapped him across the face; his glasses went flying to the floor. He reached down to pick up his glasses and she slapped him again.

He had the nerve to show up a couple of times after that, but I haven't seen him now in a few years.

The creepy thing about this story is that the massage girl told me that he told her he was married and has four children.

30) Pockets-full

A regular who occasionally comes in to visit has his favorite dancers that he likes to follow from club to club. When certain girls are dancing at the club for the week, he shows up lugging around an extremely full and heavy backpack. We started calling him "Pockets-full" years ago because he would show up with his back pockets jam-packed full of flyers from different strip bars.

Once, I caught him taking a stack of our flyers from beside the till. I told him to take only a couple as we need them to place on the tables for advertising. Staff often jokes that he wallpapers his house with all these little promo flyers from all the different clubs.

Yes, his back pockets are still full.

31) Miss BJ

Last year while I was leaving the bar at night, my manager let me out the side door of the building to get to my car. We opened the door and kneeling on the ground behind my truck was a heavy-set girl. Standing in front of her was a young guy and he was just starting to unzip his pants. As we opened the door, she started to laugh and covered her face. The guy just stood there with his hands on his zipper, staring at us with a dumb look on his face as we just interrupted them.

I gave them a disgusted look and said, "This is wicked!" Then I unlocked my truck, hopped in, and drove away.

The next day, my manager said that he had gone next door to the nightclub to check on things. As he was standing at the front door with the doormen, he noticed that the same girl from earlier on in the evening was ready to leave the bar with a different guy!

My manager said to her, "Going for round two, eh?"

Guess she got embarrassed and ran back into the bar leaving her partner standing at the door.

32) The Rolled Coin Scammer

I still remember the day some guy walked in off the street about ten years ago. He went up to the bartender and asked if he could exchange a roll of dimes for a five dollar bill. My bartender did the exchange, not thinking too much about it as he was busy serving customers. Later on, he opened the end of the roll and noticed it was a roll of pennies.

To this day, I don't take people's rolled coin unless it's a regular that I know. I tell the customer to take it to the bank.

33) The Old Transvestite

If I had to give an award to my most unusual customer, this man would receive it. I've seen him on my Saturday nightshift at least half a dozen times, about every six months or so.

He slips into the room wearing women's high heels and a bra type of bustier with a dark jacket zipped up to above the belly button. He wears poorly outlined tacky red lipstick, with white socks that have fluorescent marker written on them "free blow jobs" and "I suck cocks for free." A gold anklet and the grey beard polishes off the look. He always orders a pint of beer with a side of Clamato and he brings a crossword puzzle in with him to work on. He keeps to himself and is very polite and quiet. The staff does worry about him as he is an older gentleman and we all wonder if he is ever mocked or threatened by others.

One of our servers had asked him once if he is ever worried about his safety. He told her that he is always aware of his surroundings and if he feels any type of bad vibes, he leaves right away. He says our bar is good and he's never had a problem there.

The clients in our bar notice him and usually ask me what his deal is, but they don't bother him.

I can say that he has nice taste in the pretty bras he wears but chooses a very bad color for lipstick.

34) A Kick in the Face

I remember the day a couple of older gentlemen came in during my shift and, as they sat at the stage, they had a couple of rounds of drinks each. There was a dancer on stage and when she whipped around the pole, her heel kicked the guy in the face and slit his eyelid. He was furious and they got up to leave as they were going to the hospital to get the eyelid stitched up.

As they were leaving, I was apologizing like crazy (as was the dancer) and the friend screamed at me, "Why the hell don't you people hire a stripper that knows how to dance without harming the customers! I'm sure you can take care of our bill!" Then they left, barging through the door.

It had happened so fast and I really didn't know how to react to their fury. If anyone gets kicked, it's because they're leaning with their face towards the stage. To this day, I wonder how he explained the eyelid to his wife?!

35) The Married Creep

I used to have a big group of regular bad boys come into the bar on Friday nights with their girlfriends. I knew all of them by name as they had been coming in for years. There were many of them so they had to push three bar tables together. At the next table over, there were two older guys (about forty years old at the time) who were drinking and getting pretty drunk and obnoxious. The guy with the wedding band was starting to bother the ladies and I knew that this was the wrong group for him to screw around with.

As I dropped off a round of drinks to the bad boy table, one of the girls said to me, "Ro, you're going to have to do something about the creeps in front of us. They keep hitting on us and it's starting to upset the guys." I told her that I would drop off the rest of my drinks and then ask the DJ or bartender for help (we didn't have a doorman in those days).

Well, when I walked away, I heard a big BANG! I spun around to look and one of the bad boys had popped the creep in the face and he fell over backwards across the ledge behind him leaving his flip flops behind! The fallen guy and his buddy stumbled out of the bar and left quickly without a word.

I ran back with my full tray of drinks and asked what had happened. I was told by one of the girls that when I started to walk away, the creep with the wedding ring did this face behind my back; he widened his eyes, stuck his tongue out, and shook his head ... the kind of look that looked like he wanted to lick my you know what. That was enough to piss off the biggest bad boy in the group and drop the guy. I thanked him for defending my honor and told him to please not punch out any more customers. Rod is glad that I'm looked after in there when he can't do it himself.

This is another dumb-ass I wonder about in how he explained the black eye to his wife!

36) Hash Smoker

A few years ago, an older regular used to come into the bar during one of my dayshifts quite frequently and we always talked about our daughters as they were the same age. He was polite, very nice, and always tipped me well.

One day during one of his afternoon visits, he went into the private dance room with one of the dancers. They weren't in there for long when a few minutes later the dancer came storming out of the room. She said the guy had pulled out a pipe and had lit it and she knew one hundred percent that it was hash.

The bartender, DJ, and I were undecided with what to do. We talked about it and decided that if we started razzing the guy and it really wasn't hash that would not be a good scene. The dancer was adamant about what she smelled. She was upset and took off when we didn't react right away.

My coworkers decided to ask him anyways, and we'd take our chance. When they did, he said, "Ya, it's hash," like there was nothing wrong with it!

Let me just say that he's another dummy that is barred forever.

37) Cigarette Butt Stealer

Years ago when we still had the smoking room, we had a tin pail that sat at the waitress station. This was where we would dump the contents of dirty ashtrays. At the end of the evening, the pail of butts was dumped into the garbage.

One night, one of the servers said to me, "Ro, did you see that?"

"See what?" I said as I turned around.

"Some guy came running into the bar, dumped our pail of ashes into a plastic bag, and then ran out again!"

When you start stealing cigarette butts and can't afford to smoke, I figure that maybe it's time to quit smoking.

38) Fake Hundred

I have always been really careful about inspecting all big bills before dropping them in my waitress box. One evening I remember a guy giving me an old hundred dollar bill. I was quite busy, so when I got to the till, I glanced over it quite quickly and then popped it in my box.

The next day I got a shortage from the office for a hundred dollars and I received the old bill that was stapled to the letter. I looked it over and my heart sank as I cursed myself for being in a rush the night before and not doing my usual checks on it.

I had thoughts of where I was going to pawn this fake bill off and who I was going to rip off doing it? I knew that I would have a hard time sleeping that night if I was to do something like that. I wondered if the jerk who gave it to me in the first place had a hard time sleeping last night knowing he just ripped off a hard-working waitress out of a hundred dollars.

One of my bad boy regulars who is like family to us around our bar came in the next day and I told him what happened. He asked if he could see the bill, so I pulled it out of my box and handed it to him. He pulled out a stack of money and peeled out a crisp new hundred and replaced it with the dud. I told him that he didn't have to do that as it was my mistake and I didn't want him stuck with it.

He said, "Ro, don't worry. I'll give it to someone I don't like."

I hugged him and I never rush looking at fifties and hundreds again.

I will never forget what he did for me... Thank you T. xo

39) The World Traveler

Years ago, we used to have an older gentleman that was a regular. We saw him a few times a week and then he'd disappear for a couple weeks and show up again. I assumed he was a salesman or had a job that took him away from home frequently.

He had dark, curly hair, was well dressed, quiet, tipped very well, and his visits consisted of no more than two or three dark pints of beer.

As I was serving him one day, he said to me, "I travel a lot for work; in fact I travel all around the world. This is my absolute favorite bar to visit as you girls provide the best service I've ever had."

I have never forgotten that nice comment!

40) "Keep the Tip ... You Obviously Need it More than I Do"

One night a girl had ordered a double vodka paralyzer from me. As I was delivering it, she had jumped out of her chair and was running out the door while talking on her cell phone. When I returned to her table, I noticed that she had a ten dollar bill and a bunch of change ready for me. I set the drink down and was starting to reach over for the money when her girlfriend said, "Ten dollars and fifty cents, right?"

"You got it." I said as she handed over the ten and two quarters. I glanced back as I started to walk away and noticed that she scooped up the rest of her friend's change and dropped it in her own purse! I couldn't believe she stole my tip out of her friend's money!

41) The Head Tripper

As I write this book, I actually had this next scenario happen to me today! I'm guessing that this guy must be just passing through town and doesn't know anyone.

He sat at gyno and seemed sort of sketchy to me as he ordered a pint of beer. Walking around the room taking drink orders, I noticed that he seemed to be switching tables quite a few times and wandering around a lot. As I came from the kitchen, he was walking back into the room from the hallway with his beer in his hand. I told him that he wasn't allowed to take his drink out of the room. Well, he did it again and I repeated myself and added that we don't have a liquor license beyond the door. I also observed him hopping around from customer to customer in quite a fast pace. I was curious and went over to a couple of my regulars and asked them what he was talking to them about. They said that he was asking them where he could buy some crack.

I was in the middle of taking out a large order of drinks when I saw him walk back into the room with his beer again and go sit at gyno. As he was disrupting a couple of regulars, I marched over with my full tray and yelled at him. "Hey! If I see you leave this room one more time with your beer, I'm going to cut you off! And one more thing, stop bugging all my customers with what you're asking them for or you're going to get kicked out!" As I walked away, he downed the rest of his beer and left. I haven't seen him since.

42) The Dickhead Who Made Me Cry

Years ago, we had a different till system and the servers had to call their orders to the bartender. When I got slammed, I would be yelling big orders like this... "Three Kokanees, three Coors Light, five

Canadians, nine Budweisers, two Rum coke, gin seven, two vodka cranberry, three Jugs, pint of dark, and five pints."

One night while I was calling out an extremely large drink order, a customer was tapping me on the arm and asking me for change. As I continued calling, I widened my eyes at him and held up my finger as if to motion, "Just a minute." I couldn't believe that he saw and heard me and still had the nerve to interrupt me for something as minor as change.

I looked at him and said, "Next time you see a waitress calling an order like that, please don't interrupt."

He leaned into my face and said, "F—k you!"

I looked at my new bartender and he looked on the ground not knowing what to do. I looked back at this idiot who was a head and a half taller than me and said, "Excuse me?"

Again, he leaned his face into mine and repeated himself. Then he walked away to sit down. I was stunned, embarrassed, and upset. I went to my manager and at this point I was teary eyed and my voice was wavering. I told her what happened and he was told to leave the bar.

Move forward to today's date, and I am a completely different person. It has been more than ten years since I've come home crying from work about how a customer upset me. Many years of waitressing makes you grow a thick skin and you learn to stick up for yourself and others.

43) Mr. L

I have a regular that comes in a few times a week. He's sweet as pie and plays a game with the servers and dancers. The game goes like this ... he folds up a five dollar bill and hides it in one of his hands. Then he holds his hands out and I have to guess which hand it's in. If I guess right, I get to keep the bill. If I guess wrong, I still get to keep the bill. It's a pretty fun game and an easy way to make five bucks!

Mr. L was holding out his fists to a new dancer as she was walking by his table one day and I guess she didn't play this game before. She looked at him, said "bicycle," and walked away. We still laugh about it to this day!

If any dancer or server from another strip bar is reading this, you know exactly who I'm talking about as he's been doing this for years.

300

44) The Duos

We used to have duo nights at our bar years ago. I remember the night we had a couple of dancers do their interesting show. In their show they pulled up a couple of young guys onto the stage. The guys were thrilled that they got picked to go up on stage with the hot girls! The girls proceeded to tie the two guys to two separate poles very tightly. Then, they pulled their pants and underwear down! The guys were surprised, mortified, and stuck. While the room laughed like crazy, they couldn't move and just stood there with their privates hanging out while the girls pretended to whip them and do a show around them.

The servers thought it was funny at first, but when it lasted a little longer than a few minutes we thought that it had gone too far. When the guys crawled off stage, I noticed that they didn't touch the rest of their drink and left shortly after. I'm sure the poor guys were scarred after that ordeal.

45) The Crowbar

In between dancer shows, customers like to go outside to their cars and smoke some weed. I know because I can usually smell it on them. When this next event occurred, we had a smoke room in our bar, so I knew the guys weren't outside just having a cigarette.

This particular day, a few young guys came into the bar and they were drinking pretty heavily. They kept leaving and coming back and continued on their drinking frenzy only to have me cut them off as they were getting completely out of hand. They were upset about me cutting their drinking off and left.

A couple minutes later, I was walking out the bar doors to go out into the hallway to use the restroom. One of the guys that I had cut off was standing at the end of the hall and he fired a crowbar down the hallway and it just missed my head! There were a few guys also standing in the hallway and they saw what happened. They chased down the guy and I heard that he got a good beating in the parking lot. I was pretty unnerved for the rest of the night.

46) The Birthday Girl

A few years back, one of my regulars was in the bar celebrating her birthday. She was drinking her usual beer and getting pretty loaded. I wanted to cut her off as did her boyfriend, but we knew that she would raise some hell if we did.

I had an idea. I got my bartender to mix me up some cranberry juice and 7-Up, I put a straw in it and a slice of lime as garnish. Then I put it in front of her and said, "Happy birthday sweetie! It's on the house!" She asked me what it was and I said, "It's one of my favorite drinks. A double vodka cranberry seven!" Her boyfriend looked at me like I was nuts.

As she turned to talk to the person next to her, I explained in a whisper that it was a virgin. He smiled and looked relieved. When the drink was low, I brought another one right away before she had a chance to order a beer. We went on like this until it was time for them to leave. He thanked me from the bottom of his heart.

The next time she came in, she thanked me for doing that for her. I have used this tactic a few times for other customers. It's easier to just go along with it than argue with someone. You do have to use your judgment though. If I have someone staggering around or starting to fall asleep, I would tell his friends that it is time for that person to go home.

47) The Gay

Years ago, we used to have a regular that would visit in the evenings during the week. He would order a pint of beer and sit in the corner of the smoke room.

My young bartender at the time would always comment to me how this guy seemed to irritate him as he always caught this weirdo staring at him from across the room. I thought that it was his imagination because I assumed that if he was interested in men, he'd go to a gay club not a strip bar where there are naked women.

One day during this guy's visit, he got punched in the face. Blood was running down his face as I handed him some towels and asked what happened. The guy that punched him (who was another regular) said that he had made a pass at him.

Boy, was I wrong about that one!

48) The Big Spender

When I first started serving many years ago, there was a heavy-set guy that came in with about seven of his friends. They sat in my section at gyno and ordered two jugs of beer at a time. He didn't tip me for more than five rounds. On the last round, he told me to keep the change; a big fifty cents!

I wanted to throw the two quarters at his head!

49) My Corona Friend

I have a couple of regulars who are older gentlemen and I have known them for years. One of them drinks a Corona and the other drinks a pint. They are fun, sweet people!

Last year was my 40th birthday and it fell on a Wednesday. A few weeks before my birthday, I was on vacation. During the week I was off, the bar had printed off tickets saying that it was my birthday on April 23 and everyone should come out as all drinks will be $4.00 and a big screen TV will be given away! (All of you reading this now know my age!)

Servers in our bar love to work on their birthday as it's a great day to make some extra money! The DJ pumps you on the mike and customers will tip you better than normal and buy you drinks.

That day I worked the dayshift and got off in the early evening. Rod, my dad, Rod's dad, and Rod's uncle came out for the big party.

I found out later that it was my Corona friend that went to all the trouble of getting the TV to give away. He also brought in the most enormous birthday cake I've ever seen with Cinderella on it!

I made tons of money that day and ended up with almost a dozen bouquets of flowers from regulars. I didn't have enough vases at home so I had to resort to using jars and glasses. Regulars brought me homemade jam, stuffed toys, baking, bottles of wine, and gift certificates. My girlfriend Kim brought in forty helium balloons for me in the afternoon tied to a bottle of wine! A bunch of my girlfriends came in to rip it up ... it was so much fun!

It was the most memorable birthday I ever had! Thank you to all that made it possible! Xo

50) Merry Christmas

Many years ago, I was working close to Christmas and when I came in for my shift I was told that I didn't pay my sixty dollar float back the day before. As my bartender told me this, a regular who was standing at the bar pulled out sixty dollars and set it on the counter. I told him that it was my responsibility and it was money I had borrowed from the bar. He said that he hadn't done a good deed for Christmas yet and this was the good deed.

Thank you, R!

51) Big Tips!

One night many years ago, I ran my tail off for two and a half hours by serving four young people who were drinking jugs of beer and shots of sambuca. They didn't leave me a single cent and when they left, they left me with a big mess. There was sticky sambuca drips and spilled beer all over the table. I was cursing at them in my head when I moved a chair and found a nice, red, fifty dollar bill! They left me a screaming tip after all!

52) The Magnet

I had to add this story as I heard it today and found it very amusing.

One of my wonderful regulars told me he was going through a drive-thru for a coffee one day. As he drove up to the window, he reached down to get his gift card and handed it over to the girl. She looked at it, then passed it back and said, "This isn't a gift card."

He took it back, threw it on the floor of his car and said, "Oh my God! That belongs to my son!" It was a little magnet that one of the dancers had given him with her naked picture on it.

53) Going Commando!

I have to laugh about this one! On a busy Friday afternoon, one of my regular customers was hanging out with her parents, having a few drinks. When dad left to go outside and have a cigarette, mom stopped me as I was walking by and said, "Ro, here's a story for your book!" Miss C pulled her underwear off and slipped them in her purse. "See!" She pulled the panties out and dangled them for me as evidence. I asked why and she responded by telling me that she felt more comfortable. In her defense, it was a hot summer day.

54) Another Crazy Person ... Literally!

One day while I was working, I had a woman come into the bar during my lunch rush.

The crazy lady asked me, "Do you take lottery tickets?"

I responded with, "No, we don't."

The woman said, "Do you know of anyone that would buy me a drink? I don't have any money."

I said, "No I don't. You gotta go."

"Well, that's not fair! Why does she get to stay and I have to go?!" she said as she pointed to the naked dancer on stage.

I yelled at her, "She's doing her job!"

55) Classy Lady

My DJ told me that when he worked one nightshift, he went to the restroom and found a very drunk, heavy-set woman in the men's room. She was standing there in a purple thong and kept repeating, "Where's my pants? Where's my pants?" There was a guy sitting on the counter watching her. The DJ proceeded to take a pee as he had to hurry and get back out into the bar.

As he was in the middle of doing his business, the manager came in the restroom and said, "What's going on in here?"

My DJ responded with a very red face, "Don't look at me. I just came in here to take a leak!"

Classy people. Enough said ...

56) The Perverted Kids

One night during closing time, I was hanging out at the bar having an after-work cocktail. While the last of the customers were leaving, there were a few young guys giggling and whispering to one another as the last dancer of the night passed by them and disappeared out the doors into the hallway. I couldn't help myself and said, "What's going on guys?"

One of them looked at me and said, "What are all the strippers doing now?"

"What do you mean? It's the end of the night. They're done with work," I responded.

"Are they all upstairs together?" All the guys started giggling again.

"Do you guys think that all the girls are upstairs partying and having an orgy together or something?" I asked.

"Ya, well ..."

"Hate to burst your bubble boys, but most dancers are upstairs changing into their baggy sweat pants, throwing curlers in their hair, and washing off their make-up." I had to have a little fun with this so I continued, "They go home to their boyfriends and husbands. Some of them even have kids at home. So, nope, not many of them are going out to party or have sex with one another." I felt a little evil but I have to admit that I got a kick out of seeing their smiles fade and their enthusiasm diminish.

57) Why are there Jeans and Underwear on the Floor?

I was working one Saturday night and had a stag group of over a dozen guys sitting at gyno. They were ripping it up pretty good and tipping me very well. The groom was wearing a tacky blue floral dress. A few hours into their stay, I was down at the stage picking up empties and cleaning up while the group was outside having a smoke break. I pushed in a chair and tripped over a pair of men's jeans. I started to wonder who was wandering around the bar without their pants while I kicked the pants under the stage. I continued on to the other side of the stage and as I pushed in a chair, I noticed black clothing on the floor and picked it up. I dropped them in shock and let out a little yelp as I realize they were men's underwear, and they were wet! I kicked those under the stage as well and moved along my route.

A short time later as I looped around the stage, the groom was standing there with three of his friends talking. I barged into their conversation and said, "Sorry to interrupt guys, but I was wondering something. There's a pair of jeans on the floor over there. Do they belong to anyone in your group?"

"Ya, they're mine" responds the groom, with a silly grin on his face.

"What about the black ginch on the floor over there? Are they yours as well?" I asked pointing to the other side of the stage.

"Yup."

I start to laugh as I asked him, "Can I ask you a personal question?"

"Sure!" he says as he takes a swig from his beer glass.

"Are you going commando?" I now have some bad visuals of him scrubbing his family jewels and nether regions all over our chairs.

"Nope. I'm wearing women's thong" he responded as he pulled his dress up to reveal a cute blue thong. I couldn't help myself, but I reached over and gave the thong a good snap.

NOW, I've basically seen it all!

58) He Pays Attention!

Most of my regulars know that I have horses and I compete in endurance rides. In the Spring of 2009, I started training my young horse Spicy and entered her in a few races during the summer.

The second race we entered, we did a thirty miler and ended up coming in sixteen out of forty-two horses, while eight didn't finish the race.

A few of my regulars had asked me how my race went and I told them. Three weeks later, the fourth guy in the group joined them and asked me how my race went. I was ready to tell him, and then changed my mind as I looked at the group and said, "Anyone remember how I did?"

Two shook their head and shrugged their shoulders as the third calmly picked at his salad while looking down and nonchalantly responded with, "Of course Romana. You came in sixteenth."

Mr. B. got one big hug!

59) A Round for the House!

I was working one mellow Saturday night serving a group of five younger guys. The guy drinking the Bacardi coke was paying for all his friends' drinks. He started buying drinks for the girls across the room and random people throughout the room. A couple hours later while I was at the bar, the shooter girl informed me that the Bacardi guy was buying a shooter for everyone in the bar.

Well, before he left for the night, he bought four rounds of shots and a round of drinks for the whole bar. He was polite, kept us busy, and tipped us well. When he was leaving, he came over to the bar to hug me and the shooter girl and thank us for the great service. I hope he'll return again soon!

60) Bathing in Our Restroom

I had a dancer come to me one afternoon to inform me that there was a woman in our restroom bathing herself in the sink. I peeked in and told her that she wasn't allowed to bathe in our washroom and she had to leave. She looked at me with wet hair, apologized, and told me that she'd be gone in a few minutes. I went back to check the restroom five minutes later and found sparkles and spilled makeup all over the counter.

307

61) Random Girl or a Hooker?

One evening a couple of young guys came into the bar and had a few drinks. A young lady sauntered into the bar, bought a drink from the bartender, and went to sit beside one of the men. I assumed that they knew each other because she walked straight over and sat down. I also noticed them talking.

About five minutes later, the woman and guy she was sitting next to disappeared. He showed up again a short time later, ordered another beer from me, downed it, and then the two men left.

A few days later, Rod was telling me that a friend of a friend was in my bar with a buddy a few days earlier. While they were there, some random girl sat down next to him and asked him if he wanted to go to the restroom and have sex with her. He left with her and just before the act, he put two condoms on.

I asked Rod if he thinks the girl was possibly a hooker. He said that if she was a hooker, she was a pretty bad one because she forgot to ask him for money.

62) Guy Taking a Leak in the Women's Restroom

One evening nature was calling and as I walked into the women's restroom where there was a customer standing in the stall with the door open and his back facing me. I heard the tinkle and yelled at him.

"Hey buddy! You're in the women's washroom!" I turned and ran back out to the bar to tell my bartender. As the bartender was ready to head to the restroom, the guy appeared in the doorway and I continued to bicker at him. Another gentleman came running over from a table and asked what the problem was. I explained that his friend was in the women's restroom doing his business. The man apologized for his friend and explained that he doesn't speak any English.

63) Too Rushed and Lazy to Wash Hands

This story isn't about any one person in particular, but for the few in general. Many times I notice the many guys in a rush as they come out of the restroom still zipping up their fly and adjusting themselves. They are probably the same people that order a messy hamburger or hot wings and lick their fingers clean! Yum!

64) The Experiment

One afternoon I had a couple guys order a bunch of appetizers. They asked me to pack up the leftovers and grab their bill. I dropped off the bill and took the leftovers into the kitchen to pack it up. A few minutes later I returned with the take-out containers and noticed the money on the table but the guys had disappeared. I thought that they would be back, so I left the containers on the table. When the guys didn't return fifteen minutes later, I took the containers of food to the bar and thought to myself that there was a whole lot of food that would be a waste to throw out. I decided to take it outside and see if it would disappear off the step outside from some of the homeless people that hang around. I ran out every five minutes and within twenty minutes, the containers were gone! I look at it as recycling!

65) "Thanks for Coming Back!!"

When I was new to waitressing, I had to learn all the rules to running tabs virtually on my own through my own mistakes.

One night, the bar was busy and I had two guys sitting at the stage wanting to run a tab.

"Sure, what would you like?" I asked them. Two beers of some sort and the tab was off and running. I didn't ask for a credit card and I surely didn't know who these guys were. Before I knew it, they had disappeared and I was stuck with their bill.

Two hours later they came back and informed me that they forgot to pay for their drinks and drove all the way home, which was located almost half an hour away.

I thanked them profusely for coming back and not leaving me to pay their bill.

66) "I Knew They Were Cops!"

It was a weekend and the bar was hopping. Two younger gentlemen in crew cuts came in and sat down for a couple drinks. I served them and then made a comment to the other servers that I had a gut feeling that those two guys were cops. The other girls shook their heads and didn't agree. One girl had said that they looked more like military men.

A short time later, the two men were leaving and came to inform me at the bar that the man in the blue baseball cap sitting next to them was harassing the guy with the Tom Selleck moustache. The guy with the blue cap was insisting that the moustache guy was an undercover cop. Then he said something to me that grabbed my attention. He said, "Actually, we're cops and because we're off duty, we don't want to deal with this." Then they left.

I went to see what the problem was. The guy with the Tom Selleck moustache was a regular of ours who was a construction worker. We ended up telling the troublemaker with the blue baseball cap that he had to leave.

67) Briefcase Con

One of my coworkers recently told me that there was a guy who came in and wanted to run a tab. She didn't get a credit card but because he was well dressed and came in with a briefcase, he seemed like a nice, normal person. He had quite a few beers and shooters on the tab and a few times he had left the room to go outside for a cigarette but had left his briefcase sitting at his table.

Eventually he didn't return. At the end of the night, the staff opened the case and it was empty.

68) Tip Jar Stealer

Many years ago, one night I had a customer upset me and I ended up crying at the bar to my bartender. As my bartender came over to my till and listened to my story, the customer that was standing and talking to him at the bar quietly disappeared.

My bartender looked over and yelled, "My tip jar is gone!" We both ran outside and the guy was already speeding out of the parking lot in his old, grey van.

69) Tip Stealer

Years ago while I worked a busy weekend night, I got slammed and was working by myself. I was struggling to keep up to my drink orders. At my last table, I was able to balance my already overloaded tray with a few more empties but didn't have the muscle power to hold that full tray any longer and scoop up all the change that was left at the same time. I thought that I would grab the money the next time I looped by, even if someone was sitting there. When I came by, the money was gone and there were two young guys waiting there for me to take their order.

310

"Excuse me guys, was there a whole bunch of change on the table when you sat down?" I asked.

The smaller of the two said, "Ya."

"What happened to it?" I asked again.

"He took it all and put it in his pocket," he replied as he pointed to his friend and said it like it was no big deal.

"Hey Buddy, do you know that you just stole from me? That was a tip left for me from the last customer and I didn't have a chance to collect it as I cleaned this table a few minutes ago. I want all my money!"

He looked horrified and started dumping change on the table. I scooped it up and said, "You ever steal a tip from a waitress again and you could get your arm broken!"

I wiped the table and said, "Now, what can I get for you?"

70) The Cheap-Ass

I have a customer that comes into the bar every now and then. He's very quiet, always orders a pint, and takes all his change back. One night while I was slammed, he came in and ordered his beer from me as usual. I had to bend over and pick up all his change off the table while I juggled my full tray. I had a really bad feeling that there was not enough money there so I proceeded to count all the nickels and quarters. I guess he wasn't expecting that I would go to all the trouble as I normally just scoop it up and go.

I stopped and said, "Hey! You're over two dollars short!" I think that he did it on purpose because I was extremely busy. I make it a point to count every nickel when he pays me now!

71) "I Don't Need Your Tip THAT Bad!"

A couple weeks ago I had a gentleman sit in my section and stay for a few hours drinking draft beer. He was well dressed, very polite, and gave me a ten for every beer he purchased. He introduced himself as Peter and asked me my name. He stayed for about three hours and the longer he stayed and the more he drank, he was starting to get kind of grabby. He would rub my arm when I set down his beer and at one point he started petting my calf as I stood near him while talking to the customer next to him. I told him that he wasn't allowed to do that and made a mental note to stay away from him.

It was almost closing time, so I knew he would be gone soon. As I delivered his last beer of the night, he asked me, "Can I pinch your ass?" and before I had a chance to move, he pinched!

"Hey! I told you that you can't touch the girls in here!" I walked away and stayed away for the rest of the night. A good tip wasn't worth some old guy touching and grabbing me.

72) A Bad Drug Trip

One Saturday night, I had a small group of guys sitting in my section. One of them had waist-length hair and I didn't even get a chance to talk to them as they preferred to go up to the bartender when they got low on drinks. I basically cleaned up their empties.

As I was leaving to go out to my car at the end of the night, across the parking lot I could hear yelling and noticed three guys fighting. I ran towards them and noticed the guy with long hair was getting kicked by a kid in a white t-shirt. I started screaming and ran towards the nightclub and yelled at the doormen that there was a fight. Running back towards the kids, I started yelling at the kid in the white t-shirt to stop kicking the guy with long hair.

He screamed, "He won't let go of my friend!"

The guy with long hair had his hands gripping on the friend's black tank top. The long-haired guy was screaming like a maniac and we yelled at the friend to wiggle out of the already torn tank top.

The doormen arrived and they yelled at long hair to stay back because he had blood all over the place. Since the doormen were there and had it all under control, I took off to my car. As I drove out of the parking lot, I noticed a police car arriving and the long-haired guy was on the ground wrestling with a buddy who was trying to calm him down and was yelling, "Jimmy, settle down!"

I drove home making a mental note to myself to tell my daughter about this creepy story. I like to scare her by informing her about the bad drug trips that people have.

I asked about the guy when I returned to work after the weekend because I was worried about him. They said that he was taken away in an ambulance that night.

73) Another Idiot on the Planet

There was a guy who came into the bar in the afternoon and ordered a short double rum coke from the bartender. I remember looking at him and thinking that he wasn't a bad-looking guy.

He went to sit at the stage and about fifteen minutes later he was up at the bar ordering another double rum. At this point he started whooping and hollering and acting a little wild. He was back at the bar ordering his third double rum when he turned to me and asked if he could order a basket of fries with some vinegar. I asked him to pay me right away as I had a bad feeling that he would either leave me with his bill or would run out of money. A short time later the fries were sitting at the stage and he was nowhere to be seen.

My bartender waved at me from the door, so I came over to see what he wanted and he said, "Ro, put your tray down and come outside. You've got to see this." We walked outside and saw the guy's minivan sitting on the curb on the other side of the parking lot.

My bartender said that he went outside looking for him in the smoke area to tell him that his fries are ready, and that's when he saw the minivan. He said that when he walked over, the guy rolled down his window and told my bartender to f-off. My bartender said, "Have a good night in jail. I came out to tell you your fries are ready."

"I didn't order any fries!" he screamed.

"Yes you did! You even paid the waitress for them already."

About ten minutes later, a dancer had gone outside for a smoke and at this point the guy was leaning against a police car doing a breathalyzer test. The dancer screamed "Whoo whoo!"

He yelled "Whoo whoo" back at her while pumping his hand in the air.

I was told a few days later that the guy was back later that night trying to buy a case of beer from our liquor store! I was also told that the manager at the liquor store said that this was the same idiot that smashed into the beer and wine store curb about three weeks earlier and the guy had a suspended driver's license.

I was also informed that this dummy is barred for life.

74) Not THE Foreman!

If you think that the crazies come out only at night, think again. One Tuesday afternoon we had three older guys in their forties come in to celebrate two of their birthdays. They were drinking pretty steadily and ordered food, and by 4:00 when the shooter girl arrived, they started on the shooters. When they started to arm-wrestle around 5:00 and one of them was taking his shirt off, I informed them that they were done for the night. I also told them that they had to chill out as they were getting louder by the minute or they had to leave because my other customers were starting to complain.

Evening staff came in and I let the other server know what was going on and mentioned that the group was cut off. I grabbed all my stuff and went to the staff room to do my cash. Five minutes later I heard banging outside in the hall and someone yelled, "You were asked to leave!" Then I heard a big bang and another crash. I ran out into the hall and saw one of the men lying in the hallway and he was out cold! A customer had punched him and knocked him out. The bartender ran out into the hall and got down to check on the guy.

The friend looked at me with wide eyes and yelled, "This isn't good. This isn't good! Do you have any idea who this is?!"

At this point I'm thinking, "Oh great! This is probably some big gang member and we're going to be in some kind of major trouble!"

Then he says, "This is my man! He's the foreman!"

75) Clean up Your Own Puke!

One afternoon a guy in his mid-thirties showed up and sat at the stage. He ordered a jug from me and I proceeded to ask him, "How many glasses do you need?" I assumed a friend or two would be joining him any minute.

"Just fill up the jug" he responded.

"Buddy, can I please see your ID?" I asked him as this was the kind of comment that would come from a newbie drinker. I checked his ID and he was about twenty-seven years old and seemed a little slow. I brought his jug and put his poutine order into the kitchen that he asked me for.

As I passed him from time to time, I noticed that out of the first glass he had poured himself, it took him quite some time to drink half of it.

A short while later while I was at the till, he came over to me and asked for some napkins. I pointed at the stack beside me on the counter and then resumed to ringing in the rest of my order. A moment later, I looked over at the stack of napkins and the entire pile was gone. I ran behind the guy with a couple of rags thinking that he spilled his beer and I didn't want him wasting a big stack of napkins for a spill. I looked at the mess and realized what he did. I looked at him and said, "Buddy, did you just puke on the stage?"

He said, "Ya, but I'm not really sick."

I said, "You can't drink anymore and you're going to have to clean up your puke. I don't do puke." I gave him a bucket with napkins and then ran off to deliver drinks. I tried not to think about the puke because if I did, I would start to dry-heave. I figured that the poutine and half a glass of beer was a lethal combination for him.

A minute later I was scooting by him and noticed him pushing the puke from the stage onto the floor. I yelled at him, "Why do you think I gave you the bucket? You can't spill it onto the carpet!"

When he was done, he brought the pail of puke and dropped it onto the counter and asked me, "What do you want me to do with this now?"

"Put it onto the floor!" I yelled at him as I gagged.

I grabbed the pail and ran it out into the hall quickly so that the smell wouldn't linger. Then I grabbed a mug of water and took it out to him. The funny thing was that he wasn't even drunk. I had taken the almost-full jug away which had only a glass poured out of it and he consumed only half the glass.

I asked him how he was getting home and he said that he was walking as he lived just down the street. Then he took his mug of water and went to sit with two younger guys. I noticed them talking for a few minutes until he got up and left with one of them. Ten minutes later the kid returned without the original guy and I asked him if he had given him a ride home.

He said, "Nope, I don't even know the guy. He asked me if he could buy some weed, so I sold him some. Then he took off. He said that this is one of the rare times his mom let him out of the house."

I must add to the story that I am a very lucky girl to work with the guys I do. My cook in the kitchen got rid of the pail of puke. My bartender took a rag and deodorizer and wiped up the stage and counter area for me. My DJ sprinkled kitty litter onto the puke that was spilled onto the carpet and then he vacuumed it all up.

76) An Unusual Place to Apply Make-up

A few years ago I was driving into our parking lot before noon as I was working my Tuesday dayshift. I noticed a homeless woman sitting in the middle of our parking lot applying her make-up and there was clothing scattered around her in a circle. I assumed that she was from the soup-kitchen across the street. I couldn't understand why she couldn't find a safer place like a park bench or even a fast food restaurant to pretty herself up in!

77) Acting Like a Child

One afternoon, a very tall gentleman with thick glasses came into the bar. He ordered a pint of beer and requested a menu. He seemed a little strange, but not drunk. I made a mental note to keep an eye on him as he was sitting at gyno near the dancers.

He ordered a cheeseburger and as I brought out napkins and ketchup, my gut was telling me to ask him to prepay for his meal. When the food arrived a short time later, I noticed some of the fries were on the floor, which may have been spilled by accident. When I looped past him a second time and found lettuce and tomato on the stage, I grabbed the plate away from him and told him it was time for him to go. He refused to leave, so I went to get my DJ. When the jerk wouldn't get up, my DJ motioned for our bartender. The three of us stood around this nut and told him we would physically remove him. The guy just sat there. The boys grabbed his chair and because the chair had wheels on it, they were wheeling him towards the door. The nut closed his eyes and pretended like he was sleeping! As the chair got closer to the doors, one of the wheels caught the edge of the carpet and he toppled out onto the floor where he lay there with his eyes still closed and he was laughing! The rest of the customers sitting in the room couldn't believe what they saw. We sure didn't find it funny.

"Hey Buddy! We can't put the next dancer on until you're gone! You're going to piss off a whole lot of our customers if you don't get up and leave!" He still didn't get up. When the boys informed him that we were calling the cops now, he finally got up and walked out.

Over the years, he's come in a few times while I was on shift and I told him he wasn't allowed to be in there. I don't need that kind of headache again.

78) Shooting Up Against Our Building

One Friday afternoon I had a regular come into the bar and inform me that there was a drug-addict shooting up outside against our building. I dropped my tray at the bar and ran outside.

316

"Hey! You can't do that here! Get the hell out of here or I'm calling the cops!"

"Really? I can't?!"

I'm always amazed at some of the comments I get from people.

79) Watch Who Befriends you!

Last summer while I was working the dayshift, an older customer walked into the bar and ordered three double rye cokes in the matter of an hour. He left and then returned a short while later with another guy. He bought another double for himself and a beer for his friend. I kept an eye on the two of them and, although the first guy was quite a big man, I could clearly see that the alcohol was starting to affect him. They wanted another round and I told them that they were not going to be served anymore that day.

"That's it for today guys. Time to go home. You can come back tomorrow." I looked at the friend finishing his beer and asked him, "Are you taking your friend home?"

"You bet!" he remarked as he stood up and grabbed his buddy's jacket off the back of the chair. He started to walk towards the door while his friend stumbled behind him.

Ten minutes later, a couple of regulars came in and informed me that there was a guy passed out in our planter in the smoke pit. The bartender and I ran outside and noticed that it was the double rye coke guy, curled up in the planter. We woke him up and I asked him why his friend didn't take him home. The guy sat up and felt around his pockets for his wallet. He said it was gone and so was his jacket. He told us that he had just met the guy outside while having a cigarette and offered to buy him a beer because the guy told him that he had no money. As payment, the scammer robbed him of his wallet and jacket. We called him a taxi and sent him home.

80) Another Tab for Over $100 Owed to Me

My husband reminded me of this episode that happened over ten years ago on a Saturday night. One night, a couple gave me their credit card to run a tab. They told me not to run it through as they wanted to pay cash at the end of their stay. During their visit, the woman gave me her business card as she got quite chatty with me by telling me that she owned a sex toy store. I popped the business

317

card into my waitress box and moved on through my shift. At one point in the night, the two had disappeared and that was when I decided to run their credit card through. As a result, it declined and that was when I felt like kicking myself for not preauthorizing it!

On Monday, I gave the woman a call at her sex store. She seemed really surprised that I called and I told her that I was driving out to pick up my money and drop off their credit card. She had my money and she really didn't have an explanation as to why they took off. I guess she forgot that she had given me her business card.

81) "Where's Your Shoes?"

Not too long ago on the dayshift while I was standing at the bar, I noticed an older gentleman looking quite frantic as he entered the bar. Since it was the beginning of November, I thought it was quite unusual that this man was sweating and seemed out of breath. As I approached him, I also noticed that he wasn't wearing any shoes and he was walking around in his socks.

"Where are your shoes?" I asked him.

"I'm in trouble! I had a bunch of guys with guns chasing me down the road!" I told him to come to the bar with me. The bartender asked him a few questions and I was feeling rather alarmed.

"We need to call the police!" I told my bartender.

"Ro, there's nobody running down the road chasing this guy with any guns. He's just high on some sort of drugs!"

As soon as we told him that we were going to call the police to come and help him, he took off.

82) Little Tough-guy

One Saturday night while we weren't overly busy, I felt some crazy energy in the room from a stag party letting loose at gyno. At one point in the night, a fight erupted near the doors between a couple guys in the stag party and another group. Our one doorman managed to get the five guys down the hall and outside, but as they were making their way out, a young kid jumped on the back of our doorman. I watched from the end of the hallway as he pulled the kid off.

Later on, witnesses told me that while outside, our doorman was surrounded by this outnumbered group and the little guy jumped on his back again to play tough guy. Our doorman defended himself by knocking the kid off onto the pavement. When the kid landed, he passed out cold and he wouldn't wake up. An ambulance was called and the rest of the guys took off. The bar's customers basically dwindled down to a handful of people because they all went outside to follow the action and then left.

When the ambulance arrived, they got out a stretcher and carefully placed the young guy on it without moving his neck. I happened to walk to the doors during this time and eyeballed the ambulance people at work from inside the doors. While this was happening, the cops arrived and took a statement from our doorman. He was handcuffed and put into the back of the police car until the cop got statements from some of the bystanders. In the bar, staff asked some of the customers if they were outside and witnessed the fight. A few said that they had, so they were given a pen and paper and asked if they would mind writing a statement for the cop. They basically wrote that the doorman was surrounded by a bunch of guys and he was outnumbered as they all looked like they wanted to fight. Some stupid kid made a dumb move by tackling a big doorman doing his job who ended up defending himself. Our doorman was released from the police car ten minutes later when the cop read all the statements and found out what happened.

When I talked to our doorman later, he said that the only thing that was annoying was how crammed he was in the back of the cop car with his knees shoved up to his chin!

83) "I'm Part of Shania Twain's Band!"

About five years ago, a middle-aged, well-dressed, thin man with glasses came into the bar. He asked for the manager and after having a talk with him, I found out that he was a member of Shania Twain's band. The manager and Shania's band mate spent a few hours together and by the end of the night, they were best buddies and all his drinks consumed that night were written off as promo. After closing, Buddy (I believe that this was his name) was hanging out and standing on our stage and telling us how Shania is going to stand here and he'll be behind her with his guitar. He was looking for a place for the band to shoot their next video. I guess that management was trying to "woo" him so they ended up dragging him around town to a few of the other clubs while paying for his drinks and introducing him to people. He was given the VIP treatment. Little did we know that he was a fake.

The next day while the manager was on the phone with the stripper agency, he was informed that this con was good because the agency was also fooled by him the week before.

84) "Can You Pay Me in Money and Not Flowers?"

Have you read my stalker story about Pinepple? Well, here's another customer that "I felt sorry" for. Years ago while I was working a weeknight, a very quiet and shy young guy showed up and told me that it was his birthday. He pulled out his ID to prove it to me as I asked him where all his friends were and why nobody else was out celebrating his birthday with him. He said that everyone was busy, so I bought him a shot and got the bar to promo a beer for him. I just felt bad for him celebrating his birthday by himself. I spent a little bit of time chatting with him and thought that he was really very nice and sweet.

Shortly after that, whenever Bob came by the bar to visit, he would bring me little gifts like candles, picture frames, and chocolates. I thanked him and told him that I appreciated the nice gifts but he had to stop buying me stuff. I also reminded him that I was happily married. Rod doesn't mind me getting gifts at Christmas and on my birthday, but this was happening a little too often and it had to stop.

One weekend, our club was having a charity carwash and Bob came by to get his car washed. We washed his beat-up vehicle while trying not to cut our hands on the rust. I thanked him for coming and supporting our cause.

The person who was voted to collect the money donations walked over to me and said, "Ro, that guy told me that he has no money and wants to give you some flowers." I went over to Bob and explained that while we were working for free, this was a way we were raising money for our charity and he had to pay us in money and not flowers. He parked off to the side and scrounged through his car to find two dollars in change under and in his seats.

85) "Thank You For the Flowers"

Every few months, one of my regulars comes to visit the bar. He's mentally handicapped and is such a sweet, well-mannered person.

He will show up with a plastic bag and gives some of the dancers and waitresses plastic flowers he buys at the dollar store. As he pulls out the plastic flowers, they smell of dust and they still have the price tag on them.

"Here. These are for you because you are my favorite waitress. I also have flowers for so and so because she's my favorite stripper," he informs me as he sits there smiling. All you can do is thank him and tell him how sweet he is. The plastic flowers are added to the others that are abandoned in the staff room alongside the stuffed animals and costume jewelry and other gifts that we receive from customers.

86) "How the Hell Did You Get in Our Cooler?!"

A few years ago while working the dayshift, my bartender cruised over to the nightclub next door and entered the walk-in cooler to grab some beer that we ran out of. He went inside and was immediately startled because in the corner of the cooler stood a haggard-looking man.

"What the hell are you doing in here?!" my bartender asked while he approached him.

The guy seemed all flustered and replied with, "I'm looking for the lobby."

"In the cooler?!" the bartender yelled as he started to pat the guy's puffy coat down to make sure he didn't stash some liquor bottles inside. He was escorted outside and from this day forward we make sure to keep all the doors closed and locked to keep any unwanted guests from entering the nightclub off hours.

87) "You're Breaking into my Waitress's Truck!"

Years ago, my bartender took a walk outside into the parking lot to have a quick cigarette. As he stepped through the doors, he saw an older gentleman and a younger woman trying to jam a key into the driver's side of my 4Runner!

"Hey! That's my waitress's truck! What the hell are you doing?" he yelled at them.

The girl said, "Ummmm, she said that we could go in and look inside her vehicle."

"I'll go in and ask her. You guys wait here," he said as he ran inside to get me. By the time we returned, they were both gone. We both knew who they were as they were sitting in the bar at the pole for a few hours that day. A few weeks later, she returned and I told my bartender that that was the girl who was breaking into my truck a few weeks ago.

"I'm going over to kick her out!" he said.

"No, please don't! She knows the vehicle I drive and I don't need her to start keying up my truck or doing stuff to it!" I told him. He agreed.

"Then spit in her drink."

"No! That's disgusting and I could never do anything like that!"

"Oh, come on Ro! Here, ..." He grabbed the straw that I had placed in her vodka paralyzer a moment earlier and he put it in his mouth. Then he licked it up and down and chewed on it. And before I knew it, he slipped it back into her drink! "Come on Ro! It'll make you giggle for the rest of the night!"

I didn't know what to say. I just placed it on my tray and delivered it to her. He was right about one thing; it did make me giggle, especially when she didn't tip me a cent!

88) The Working Girl

When I used to work the nightshift, every few months a dark-skinned woman would show up in the corner of our bar. When I asked to take her order, she would tell me to come back as she was waiting for a friend. The *friend* was always a different older gentleman. As they sat there side by side, I never saw them speak to one another while they had a few drinks and a bite to eat.

I have come to the conclusion that she must be a "lady of the evening."

89) I Get a Kick in the Face

About ten years ago while I was working the nightshift, I was at gyno row picking up some empties. While I was wiping up the counter, the dancer on stage leaped at the pole I was standing near and she whipped herself around. As she was kicking her leg, her heel grazed my cheek! She stopped and I froze. We both just stood there staring at each other and I remember the people in the room stopping to stare. Then she started to apologize like crazy to me.

"Oh my God, Ro! I'm so sorry!"

322

I told her that it was okay and not to worry. I was told later by many customers that the look on my face read that I was ready to dump my tray and hop on stage and start pummeling her. I have to admit that the thought did go through my mind!

90) "The Annual Organic Meat Gathering"

One afternoon while one of my regulars was paying his bill, I had asked him what his plans were for the weekend. He responded with, "Oh, my buddies and I have our annual organic meat gathering."

"What?" I asked as I looked up from my till.

"Ya. It's a comprehensive environmental study."

"Speak English. What are you exactly doing, Bill?"

"Ro, we're going hunting!" He laughed as he waved and walked out the door.

91) Someone Shit All Over the Toilet!

Why are people disgusting? One dayshift last year, a customer came into the bar and said that someone had sprayed diarrhea in the men's washroom all over the toilet and the wall! The bartender and DJ went in to investigate. I was glad that it wasn't me that had to go in there! I can't remember if it was the DJ or the bartender that ended up cleaning up the mess, but I know that it was one of the two as we couldn't leave it until a cleaning person showed up at 2:00 am!

92) "The New Doorman is Gooned!"

Good help is hard to find ... this hit home the night the new doorman started working for us. He kept disappearing out the front doors to *have a cigarette* and ended up getting so drunk on his first day on the job that he couldn't even stand. Pretty soon, he was sitting down at the closest table near the doors and he was swaying in his stool! As I walked by, I realized he had a blank stare in his eyes and I asked him if he was ok. Too late! Our manager noticed it at the same time I did and pulled him aside where he was fired on the spot.

The fired doorman said that he had some friends show up and they were giving him alcohol outside and he didn't realize the amount he must have had to drink.

93) Creepy Eyes

Years ago we had a shooter girl that told one of our young regulars that he had creepy eyes. I have no idea as to why she would say this to him if she's trying to persuade him to buy shooters and win a tip out of him. The poor guy was so panicked about it that he asked me if I agreed with her.

"Of course you don't! I think you have very nice eyes!" I would say that even if he had the eyes of the devil. After all, I don't want to upset a regular and I'm still hoping for any future tips!

94) The Missing Wallet

A customer came into the bar one afternoon and ordered a drink. I looped around the room, went to ring in more drinks at the till, and continued to drop them off. I ended up back at the customer, set his drink down, and let him know how much he owed me. He reached into his jacket pocket for his wallet and his face distorts into a panicked look.

He looked at me and said, "My wallet is missing!"

"Did you forget it at home or in your car?" I asked.

"No. Oh no ..." he said as he jumped up and ran out the door.

I left the beer on the table and continued to deliver the rest of the drinks on my tray. The next time I looped around the room, he was back at his chair with the wallet in his hand.

He said, "I went into the restroom when I first got here and left my wallet in there! I have over three hundred dollars in it and all of it is still in here!"

"Consider yourself lucky, my friend!" I told him.

95) "I Hope You're Wearing Underwear!

About thirteen years ago, one of the nighttime waitresses caught some older guy trying to look up her skirt with a small mirror! She got him kicked out of the bar and I asked her, "I hope you're wearing underwear." She informed me that sometimes she doesn't!

96) "Why don't YOU F-off?!"

A few months ago, an older customer was sitting at the corner of a table and as he chatted with his buddy, he was acting quite animated by waving his hands all over the place. Just as I was passing by with a full tray of drinks, he popped his hand underneath my tray and knocked over two drinks, which fell to the floor. He looked at me and didn't say anything, not even to apologize! I explained that I'm responsible for all the drinks on my tray and I would pay for one of the spilled beers, but he'd have to pay for the other. He refused and said that he did nothing wrong. I was now getting upset.

"Buddy, you're going to have to pay for one of these drinks! You were the one who hit my tray with your hand!"

"F-off." He said to me.

"Get the hell out of this bar!" I yelled at him as I moved to the bar to explain what happened to my bartender. After hearing the story, my bartender started to walk towards the rude man and the jerk jumped out of his chair and left.

A month later as I was moving around the bar on a busy Friday afternoon, I looked at an older customer with a thick moustache and curly black hair. I said, "Hey! You're the guy who told me to f-off after you knocked two beers off my tray!"

He looked at me with a stupid smirk on his face and said, "So?!"

"So, you didn't pay for the beers or even apologize for being rude to me!"

"You know what? Why don't you call your manager over and I'm going to have a few words with him. He'll put you in your place!"

"Oh, is that so?!" I was furious as I ran to my manager and told him my story and then informed him that this sucker wanted to talk to him so that *I would be put in my place.* My manager walked over and the jerk-off was talking and waving his hands like mad trying to explain himself. I could see that he gave a thirty-second explanation and then my manager was pulling the guy's chair out as an indication for him to leave. When my manager returned, I asked him what the creep said.

"I don't know and I don't care. I just said to him that you've been here for over fifteen years and I believe you over a guy like him. Then I told him to shut up and get the hell out of our bar!"

97) "Who Wants Free Money?"

One of my bartenders used to work at another strip bar that is now long gone. He said that the bar used to raise money for a children's cause every year around the Christmas season, just as our bar does.

Well, the children's cause caught wind of that bar being a strip bar and they told them that although they would like the money, they can't take it as it links them to this industry.

So, the bar put an advertisement in the paper saying that they have this money raised and if any cause out there can prove that they need it, they would give them the money. Can you believe the advertisement ran for a few months? After this amount of time, a local fire department called and said that they would love the money if nobody else wants to claim it as they need to do some work to the trucks and update their firehouse. They were given the money.

98) Money Comes Easily and Frequently

A few years ago when "The Secret" came out, I was one of those people that got excited about changing my life and living it in a more positive way. In one part of that movie, a woman stated that if you want money to come your way, you have to think positive and reinforce that "money comes easily and frequently." Say this many times in the day and believe it in your heart and it will come your way! So, on my way to work I list off and thank the universe for all the good things that are in my life and then I will end it with, money comes easily and frequently.

One day I decided to grab a blank guest cheque that we write customers' tabs on and I wrote on the back in fancy font, money comes easily and frequently.

I came into work a few days later and was told that one of the other waitresses had grabbed this guest cheque and wrote a regular's tab on it without knowing. Then she dropped it off at the table, thanked them, and walked away. Well, I guess the guys flipped it over, read it, and got really mad. She didn't get a tip and they freaked on her about it. While I knew who they were, I had to wait for them to come back and explain the story. I still have to laugh when I think about this story!

99) The STARS

Working where I do, I am fortunate to meet and serve some famous people. I don't want to mention names as I like to keep the privacy factor in place. But I will give you little indicators as of whom I've met and served at our bar.

326

- A baseball star that plays for the big leagues in the USA
- A pro skateboarder
- A pro motorcycle racer who races for Canada
- A television and movie star who was on a very popular law show on TV
- A movie star who was in a few movies and lives locally
- A movie star who was in a Rocky movie and he is now a producer. He was filming a movie at the nightclub next door a few years ago
- A few porn stars

100) My Regulars

I dedicate the #100 spot to each and every one of my regulars! As I wrote this book, many of you asked me if you were in it. My response was always, "No, because you're normal. You really haven't done anything unusual, stupid, weird, or illegal. Nobody really wants to read about people like that."

So, this is your spot in my book! I thank you all for being nice, normal guys who treat me with respect. I enjoy the slow times in the bar when I can stand around and exchange stories with you. I've had some nice conversations with people about traveling, horses, motor homes, and pets. I've also had some interesting conversations with regulars about death and even psychics.

As you thank me for the service, I thank you for coming into our bar and becoming a friend!

Romana
www.howtobeawaitress.com

LaVergne, TN USA
06 June 2010

185049LV00005B/2/P